A HISTORY OF ZEN BUDDHISM

A HISTORY OF
ZEN BUDDHISM

Heinrich Dumoulin, S.J.

Translated from the German by Paul Peachey

BEACON PRESS

Boston

Preface

Interest in Zen Buddhism has grown continually since this book was first published in German. Although it was then thought necessary to preface the work with some remarks for the benefit of Western readers about Zen and its living values, a general knowledge of Zen Buddhism can now be presupposed. To be sure, this knowledge is often and in many respects inadequate, distorted, or even altogether false. In the wake of the "Zen boom" in the United States, there originated "Beat Zen," "Square Zen," and other distorted forms which must be considered caricatures rather than true expressions of Zen Buddhism. A French scholar who had lived in Asia for many years once said to me: "One has to distinguish between Buddhism in Asia and Buddhism for Europeans." This very relevant remark applies to Zen Buddhism as well. Zen Buddhism in Asia can only be understood in terms of its Asian development—its origin in China, most likely in the sixth century, the meditation tradition of a thousand years' duration upon which it was based, and its thirteenth-century transplantation to Japan where it reached its fullest and highest development. Hence, in order to obtain a reliable and correct knowledge of Zen Buddhism, our interest is directed towards a study of its history.

I feel very grateful to my Japanese friends who, shortly after my entrance into the postgraduate course of the Science of Religions Department of the then Tokyo Imperial University in 1936 (one year after my arrival in Japan), introduced me to Zen Buddhism and encouraged me to study its history, for I have continually found this a most fascinating subject of study. Two of my fellow students, themselves believers in Zen, used to accompany me on visits to Zen monasteries in Tokyo and its vicinity, and invited me to read with them a Zen text, the famous *kōan* collection *Mumonkan*. This *kōan* collection presents a vivid reflection of the history of Zen Buddhism in China during a span of nearly five centuries. Out of this study came a short summary of the history of Chinese Zen Buddhism, which was written in German and first published in *Monumenta Serica* (Vol. VI, 1941, pp. 40-72).*

At our first meeting Mrs. Ruth Fuller Sasaki suggested that I write a complete history of Zen Buddhism. At that time I declined laughingly. However, the importance of such a scholarly endeavor always remained in my mind, and from that time on I tried to extend my studies of the history of Zen Buddhism in different directions, and when time was available, I began to work upon a synthesis of these studies. Whenever possible I tried to fill in gaps and to indicate the connection of movements and events. Naturally, it was impossible to shed light on all the obscurity, for in the history of Chinese Zen Buddhism, as in the whole of the history of Chinese Buddhism, there is still much unexplored territory. The personality of Bodhidharma as well as the beginnings of Zen (Ch.: *Ch'an*) in China remains uncertain. The fusion of Buddhist and Taoist elements had probably already progressed far in the schools of contemplation which preceded Zen. The precise proportion of Taoist influx

* Later, Mrs. Ruth Fuller Sasaki translated it into English and published it with her admirable annotations and indices (*The Development of Chinese Zen after the Sixth Patriarch, in the Light of Mumonkan*, New York, 1953).

into Zen Buddhism can as yet hardly be gauged. Even more important would be to ascertain the exact character of this influx. Further investigation will certainly enrich as well as correct our picture of the history of Zen.

This book is of an historical nature and is intended to give to the reader a faithful account of the historical development of Zen Buddhism as far as this is possible at the present time. The German edition was well received by the specialists in this field. The historical accuracy of the work was acknowledged by Buddhist scholars of the first rank. The title of the American edition, A *History of Zen Buddhism,* stresses even more clearly its historical orientation.

However, Zen is not merely of historical interest; it has importance for the present day. This conviction never left me during my historical studies. At the same time I am convinced of the eminently spiritual function of history. In the preface to the German edition I expressed this in saying: "Perhaps there is no other way that leads as surely to the very essence of things as inquiring into their historical development. Certainly, by its very nature, historical presentation will always be imperfect, for history in its complex interrelationships is mysterious and enigmatic, but at the same time sobering and disenchanting. . . . History reveals the form and leads to the essence of things. In historical research we are guided by the things themselves, and we try to comprehend their response and their teaching. The object of this book is to put the reader into as close a contact with Zen as possible, to elucidate its inner form from history, and to make its living values apparent."

It is impossible to thank one by one the many persons who were of help to me during the long years of preparing the German original of this book and translating it into English. Only a few names can be mentioned. The Japanese professors Reihō Masunaga, Hajime Nakamura, and Shōkin Furuta have helped me in my Zen studies in many ways and contributed much useful information. Through the kind offices of Mrs. Sasaki the doors of the Zen monasteries of Kyoto with their memorable art treasures were opened to me. Mrs. Sasaki, moreover, not only put her library at my disposal during the writing of the original and its rendition into English, but also had the kindness to assist in the revision of both. Thanks to the co-operation of Fr. Heinrich Busch and Fr. Gerhard Schreiber, I was able to make use of the Oriental Library of the *Monumenta Serica*. Fr. Wilhelm Schiffer and Fr. Franz Mohr assisted me in procuring the illustrations. Last, but not least, I am deeply grateful to the Reverend Mr. Paul Peachey who undertook the wearisome task of making the basic English translation of the entire book. To all these and the many others who helped in the composition and publication of this book, hearty thanks.

Heinrich Dumoulin

Tokyo, 1962

Contents

Illustrations

We would like to thank the following for the photographs which they made available to us: the Reverend F. Mohr for photographs number 1, 2, 3, 4, 7, and 8; the Reverend W. Schiffer for photograph number 5; Mr. T. Okamoto for photograph number 9; Benridō Publishing Company, Kyoto, for photographs number 11 and 12; Daihōrin Publishing Company, Tokyo, for photographs number 13 and 16; the Japan Travel Bureau, Tokyo, for photographs number 14 and 15.

A HISTORY OF ZEN BUDDHISM

1 *The Mystical Element in Early Buddhism and Hīnayāna*

Buddhism and Mysticism

When, in the nineteenth century, Buddhism for the first time was disclosed to the West, the rationalist scholars of Europe thought they had found in it the coveted credo of reason, without God and revelation, without heaven and hell, or soul and immortality. Further research, however, soon taught them otherwise. Not only did the later Buddhism of the Great Vehicle (*mahāyāna*) exhibit all the despised "irrational" phenomena of religiosity such as miracles, saints, the cult and veneration of images and relics, and superstition and magic as well, but also the Buddhism of the canonical writings showed itself, on closer study, to be a religion which transcended the worlds of sense and reason. Everything that the sutras relate of the life and work of Shākyamuni—his words to his disciples, his profound contemplation, his sayings and demeanor—all bear witness to a man mightily stirred by religion, who, with a high sense of mission, opened a new way to knowledge and final release. Thus Buddhism could not be fitted into the mold of a religion of pure reason.

But Christian scholars likewise had to concede to the force of the facts and recognize the religious character of Buddhism. Up until that time the term "religion" had designated the relationship of man to a transcendent personal God or to a Divine Being. Now the concept had to be broadened to embrace the phenomenon of Buddhism. Today Buddhism is generally recognized by scholars as a religion, and, because of its historical and contemporary significance, it ranks among the world's great religions. The basic trait of Buddhism is its striving for otherworldly salvation.[1]

At the same time, the concept of mysticism has been considerably enlarged. Since the definition of mysticism developed within Christianity, which calls for the immediate experience of the personal God through the knowing and loving soul, does not apply to many unmistakably mystical phenomena in non-Christian religions, it has become necessary to place alongside the supernatural mysticism of grace the concept of natural mysticism. Admittedly this concept entails certain difficulties, and frequently it is not sharply enough defined and differentiated. For the moment we shall content ourselves with a general description, and designate as mysticism all efforts of man to elevate himself to a supercosmic, supersensory sphere which he experiences immediately. The supercosmic domain stands in necessary relationship to the Absolute with which man in mystical experience establishes some kind of contact. Where these three essential elements are manifest—namely, where man transcends the sense realm, breaks through the limits of normal psychic experience, and reaches the Absolute—there we can speak of mysticism. The respective strength of each of these three elements varies greatly from case to case, but none must be missing entirely. The sphere of mysticism is thus clearly differentiated from phenomena such as sorcery, magic, and even speculative metaphysics. Since contact with the Absolute becomes, in mystical experience, a means of salvation, Buddhism, precisely because of its mystical element, must be regarded as a religion. Buddha, and those who followed him, saw in mystical enlightenment the "vehicle of salvation" that carried them beyond this world to the "other shore."

The mystical element is an essential part of Buddhism. The multiplicity of phenomena in the religion of Buddha has often amazed scholars and laymen. There is hardly a religious motif or manifestation which has not been used down through the centuries by one Buddhist sect or another. In vain does one seek a bond that would embrace all these numerous contradictory forms. And yet, despite the absence of a common denominator, Buddhism constitutes a whole. The specific essence of Buddhism is nowhere so clearly apparent as in the mysticism that pervades the whole of this religion. The manifold Buddhist manifestations—the rigorous moral code of the early monastic communities, the daring metaphysical speculations of the Great Vehicle, the intimately confident prayer of the believers in Amida, the magic rites of Shingon and Tendai—all these are immersed in the mystic twilight that envelops the disciples of the Buddha, each in his own way.

Shākyamuni, the Enlightened One

The nature of Buddhist sources does not permit us to distinguish clearly between history and legend in the life of Shākyamuni.[2] According to the majority of Buddhologists, those incidents which are transmitted alike in the Pali Canon and the Sanskrit sources can be regarded as containing a historical core. All records tell us that the decisive turn in the Buddha's career was brought about by a mystical experience. As the early sutras relate, Prince Siddhartha of the house of Shākya chose a life of wandering to learn the meaning of suffering, and became the Wise (*muni*) and Enlightened One (*buddha*), who teaches the path of redeeming knowledge. The accounts all stress that only after long ascetic exertions was Shākyamuni able to enter the true way of liberating meditation, and emphasize thereby the Buddhist manner of meditation as distinct from the practices of self-castigation in Yoga. The renowned Brahmans to whom Shākyamuni first went recommended to him dangerous austerities which he carried out fearlessly to utter exhaustion. But he did not reach liberation. Only after he took nourishment again, which occasioned the departure of his five fellow ascetics, and entered the new path of meditation, did he achieve his goal. While he sat beneath the pipal tree, dead to his senses and absorbed in deep meditation, his spiritual eye of illumination was opened. According to the account in the *Mahāsacca Sutta* he thereupon went immediately to Benares, where he "set in motion the Wheel of the Doctrine," basing his authority directly on his illumination. When he met his five comrades in asceticism, they mocked him. But Shākyamuni faced them in his newly acquired dignity as the Enlightened One, declaring: "The Perfected One is the holy, highest Buddha." This word, from now on recurrently on his lips, establishes his authority as the founder of a religion and a leader of men to salvation. In the sermon at Benares, Buddha developed the doctrines of the Four Noble Truths and of the Middle Way between the two extremes of asceticism and indulgence. We may assume that these doctrines comprise the content of his enlightenment.

Legend has removed Shākyamuni from the realm of the merely human and has attributed extraordinary powers to him. The Exalted One is said to have possessed the capacity to penetrate bodies and to read thoughts. The might of his spirit was such that it gave him power over sickness. He communicated with supernatural beings and was able to recall his previous incarnations. Indian imagination elevated the figure of Buddha to a superhuman level. His miraculous powers made him "the greatest of all Yogis." [3] The mystical element comes strongly to the fore in the legends. The Bodhisattva, who in "thoughtful consciousness" entered his mother's body, relaxes there in the posture of Yoga meditation, sitting with crossed legs. There his mother, Māya, sees him—herself caught up in a state of higher consciousness. As a youth, the Prince once went with his companions into the country and, beneath a rose tree, sank into a deep meditation in which he ascended from the lowest to the fourth *dhyāna* stage. The youth, encircled by the "halo of contemplation," aroused the admiration of all. Tradition also tells of the many Yoga-like practices of Shākyamuni before he achieved Buddhahood. As he lived, so he died, a mystic.

The sutra relates how the Enlightened One at an advanced age, after he had for a time postponed death through the power of his conscious will, decided to allow nature to run its course and voluntarily relinquished the will to live. The Master now spoke his final words of admonition to his disciples. While his body lay in mortal illness beneath a *sāla* tree in the grove of Kusinārā, his spirit was absorbed in contemplation. He ascended through the four stages of *dhyāna,* then hastened through the five ecstatic states, returning finally through these same stages to the first *dhyāna*. His spirit now mounted a second time to the fourth *dhyāna* and from there entered perfect *nirvāna* (Pali: *parinibbāna*).[4]

The mystical elements, which in legend and tradition permeate the figure of the Buddha, obscure his person as much as the miraculous and the supernatural attributes. Even though the accounts in the Pali Canon reflect a distinct historical reality, the Buddha does not emerge as a perfectly tangible person. The mystic traits veil his human countenance. Since we cannot know with complete certainty a single actual word or event from the life of Shākyamuni, the original Buddhism cannot be fully reconstructed. But one thing is certain. Buddha lives in his religion as the highest, most perfectly Enlightened One, who through his mystic vision gained the supreme and saving knowledge. Throughout all Buddhism the mighty confession of his disciple Sāriputra sounds forth like the roar of a lion: "This, Lord, is my faith in the Holy One: that there never has been nor will be, nor is there at this time any other ascetic or Brahman greater or wiser than he, the Enlightened One." [5] Artists have hit upon his essence when they have presented the Buddha of the house of Shākya as the great contemplative who has entered *nirvāna*.

Hinayanist Meditative Exercises

Buddhology for some time has devoted its best energies to probing the original character of Buddhist doctrine, but though achieving valuable results it has not succeeded in reaching its major objective. Critical textual studies of both the Pali Canon and the Sanskrit works do not permit definite or final conclusions regarding Buddha's life and teaching in precanonical Buddhism. Usually the Four Noble Truths and the Eightfold Path are regarded as the primitive Buddhist credo. Undoubtedly certain Yogic elements also belong to the primitive substance of the Buddhist religion. Even in the earliest times the Four Truths were practiced and experienced in meditation.[6] Indeed, the exercises of Buddhism are to be distinguished from Yoga chiefly in that the Buddhists, remaining true to the Middle Way, reject violent exertions and bodily chastisements.

The sutras of the Pali Canon present a wealth of descriptive accounts of mystic stages and states which are to be achieved by systematic exercises. This textual material, though engulfed in repetition and accretion, has been examined and put into order by Buddhist research.[7] By placing the four *dhyāna* stages at the center and grouping all other phenomena about them, Heiler sketches a logical over-all figure that far outdoes reality. For the impartial reader of Buddhist literature, many disharmonies, tangles, and contradictions remain. Thus, for example, the thirty-seven elements which, according to the *Mahāparinibbāna Sutta*, the Buddha is said to have explained to his disciples

shortly before his death as the essence of the way of enlightenment, are anything but a systematic summary of the mystical
doctrine of Buddhism. We will limit our discussion here to a
brief evaluation of those fragments most important for the
further development of our present study.

The Eightfold Buddhist Path of salvation leads to "right concentration" (*samādhi*). Thus the impression could be created
that the first seven stages are the means to this final goal.[8] But
on the other hand, one finds in the Hīnayāna sutras another
more comprehensive formulation according to which the way
of salvation begins with observance of the rules of morality
(*sīla*) and then leads to concentration (*samādhi*) in which the
saving knowledge (*paññā*) is acquired, which in turn is inseparable from liberation (*vimutti*). This fourfold formula,
which occurs in many texts and is repeated eight times in the
Mahāparinibbāna Sutta, represents a blueprint of the mystical
doctrine of salvation in Hīnayāna Buddhism. While contemplation is merely the means, it occupies as such the central
position. Moral discipline is directed toward concentration, for
it is the knowledge acquired in concentration that leads to final
salvation. In addition to the familiar five commandments, the
Hīnayāna Buddhist moral code demands the monastic celibacy
of religious life (*brahmacarya*), the bridling of the senses, vigi-
lance of the spirit, and self-control as prerequisites conducive
to concentration.[9] In the meditative scheme recommended by
the Pali Canon, the Four Immeasurables (*appamaññā*), which
are also called the Four Brahma Abodes (*brahmavihāra*) or
Awakenings (*bhāvanā*), exhibit especially close relations to
morality. In this exercise, the monk extends successively, in the
directions of the four cardinal points, the powers that fill his
heart: first, the power of benevolence (*mettā*); then of compassion (*karunā*); then, of sympathy (*muditā*); and finally, of
equanimity (*upekhā*). Thus "he permits the power of benevolence (of compassion, sympathy, equanimity), which fills his

mind, to extend over the whole world." [10] Through these exercises the virtues of benevolence, compassion, sympathy, and equanimity are acquired. This meditation is similarly recommended in the *Yoga Sutra*.

"Concentration is a purely spiritual activity; the seated posture of the body has merely auxiliary significance," Heiler emphasizes,[11] and yet Buddhism knows of no advanced meditation or higher mystic state apart from the cross-legged posture. This posture has belonged to the heritage of India from time immemorial. The search for its origin takes us to the dawn of history, as is shown by the figure of a meditating god excavated in Mohenjo-Daro on the Indus River.[12] The Upanishads and the early Hīnayāna sutras tell of pious ascetics and disciples of Buddha who sat in meditation beneath shady trees in cool groves and there experienced unity with Brahma or recognized the sorrow and vanity of all things earthly, thus acquiring a foretaste of *nirvāna* repose.

Quite similarly, breathing exercises belong to the ancient Indian Yoga heritage. Whereas some Yoga practices seek to suppress the awareness of breathing as the basic vital function, the "excellent and joyful" control of breath praised by the Buddha in the Hīnayāna sutras makes respiration conscious. "The monk breathes in and out consciously. When he breathes in long, he is conscious—'I will breathe in long.' When he breathes out long, he is conscious—'I will breathe out long.' When he breathes in short, he is conscious—'I will breathe in short.' When he breathes out short, he is conscious—'I will breathe out short.'" [13] The Buddhists reject the coercive inhibition of breathing practiced in Yoga. At the fourth stage of *dhyāna* breathing automatically becomes imperceptible.

The four stages of *dhyāna* (Pali: *jhāna*) and the four realms of infinity (*arūpa*), which in the Pali Canon are combined frequently in a series with a ninth stage of the destruction of consciousness and sensibility (*nirodha*), form the core of the

mystic practices in Hīnayāna Buddhism. After the conquest
of the five hindrances (*nīvarana*)—desire, hatred, slothfulness,
fear, and doubt—begins the ascent through the four stages of
dhyāna. In the first stage, that of inner composure and cessation
of desire, there still remains the image of objects, and a feeling
of delight arises. In the second stage, the release from the outer
world is accomplished and the consideration of objects has
disappeared, but joy permeates the body. In the third stage, this
feeling of joy gives way to equanimity, and spiritual contemplation becomes consummate. The fourth and highest of the
dhyāna stages is the world-removed state of equanimity
(*upekhā*), free of joy and suffering alike. Meditating on infinity,
the monk strides successively through the realms of the infinity of space, of the infinity of consciousness, of nothingness,
and of the sphere beyond consciousness and unconsciousness.
The subsequent "destruction of consciousness and sensibility"
signifies, not the final liberation in *nirvāna,* but an ecstatic state.

Among the various ways of meditation the four stages of
dhyāna take priority. According to tradition, the Buddha passed
from the fourth *dhyāna* stage into *nirvāna.* This stage opens
the door to all the higher spiritual powers which, in the manner
of Yoga, play an important role in Hīnayāna Buddhism. Among
the magic powers (*iddhi*) acquired in meditation are included
extraordinary states of consciousness and unusual bodily capacities, such as levitation, self-duplication, bodily penetration,
invisibility, touching of sun and moon, clairaudience, and
others.[14] A further miraculous fruit of the *dhyāna* states is
threefold knowledge (*tevijjā*), namely, the recollection of previous existences, a knowledge of the destiny of all beings in the
cycle of rebirths, and the knowledge of suffering and its conquest. This supreme knowledge, which is the point of departure
in Buddhist doctrine, is now perfectly comprehended on the
higher mystical level; thus the state of the saint (*arhat*) is
reached.

In this connection mention must still be made of two aids to contemplation which survive in Zen, though all other practices of Hīnayāna have disappeared completely. The schematic objects of consideration (*kammatthāna*), detailed especially in the *Mahāsattipatthāna Sutta*, are directives to psychic technique rather than to spiritual reflection. And yet they place the monk in that grave mood, engendered by contact with the fundamental truths of the transitoriness of life (*anicca*), the unreality of existence (*anattā*), and universal suffering (*dukkham*), which is a prerequisite to success in all Buddhist meditation. Zen knows no thematic considerations similar to the Hinayanist approach. However, the beginner is taken through exercises which, in a fashion similar to the recommendations of the sutras to fix the attention on the impurities and ugliness of the body, are designed exclusively to unmask beauty and to lead to an experience of human frailty. The Zen masters speak much of death and renunciation to their disciples, so that through their grasp of these basic truths illumination may come the more easily. The Zen monastery is as much pervaded by an awareness of transitoriness as are the meeting places of the *bhikkhu*.

The *kasina* exercise, likewise, leads to the state of contemplation. In this exercise an extreme degree of concentration is achieved through fixing the attention on a physical object. The monk gazes steadfastly at a circle or disk of clay or earth, or into a vessel of water, or into a fire, or at a treetop waving in the breeze (*kasina* of the four elements). Or he fastens on a spot of color, space, or light. He gazes until the "sign" has been impressed so deeply into his consciousness that he can see it as an afterimage with closed eyes as clearly as he had seen it with his eyes open.

In the meditation of Tantric Buddhism the *mandala*, which may have developed from the *kasina*, plays a similar role.[15] Zen also makes use of symbolic representations of spiritual realities which are appropriated through concentration by sensory means. Among the masters of the Wei-yang sect of Chinese Zen we encounter the exercise of the "circular figures," which is related to early Buddhist *kasina* practice. Elsewhere in Zen, symbolic representations of metaphysical truths likewise occur frequently. Often the signs serve not merely to illustrate abstract truth but also as a means of concentration.

A survey of the kinds of meditative life in Hīnayāna Buddhism reveals the extent to which mystical elements pervade the whole. Indeed, it has been maintained that "all Buddhism is permeated throughout with Yoga." [16] For every individual phenomenon in the early Buddhist meditative practice, one can find parallels in the old Indian Yoga tradition.[17] If, then, this historical setting gives rise to the conjecture that in the exercises of Hīnayāna Buddhism we are dealing chiefly with psychic techniques, so in the stages and systems of meditation we can readily recognize descriptions of mental states. Nowhere does a way open into transcendence. Hīnayāna Buddhism achieves a spiritualizing of Yoga by uniting its psychic exercises to a moral and religious quest for salvation, but it is unable to introduce any element of metaphysical knowledge. The knowledge acquired by meditation is of a practical nature and pertains to the way of salvation, namely, the cycle of rebirth and the conquest of suffering. We therefore cannot recognize the Hinayanist meditative exercises as genuine mysticism, since true mysticism, whether natural or supernatural, signifies an immediate relationship to absolute spiritual reality. In Hīnayāna Buddhism the question of the Absolute arises first in connection with the doctrine of *nirvāna*, which is of decisive significance for the whole system as well as for a possible Hīnayāna mysticism.

Nirvāna as the Goal of the Mystic Way

Etymologically, *nirvāna* signifies something negative. Derived from the verb *va*, "to blow as the wind," with the negative prefix *nir*, it denotes motionless rest, where no wind blows, the fire is quenched, the light is extinguished, the stars have set, and the saint has died.[18] "The extinction of desire, of hate, and of delusion—that, O friend, is called *nirvāna*." [19] "The body is broken, consciousness has ceased, sensibility has vanished, the forces of imagination have come to rest, and cognition has ended." [20] The saint vanishes into *nirvāna*, to use the Buddha's famous simile, as the flame of an oil lamp sinks in upon itself and expires when its fuel has been consumed. Such words and images evoke the concept of complete annihilation.[21]

At the same time, it is certain that Buddhists persistently regarded *nirvāna* as the supreme goal for which they yearned as for heaven. In the ancient collections of hymns composed by Buddhist monks and nuns, the state of final deliverance is lauded with enthusiasm. *Nirvāna* is regarded as consummate salvation, supreme blessedness, the haven of peace and isle of deliverance. Could such figures be veils without substance, enshrouding nothingness? Or do they not rather conceal a positive core? Attention was called to this contradiction in the teaching of Buddha, and he was asked whether the Perfected One would or would not exist beyond death. Buddha declined to answer this question, apparently because it is theoretical in nature and its solution is irrelevant to the one thing required, namely, the achievement of salvation. He was therefore accused of philosophical agnosticism.[22] It is possible, however, that Buddha did not wish to express himself regarding life in the beyond, since our conceptual language is not adequate to that purpose. Regarding the "other shore," the immortal sphere removed from death, nothing can be expressed with certainty in human words. That realm is accessible only in mystic ascent.

He who seeks to resolve the paradox in the Buddhist doctrine of *nirvāna* logically must resort to either a nihilistic or a realistic explanation. Both, however, are refuted by Buddha. Shākyamuni rejected as heresy both the materialistic-nihilistic ideology (*uccheda-vāda*), which knows nothing of *karma* or of deliverance, and the metaphysical doctrine of substantiality (*sassata-vāda*), which accepts the view of indestructible bodies. Perhaps the final word in Buddha's philosophy is that same Middle Way which Mahāyāna metaphysics was later to teach as the supreme wisdom. According to the Japanese Buddhologist Ui, the twelve-linked causal chain (*paticcasamuppāda*), which became transparent to Buddha in his liberating knowledge, does not signify a causal sequence in the origin of things, but rather the general law of becoming and dissolving in reciprocal dependency.[23] Like Heraclitus and Nietzsche, Buddha may have become intoxicated with "the innocence of becoming," but with this difference—that Buddha saw by mystic insight what these philosophers believed themselves to grasp by metaphysical intuition. Significantly, Buddha, just before leaving this world, comforted his followers, not with the prospect of *nirvāna*, but by pointing to the immutable law that all who are born must die and that all compounded things are subject to dissolution.[24] If, however, the usual Hinayanist view is valid, which regards the twelve-linked causal chain in the doctrine of *karma* and *samsāra* as the explanation of a continuous engendering influence working through past, present, and future, then *nirvāna* signifies liberation from the round of birth and death and hence the way out of the suffering of existence subject to *karma*. In Buddhist terminology, existence falls within the categories of the Five Elements (*skandha*),[25] which occur only in the cycle of reincarnations (*samsāra*). The land of freedom, the opposite shore, is beyond our intellectual comprehension.

The philosophy of early Buddhism, inclined as it is to skepticism and pessimism, makes no attempt at a higher ascent. The exalted words that we find in Hīnayāna Buddhism come from the lips of religiously inspired monks and nuns. Here we are in the domain of mysticism. We read: "There is an unborn, an unbecome, an unmade, an uncompounded. If there were not this unborn, unbecome, unmade, uncompounded, there would be no escape from the born, the become, the made, the compounded." [26] "The great ocean is profound, immeasurable, unfathomable. . . . So also is the Perfected One; he is profound, immeasurable, unfathomable." [27] Negations here signify complete transcendence of human thought and speech.

Similarly, the Upanishads speak of the All and the Nothing of the eternal Brahma. In the following verses, likewise cited by Oldenberg, we observe the same mystic note:

> He who has gone to rest, no measure can fathom him.
> There is no word with which to speak of him.
> What thought could grasp has been blown away,
> And thus every path to speech is barred.[28]

So too, in Hīnayāna Buddhism, the meditative techniques and the psychic training of the Yoga exercises are vitalized by the mystic *élan* nourished in the best Indian tradition. *Nirvāna* is not a remote state in the distant beyond, but can be attained now, on this side, in "the visible order" (*ditthe dhamme*). The this-worldly *nirvāna* is to be distinguished from the other-worldly one only by the persistence of the bodily substratum (*upādhi*), which no longer inhibits the Perfected One.[29]

Hīnayāna Buddhism is indebted for much of its vitality and its resilient power to the mystical element striving within it toward the Absolute, despite its theoretical negation of the Absolute. All mysticism, in keeping with its nature, maintains a relationship to ethics and metaphysics. Ample provision is made in Hīnayāna for ethical preparation. The wise control of sense and sensual desire, which the Middle Way between pleasure and mortification demands of its disciples, lays the foundation for the higher ascent of the spirit. The absence of a genuine metaphysics must have been felt as a real deficiency until the keen philosophical speculations of the Great Vehicle, vibrant with mystic spirit, appeared on the scene. In Mahayanist metaphysics a new element breaks forth, but the coherence with original Buddhism persists.

2 *Mysticism Within Mahāyāna*

Perception of Life and Mysticism

The peculiarly Buddhist perception of life tends toward mysticism, for it appears that the two sorrowful convictions upon which it rests can be resolved only in a higher knowledge. In the first place, the Buddhist believes that by the nature of things, true reality is hidden from man, and that the senses as well as ordinary understanding lead him astray and entangle him in insoluble confusion. Man lives in ignorance and deception, and only with the greatest effort and the exertion of the hidden power of his inner being can he break through the veil of illusions which his greed weaves ever more thickly about him. True reality is accessible only to the mystic view. In the second place, the common human awareness of the frailty of earthly things, so powerful in the Oriental search for truth, impels one to mysticism. The Hīnayāna Buddhist reaches the other shore, beyond desire and pain, in that he sees through the causal chain of sorrowful human existence and thus destroys ignorance. In Mahāyāna the insubstantiality of human suffering is comprehended in transcendent knowledge. Not philosophical insight but salvation is mediated through the intuitive view.

The experiences at the root of the Buddhist Way give rise to awareness of the sorrowful character of human existence, of the deceptive appearance of things, and of the ignorance of the selfish ego. The extreme human need of salvation thus becomes evident. For all Buddhists, salvation lies in the absolute knowledge which is prepared for by meditation and comprehended in mystical experience. Without this saving knowledge man is inescapably set adrift on the sea of inconstancy, which the Indian imagination has stretched to infinity. Neither logic nor piety nor asceticism, but only a higher, hidden, mystic vision, difficult to attain, can carry man to the shore of eternal liberation.

How did this view of life express itself in the new forms of Mahāyāna? What stamp did the Buddhist mysticism of the Great Vehicle receive in its peregrinations through the countries of Asia?

The Beginnings of Mahāyāna

For a long time Buddhology has struggled to distinguish between the several phases of Buddhism and to classify them in terms of their historical succession. The customary division according to the two Vehicles has had to yield more recently to a threefold division, namely, primitive Buddhism, Hīnayāna, and Mahāyāna;[1] the designation "Hīnayāna" proved to be ill suited to include the earliest Buddhist development. It was also recognized that its origins went further back than had generally been assumed. Obviously, the claims of the Mahāyāna sutras to stem directly from Shākyamuni, the founder of the Buddhist religion, cannot be upheld. Apparently the Pali Canon contains the oldest extant writings by which primitive Buddhism is to be evaluated, while the beginnings of Mahāyāna go back to the time of the early formation of the Buddhist schools.[2]

Out of bias for Pali Buddhism, the first generation of Buddhologists saw all other developments as defections from the sober and ethical spirituality of their origin. Mahāyāna was regarded both as a degeneration of and as a radical break with the original stream. Stcherbatsky depicts the departure of the new movement in terms of almost dramatic fervor:

> When we see an atheistic, soul-denying philosophic teaching of a path to personal final deliverance consisting in an absolute extinction of life, and a simple worship of the memory of its human founder—when we see it superseded by a magnificent "High Church" with a Supreme God, surrounded by a numerous pantheon and a host of saints, a religion highly devotional, highly ceremonious and clerical, with an ideal of universal salvation for all living creatures, a salvation by the divine grace of Buddhas and Bodhisattvas, a salvation not in annihilation but in eternal life— we are fully justified in maintaining that the history of religions has hardly ever witnessed such a break between new and old within the pale of what nevertheless continues to claim common descent from the same religious founder.[3]

Other scholars reached similar conclusions, their view being obscured by philosophical prejudices which prevented them from seeing the common religious life-stream that flows through apparently different forms.

At no point in the history of Buddhism is it actually possible to demonstrate an upheaval which might have brought about a radical break. Could there have been external pressures that precipitated profound changes? Or did the innovations stem from a personality of genius? Today Buddhist research is inclined to regard the transition as gradual—so gradual that contemporaries of the change were initially unaware of it.[4] This assumption is justified by the many traces of Mahāyāna doctrine which appear here and there in early Buddhist literature. Much that is new in the Mahāyāna movement does not present itself as wholly original thought. It appears likely that in the period from Alexander to Augustus, intellectual and religious influences reached India from the Occident. The development is highly complex. But it can be regarded as certain that Mahāyāna developed in organic connection with the whole of Buddhism, i.e., that it arose directly out of the Hinayanist schools. From the sources it can be seen that for a long period of time the followers of both Vehicles lived peaceably side by side in the same monasteries of the Hīnayāna observance. Intellectual-historical examination of the philosophic schools of Mahāyāna reveals that the new movement received important influences from without.

Early tendencies toward Mahāyāna teachings are to be found in the philosophically inclined Hīnayāna schools whose writings are composed in Sanskrit. The major work of Hinayanist philosophy as set forth by the Sarvāstivādins is the *Abhidharma-kośa* of Vasubandhu, a dishearteningly lifeless product without metaphysical *élan*. This *Summa* of Hīnayāna dryly catalogues all the constituent parts of reality. The materialism of the pluralistic *dharma* theory is mitigated to some extent only by the moral law of *karma*. For if even *nirvāna*, which is listed as one of the constituent elements of reality, is conceived material-istically as a lifeless residue of the processes of living, nothing is left in the end but sheer materialism. Some expositors, indeed, regard this as the real substance of Buddhism.[5] The process of salvation is divested of its metaphysical character and is pressed into a mechanistic scheme.

This materialistic-pluralistic philosophy, however, exhausting itself in a maze of innumerable hairsplitting definitions and classifications, can hardly do justice to the religious experience of Hīnayāna, Both the meditative practices and the striving toward the absolute state of *nirvāna* give evidence of the genuine religious vitality in Hīnayāna, without which the development of Mahāyāna obviously could not be explained.[6]

The gradual growth of Mahāyāna thought brings about a complete change which touches practically all the basic Buddhist concepts. In philosophy, the theory of *dharmas*, shattered by criticism, gives way to an exclusive monist doctrine. The new doctrine of virtue (*pāramitā*) with the contemplative summit of knowledge, is placed in the service of a higher wisdom. *Nir-vāna* is coupled to the cosmic Buddha-vision and, as the goal of salvation, is equated with achieving Buddhahood. Buddha, *nirvāna*, and enlightenment express the absolute side of reality, whose manifestation is the phenomenal world of *samsāra*, in which all sentient beings go astray in their search for salvation. The Bodhisattva is presented as the embodiment of enlighten-ment. All these thoughts and motifs converge. And yet Mahā-yāna proper comes into existence only when the Great Vehicle is proclaimed in conscious opposition to the less valuable Small Vehicle. It is significant that this should occur in the sutras, which claim religious authority. The power unleashing the movement stems, not from philosophical speculation, but from the inspiration of spiritual men. The sutras as the expression of the new religious consciousness are the directing force.[7] The predominant position of the mystical element becomes markedly apparent.

The Bodhisattva Ideal

As the religious way of salvation for all sentient beings, Bud-dhism possesses the appropriate vehicle (*yāna*) which ever carries man from this sorrowful earthly existence to the opposite shore. The first means of salvation is provided by the vehicle of the hearer (*śrāvaka*). The hearer who comprehends the Buddhist teaching, and follows it, acquires in contemplation (*samādhi*) his own salvation and becomes a saint (*arhat*). All the early dis-ciples of Buddha followed Shākyamuni and entered *nirvāna*. In the Pali Canon, self-enlightened Buddhas (*pratyekabuddha*) are mentioned occasionally who, through their own power, achieved perfect Buddhahood independently of the teaching of Buddha. The third vehicle, that of the Bodhisattva, is far superior to the two preceding ones; it alone is great and assures all sentient beings perfect salvation. With the highest authority the Mahāyāna sutras disclose the absolute perfection of the Bodhisattva vehicle.

Mahāyāna doctrine is developed, religiously and philosophically, with the Bodhisattva ideal as its center. The term "Bodhisattva" signifies a being "attached [*sakta*] to enlightenment" or, simply, a "being [*sattva*] of enlightenment." [8] Though perfectly enlightened and in possession of the omniscience of a Buddha, the Bodhisattva forgoes final entrance into *nirvāna* in order to aid sentient beings on their path to enlightenment. For indeed all beings participate in the Buddha-nature and can achieve total enlightenment. The Bodhisattva ideal receives its significance from the basic Mahayanist doctrine of the innate Buddha-nature of all beings.

The way of the Bodhisattva to final enlightenment, the so-called "Bodhisattva career" (*bodhisattvacarya*), could be said to correspond to the Christian way of perfection, if the Bodhisattva were nothing but the image of the perfect disciple of Buddha. But in Mahāyāna Buddhism the Bodhisattva also performs a dogmatic function, without which the salvation of sentient beings could not be realized. Therefore the Bodhisattva is accorded a religious veneration second only to Buddha himself. Removed to the realm of the miraculous and magic, his contours are often effaced and are lost in cosmic dimensions. The mystical element is thus clearly discernible, both in the way of achievement and in the final state of the Bodhisattva.

A Bodhisattva is totally dedicated to the Law of Buddha. The Bodhisattva career begins with the awakening of the thought of enlightenment (*bodhicitta*) and the taking of the vow (*pranidhāna*) to ascend tirelessly through the perfections of all the stages until supreme enlightenment is attained in order to assist all sentient beings to obtain salvation. Various Mahāyāna scriptures explain the ten stages of the Bodhisattva's career.[9] According to the *Daśabhūmika Sutra*, the first six stages consist in the mastering of the different degrees of contemplation aimed at in Hīnayāna mysticism, and especially of the four *dhyāna* stages. A meditation in ten stages on the twelve-linked causal chain is also mentioned. Having reached the seventh stage, the Bodhisattva now moves on (*dūramgamā*).

The peculiarity of the Mahāyāna Bodhisattva career in distinction to Hīnayāna is revealed in the practice of the Ten Perfect Virtues (*pāramitā*).[10] Originally, only six were named. In Mahāyāna the first five of these—namely, giving (*dāna*), morality (*śīla*), patience (*kshānti*), energy (*vīrya*), and meditation (*dhyāna*)—are directed toward the sixth, wisdom (*prajñā*), as the goal and fruit of all endeavor. Later, four further perfect virtues were added. Again the goal is excellence of knowledge (*jñāna*). *Jñāna* appears to connote primarily intellectual cognition, while *prajñā* points more to intuitive insight.[11] Evidently in the Mahayanist scheme of virtues the intellectual proficiencies occupy the key positions. With the practice of these perfections, the Bodhisattva in the seventh stage has entered the ocean of omniscience. He strides on, in his comprehension of the emptiness and unbornness of all things, to the tenth stage (*dharmameghā*), where he achieves "all forms of contemplation." Seated on a vast lotus, he possesses the concentration called the "knowledge of the Omniscient One." The sutra describes the magnificent scene of his consecration (*abhisheka*) in which he becomes manifest as the fully enlightened Buddha. But great compassion compels him to descend by skillful means from the Tushita heaven to earth, and without entering *nirvāna*, he sets out to save all sentient beings.

The Bodhisattva state is characterized by the Perfection of Wisdom (*prajñāpāramitā*). Without wisdom, the other five virtues, as well as skill in expedients, are worthless. *The Sutra of the Perfection of Wisdom* says: "Though a Bodhisattva should bestow gifts through aeons as numerous as the sands of the Ganges, and should observe morality, practice patience, apply energy, and persist in meditation . . . if he were not embraced by the Perfection of Wisdom and emptied by skill in expedients, he would fall to the level of a hearer (*śrāvaka*) or a *pratyeka-buddha*. . . ." [12] The Perfection of Wisdom is not to be realized without emptiness of the spirit. The unenlightened person hears the word "emptiness" and expresses his concept in signs. "The Way of the Bodhisattva is emptiness, or the way of that which is without sign." [13] The Perfection of Wisdom is beyond all concepts and words. But above all, the Bodhisattvas, who "find rest in one thought" (*eka-citta-prasādam*), are freed from the concept of self. "In these Bodhisattvas no perception of a self takes place, no perception of a being, no perception of a soul, no perception of a person." [14] Nor is their spirit hampered by the concept of Dharma or of the nonconcept. The Bodhisattva does not grasp at any concept; he clings to nothing. His Perfect Wisdom is void. This is the essence of highest wisdom: "A Bodhisattva-Mahāsattva should abide himself in the Perfection of *Prajñā* by abiding in emptiness." [15]

But though the Bodhisattva in possession of Perfect Wisdom sees through the emptiness of all things, he does not consummate his insights. For the sake of the salvation of sentient beings, he forgoes entrance into the eternal rest of *nirvāna*. He keeps close to the "borderline of reality" (*bhūtakoti*), never taking the step into *nirvāna* nor yet clinging to the unenlightened restlessness of *samsāra*. Though aware of the nothingness of all things and of the ultimate irrelevance of all exertions of the spirit, he never ceases to work for the benefit of sentient beings. "This logic of contradiction is what may be called the dialectics of *prajñā*." [16]

Suzuki sees in the psychology of the Bodhisattva one of the greatest achievements in the life of the spirit. He describes this curiously suspended attitude by comparisons approximating the paradox of Zen. The Bodhisattva holds "a spade in his hands and yet the tilling of the ground is done by him empty-handed. He is riding on the back of a horse and yet there is no rider in the saddle and no horse under it. He passes over the bridge, and it is not the water that flows, but the bridge." [17] The interconnection of illuminative knowledge (*prajñā*) and compassion (*karunā*) in the Bodhisattva is logically inexplicable. It remains an unsolved riddle. In vain does one seek an ontological basis. "It is again like the shooting of one arrow after another into the air by a man whose mastery of archery has attained a very high degree. He is able to keep all the arrows in the air making each arrow support the one immediately preceding. He does this as long as he wishes." [18]

In his description of Bodhisattvahood, Suzuki emphasizes the kinship of *prajñā* with Zen. At the same time, the difference between Oriental and Western mysticism becomes evident. The Bodhisattva riddle is not solved in a *coincidentia oppositorum*, a unity of opposites, nor is it resolved by the shifting to a higher level. The contradiction remains, unsolved and insoluble, but enshrouded in a veil of unreality.

The ideal of Bodhisattvahood is engendered by the spirit of India, which is indifferent as to whether or not its concepts correspond to reality. Or rather, concepts, desires, wishes, and vows are considered to be realities as fully as are men and their deeds. In the face of Buddhist negativism and idealism all things vanish into the Void. What does it matter whether a Bodhisattva ever existed or whether he can exist? In the climate of *māyā*, creative fancy generated the Bodhisattva figure, something between Buddha and man, neither male nor female, the embodiment alike of illuminated knowledge and of great compassion (*mahākarunā*). The attraction of this concept for the people proved enormous. In Mahāyāna Buddhism the Bodhisattvas became the highly praised gods of salvation for all of erring mankind. Their compassion and miraculous power were soon esteemed more highly than their illuminated knowledge, though this was the root of their acts of salvation.[19]

The unreality of the Bodhisattva ideal impairs considerably

the value of the great compassion. The admirable heroism of these enlightened beings shows itself primarily in wishes and vows. Their deeds, which achieve the salvation of sentient beings, are magic wonders performed by fantastic powers. While the Bodhisattva saves all beings, no form of a sentient being enters his mind since his knowledge abides in emptiness. As an embodiment of the cosmic Wisdom, he is, at least theoretically, an impersonal being. For the same reason, the suspended attitude of the Bodhisattva is basically different from the detached love of the Christian saint. For the saint who remains unattached to his acts of charity, looking alone to God, whose right hand knows not what his left hand does (Matt. 6:3), realizes within himself full personal freedom. He recognizes and loves his fellow man as a person, in the God to whom his spirit ascends in untrammeled flight. The act of love which he performs for the sake of God is not for that reason any less real. The recipient is indeed enriched. Something actually happens; and that it should happen, and the manner in which it happens, are important.

The Bodhisattva ideal exercised a persistent influence on the whole of Buddhism, and particularly in Zen did it bear rich fruit. Up to the present day, the Bodhisattva's vows play an important role in the life of the Zen disciple. These vows are pronounced with fervor at the very outset of the spiritual career and are constantly repeated throughout the long years of practice:

However innumerable the sentient beings, I vow to save them all.
However inexhaustible the passions, I vow to extinguish them all.
However immeasurable the *dharmas*, I vow to master them all.
However incomparable the truth of Buddha, I vow to attain it.

In the last of these four sentences the initiate binds himself to supreme enlightenment. Through his omniscient knowledge the Bodhisattva abides constantly in the realm of the Absolute.

The mystical character of intuitive insight is proper also to the enlightenment to which the Zen disciple aspires as he proceeds on the path to Bodhisattvahood.

Buddhology and Nirvāna

The Bodhisattva ideal is the new creative force motivating Mahāyāna. The Mahāyāna development, which first proceeds without break from Hīnayāna, ends by transforming all basic Buddhist concepts. Japanese scholars regard the evolution of Buddhist dogma as the chief characteristic of Mahāyāna. For this reason they place the beginning of the new movement in the Docetic tendencies of the Mahāsāmghikas.[20] The various embellishments of the Buddha figure, an early outgrowth of a natural impulse of veneration, at the outset scarcely touched the substance of his teaching.

The dogmatic concepts of Western Docetism are remote from Buddhist thought. Buddhism draws no boundary between man and God.[21] The divine beings who appear in the sutras, in cult, and in art stem mostly from mythology and are classified with the sentient beings who move in the birth-and-death cycles. The elevation of Buddha into the superhuman realm takes on significance when it gives rise to metaphysical speculations about the Absolute. Emerging originally from the multitude of errant beings in need of salvation, the Buddha transcends the boundary so definitively as to belong to absolute reality. He ceases to belong to the merely human side. His earthly origin, though not forgotten, is nonetheless reduced to an insignificant phase in the endless history of his acts of grace. Essentially, he *is* the Absolute.

This is the potent new discovery of Mahāyāna, which was anticipated religiously by the growing tendency toward ritual worship, and philosophically through an influx of Indian monistic pantheism. In the Mahayanist view, the Buddha is pri-

marily and essentially a transcendent being. But since Buddhism
permits no logical categories for the description of otherworldly
reality, and since it denies substantiality and limits causality to
the realm of becoming in *samsāra,* the Mahayanists could not
regard Buddha as God and Creator. His being lies beyond all
conceptual expression and is ineffably mysterious. The identification of the final absolute mystic state of *nirvāna* with the
Buddha arose consistently out of Mahāyāna Buddhology. But
the world of becoming also is veiled in the mystery of Buddha.
The enlightened eye of *prajñā* beholds the universal reality of
Buddha, namely, the unity of *samsāra* and *nirvāna.*

The consummate expression of the new Buddhology is to be
found in the doctrine of the Three Buddha-Bodies, which belongs to the central dogma of Mahāyāna and is accepted by all
schools.[22] The diverse and contradictory aspects of Buddhist
doctrine were systematized and brought into final form only at
a late date in the philosophical school of the Yogācāra. As a rule
the three Buddha-bodies are designated as (1) "the Transformation Body" (*nirmanakāya*)—later sects here distinguish the
complete manifestation of the Perfected One (e.g., that of
Shākyamuni) and the partial manifestations (as the appearance
of the great Buddhist teachers); (2) "the Body of Enjoyment"
(*sambhogakāya*)—the idealized figure of Buddha, which invites
personification (e.g., the famous Buddha Amitābha [Jap.:
Amida]); and (3) "the Cosmic Body" of the Dharma (*dharmakāya*)—which is none other than the ultimate reality of
Buddhahood itself.

Obviously, in this Buddhist view the most diverse concepts
can be satisfied. The infinite phenomenal possibilities invented
by fantasy provide the substance for a pantheon of numerous
Buddhas, which nonetheless possesses its unity in the single
Buddha-nature of the *dharmakāya.* The urge to virtual worship
was enabled to clothe the blessed body of Buddha in an in-
effable splendor of light and beauty, to endow it with infinite

wisdom, power, and compassion, and to depict the Pure Buddha-Land as the home of all human yearning. The basic metaphysics of this Buddhology is pantheistic or, as the Buddhists prefer to say, cosmotheistic. The corresponding anthropology is mystical. The deepest concern of man must be the attainment of the enlightened view, for only the illumined one can grasp the perfect Buddha-reality. Enlightenment signifies at the same time the realization of man's own deepest self, namely, the Buddha-nature inherent in all life.

The superiority of Mahāyāna to Hīnayāna derives chiefly from its teaching of a mystic, monistic vision which promises to satisfy to a large extent the fundamental yearning of the human spirit for unity.[23] The concept of a double truth, one exoteric and involved in the plurality of things, the other esoteric, in which All and Nothing coincide, permeates the whole of Indian thought, and is especially pronounced in Mahāyāna. This problem is most advanced philosophically in the dialectics of Nāgārjuna, whose radical, logical, and ontological criticism pushes Buddhist philosophy close to the borders of nihilism. Significantly, it is saved from this conclusion, not by philosophical speculation, but through mystical intuition alone. Here lies the difference from the genuine philosophical position of Shankara. The philosophy of Nāgārjuna rejoins the Buddhist mystic way of salvation.

Among the religious practices of Mahāyāna, meditation stands out, since it alone can lead to the realization of the monistic vision. The personal veneration as an outgrowth of popular piety, no matter how preponderant in terms of the essence of Mahāyāna, remains on a secondary plane. In all the Mahayanist schools, the meditative element plays a more or less important role. This is also true in Amidism, where the endless repetition of the Buddha's name lulls the soul into a state of complete rest.[24] Tantrism and Zen in different ways pursue the same objective, namely, the breakthrough to a higher, hidden truth, the knowledge of which transfers the illuminated one into the sphere of the Absolute, where All is One and Buddha is the One.

3 *The Mahāyāna Sutras and Zen*

The Position of Zen in Intellectual History

Ever since Zen was introduced to the Western world, it has
aroused increasing interest and esteem, not merely among a few
Orientalists but among wide circles of the intellectually alert
who are concerned with the inner renewal and spiritual growth
of man. In their promotion of Zen, its admirers fall into differ-
ing groups in accordance with their viewpoints.

The Buddhist societies working in America and Europe seek
to adapt themselves to Western understanding. Nonetheless the
tie with Buddhism seems to them to be disadvantageous to the
Zen movement. Therefore some advocates of Zen in the West
seek to extract its true kernel from the Buddhist shell.

The representatives of modern psychology, who detect a relationship between Zen and depth psychology, believe that the
introduction of Zen methods will help in the guidance of men,
both the healthy and the psychopathic, toward true individua-
tion. The question arises, of course, whether Zen can be separated from Buddhism without harm to its real substance, and
whether without religious bonds it will remain meaningful
and effective. In other words, can Zen be used simply as a
method toward man's self-realization, in the same way as Yoga
is employed?

A comparison between Zen and Yoga forces us to notice the substantial differences in their historical settings. Admittedly, in its origin Yoga was bound up with the religion of India, but it allied itself readily with varied philosophical and religious systems, such as Sāmkhyā, Bhakti Yoga, and Hīnayāna Buddhism. Since it lacked a sharply defined religious character, it could easily be secularized by a psychology which sought to enhance its own "doctrine of salvation" by the assimilation of ancient Oriental wisdom. In any event there remain some unclarified problems in the relationship of Yoga to religion and psychotherapy.

With regard to Zen, however, the historical situation is different. Sprung out of Buddhist soil and cultivated as a school in its own right, with a hierarchical organization and an established temple system as it flourishes today in Japan, Zen is completely Buddhist. Suzuki, who knows the real situation and rightly maintains the unity of all Buddhism, regards Zen, whose "main ideas are derived from Buddhism," as "a legitimate development of the latter." [1] His books, however, being distinguished by lively suggestiveness, abundance of material, and absorbing exposition but not by clear order and transparent logic, have contributed to conceptual confusion. Over and over Suzuki stresses the independence and incomparability of Zen as nothing other than personal experience which, in its pure subjectivity, forgoes all sub- and superstructures, appears spontaneously without cause, and is inexpressible in words. Indeed, this experience is so far beyond words that it transcends and embraces all philosophy and theology. All clear delineations vanish in Suzuki's expositions for his European-American audience. For him, Zen is an absolute, and one cannot define its place in intellectual history.

Suzuki's scholarly works contain much valuable material regarding the relationship of Zen to Mahāyāna Buddhism. These works have proved helpful in the attempt to trace the roots of

Zen to the early Mahāyāna sutras, out of which soil it arose under the influence of Chinese thought. For, to comprehend the formative forces of Zen, one must consider equally its origin in Mahāyāna and the peculiar impulse of the Chinese spirit.

We set forth first the mystic utterances in the Mahāyāna sutras which later crystallized in Zen. This inquiry is important, not merely historically, but also for our understanding and evaluation of Zen. All mysticism is conditioned in character by the spiritual setting in which it originated and flourished. Thus Zen is stamped with the Chinese and Japanese religiosity of Mahāyāna Buddhism.

Prajñāpāramitā—Transcendental Wisdom

All the schools of Mahāyāna Buddhism are based on a group of sutras known by the name of *Prajñāpāramitā*—the *Sutras of Transcendental Wisdom*—the oldest portions of which apparently go back to the first century B.C.[2] These sutras are not philosophical treatises but a religious message. The new doctrine is proclaimed authoritatively and is couched in fanciful and magical images and symbols, but lacks a metaphysical basis. The very word is the "Void" (*śūnya*), and its assertion goes far beyond the Hinayanist negation of substantial reality and the doctrine of Nonego and the inconstancy of all things. All phenomena as such, including the external, visible world as well as the subjective inner world with its rational knowledge, are declared "void."[3] This emptiness of all reality is beheld by the enlightened eye of wisdom (*prajñā*), the organ of intuitive knowledge, which brings about all-knowing (*sarvajñatā*). The psychic process is designated as enlightenment (*bodhi*), and enlightenment brings with it omniscience as its fruit. Thus wisdom, enlightenment, and omniscience are regarded as coordinate and inseparable. When the Bodhisattva, in the possession of supreme enlightenment, nonetheless forgoes its fruit, omniscience, he does so out of compassion for errant sentient beings to whose salvation from the cycle of rebirths he has dedicated himself.

Negativism and paradox are the striking characteristics of the proclamation of the supreme transcendental wisdom. With incomparable emphasis and countless repetition, the sutras inculcate the paradox of "the Void." In the *Diamond Sutra* we read:

> The Lord continued: "What do you think, Subhuti, can the Tathāgata be seen by the possession of his marks?"—Subhuti replied: "No indeed, O Lord. And why? What has been taught by the Tathāgata as the possession of marks, that is truly a no-possession of no-marks."
>
> The Tathāgata spoke of the "heap of merit" as a non-heap. That is how the Tathāgata speaks of "heap of merit" . . .
>
> The Tathāgata has taught that the dharmas special to the Buddhas are just as not a Buddha's special dharmas . . .
>
> Just that which the Tathāgata has taught as the wisdom which has gone beyond, just that He has taught as not gone beyond . . .
>
> The Tathāgata has taught this as the highest (*paramā*) perfection (*pāramitā*). And what the Tathāgata teaches as the highest perfection, that also innumerable Blessed Buddhas do teach . . .[4]

No effort is too great to grasp the emptiness of all things, for "deep is the designation of the empty, the markless, the inclinationless, the nonachieving, the nonoriginating, the nonbeing, the passionless, the annihilation, the extinction, the expiration."[5]

In the "Religion of the *Prajñāpāramitā*,"[6] negativism and paradox are not to be understood relativistically or nihilistically, nor yet dialectically; rather, they stand in the service of the mystical intuition of truth. After the eye of wisdom has comprehended the Void, has unmasked all false appearance, and has destroyed attachment to illusory concepts, it beholds, in enlightenment, things as they are, and also the human spirit, in the simple *thusness* of being. "Thusness" (*tathatā*), in

the *Prajñāpāramitā Sutras,* is the only positive expression regarding reality. All other assertions are stated negatively. And
even regarding thusness, the sutra is able to say that it "has not
come, not gone," is "not past, not future, not present," "without change and without distinction," "a thusness without
duality . . . a nondualistic thusness." [7]

The *Prajñāpāramitā Sutras* lead to the religious experience
in which both the emptiness of things and their thusness are
comprehended, simultaneously and in one, as the passing darkness and the coming light. The Void is unutterable and unfathomable, without growth or diminution. "Thusness is this
matchless, perfect enlightenment. And this thusness neither increases nor decreases." [8] In the same way the sutra speaks of
enlightenment: "The perfection of knowledge is empty; it neither increases nor decreases." [9] Emptiness, thusness, and the
wisdom of perfect knowledge all stand on the same plane, exalted above the fluctuation of change, and thus compose the
absolute state attained in mystical experience.

Zen regards itself rightly as the legitimate heir of the wisdom
of those deep and mystically dark sutras which, according to
the legend, could not be comprehended by contemporaries
and were preserved in the Serpent Palace until the time when
they were brought forth by Nāgārjuna, the bold thinker and
enlightened saint.[10] Nāgārjuna, probably in the second century A.D., built up his philosophy of the Middle Way (*mādhyamika*) on the *Sutras of Transcendental Wisdom,* which have
as their apex intuitive enlightenment. Revered as a Bodhisattva
throughout all Mahāyāna Buddhism, Nāgārjuna is reckoned
among the patriarchs by both mystical schools, the Tantrist
Shingon and Zen, and is regarded as the most important Indian link in the long chain of witnesses since Shākyamuni.
The chief elements in the doctrine of Transcendental Wisdom
—negativism, paradox, religious experience in intuitive cognition, the comprehension of things in their thusness—all flowed

from the *Prajñāpāramitā Sutras* through Nāgārjuna into Zen, embedding themselves deeply in its substance.

Paradox could unfold with virtuosity in the peculiar spiritual climate of Zen. The comprehension of things in their thusness is what the Chinese Zen masters were to call enlightenment in daily life. The stating of a simple fact in ordinary life as the answer to the profound inquiry of a *kōan* frequently leads to sudden insight.

> A monk once asked Chao-chou, "Master, I am still a novice. Show me the way!" Chao-chou said, "Have you finished your breakfast?" "I have," replied the monk. "Then go wash your bowl!" Thereupon the monk was enlightened.[11]

Suzuki cites as illustrations of *"prajñā* as handled by Zen masters" a number of similar instances, among them the following pregnant pronouncement of a Chinese Zen master from the early Ming period (fourteenth century):

> Yün-mên one day produced his staff before an assembly of monks and said: "Common people naïvely take it for a reality; the two Yānas analyze it and declare it to be non-existent; the Pratyekabuddhas declare it to be a Māyā-like existence; and the Bodhisattvas accept it as it is, declaring it empty. As regards Zen followers, when they see a staff, they simply call it a staff. If they want to walk, they just walk; if they want to sit, they just sit. They should not in any circumstances be ruffled and distracted.[12]

Here metaphysical insight into the thusness of things has been made into a concrete way of life, which derives its validity from the Mahayanist doctrine of Transcendental Wisdom. Hui-nêng, the Sixth Patriarch and one of the greatest figures in Chinese Zen, was awakened to the great enlightenment by this verse from the *Diamond Sutra*: "Let your mind take its rise without fixing it anywhere." [13]

The *Prajñāpāramitā Sutras* are eagerly studied and recited in Zen monasteries even today, especially the brief *Prajñāpāramitā-hridaya Sutra*. The magic formula at the end, which seems

to contradict the metaphysical spirit of the sutra, is regarded by
Suzuki as a *kōan*.[14] Indeed, he regards the whole sutra as an introduction to religious experience in accordance with the *kōan*.
By means of negation and paradox, the inadequacy of rational
understanding as a cognitive channel for the realization of actual reality and ultimate truth is driven home. The negations
are the indispensable prerequisite for a breakthrough to the
affirmation which arises in the comprehension of thusness.
Thus sutra and *kōan*, each in its own way, arouse the same
psychic process of enlightenment.

Religious Cosmotheism in the Avatamsaka Sutras

European literature gives scant information regarding the content of the many volumes in the group of the *Avatamsaka
Sutras*, which in China gave rise to the school of Hua-yen.
This school, transplanted to Japan as the Kegon school, played
an important role in the Buddhism of the Nara era. Even
down to the present, none of the *Avatamsaka Sutras* has as yet
been fully translated into a European language. Isolated quotations alone cannot convey the full religious impact of these
sutras.

Here again the essays of Suzuki offer the European reader
considerable insight.[15] Couched in light, paraphrastic form,
they not merely set forth the basic ideas of the *Avatamsaka Sutras* but also make the poetic texture of this religiously inspired
work vividly evident. The connection between Zen and the
Avatamsaka Sutras thereby becomes clear. To Suzuki, Zen "is
the practical consummation of Buddhist thought in China and
the Kegon (*Avatamsaka*) philosophy is its theoretical culmina-
tion." The two are related in this manner so that "the philosophy of Zen is Kegon and the teaching of Kegon bears its fruit
in the life of Zen." [16]

The basic core of the religious proclamation of the *Avatam-saka Sutras* is the central Mahayanist doctrine, i.e., the Buddha-hood of all sentient beings, the identity of the absolute state in *nirvāna* and the relative phenomenal world in *samsāra*, and the enlightened way of the Bodhisattva, who is endowed with wisdom (*prajñā*) and compassion (*karunā*) in order to guide errant beings, caught in the cycle of rebirths, to Buddhahood. The *Avatamsaka Sutras* also prefer the negative mode of expression, the *theologia negativa* of the school of Transcendental Wisdom, which stems from the knowledge of the emptiness of all things.

The conviction that the supreme liberating knowledge is attained by intuitive insight is likewise common to all Mahāyāna. The *Avatamsaka Sutras* state impressively the reciprocal relationship and interpenetration of the absolute Buddha-nature and the world of individual phenomena. The Buddha is all, and all is the Buddha. But this inclusive unity does not rob the phenomena of their individual character. Certainly things do not possess a self-nature, for all self-nature is swallowed up in identity with the Buddha. And yet each individual thing has its special meaning in the universe.

Examples help to make clear this interpenetration. There is the analogy of Indra's net, made of precious gems, hanging over Indra's palace. "In each of these gems are found reflected all the other gems composing the net; therefore, when it is picked up, we see in it not only the entirety of the net, but every one of the gems therein." [17] Or, here is a burning candle, surrounded on all sides by mirrors which reflect in a perfect interplay of lights the central light of the candle and the light as reflected by the other mirrors. [18] The *Avatamsaka Sutras* do not weary of depicting the interrelatedness and interpenetration of all things. In every particle of dust the whole universe is contained, and every particle of dust engenders all the powers of the cosmos. For every particle of dust is the Buddha, who in a single pore of his skin can reveal the history of all the worlds from their beginning until their destruction.

The *Avatamsaka Sutras* depict the universal reality of the Buddha under the figure of the Tower of Maitreya, the Buddha of the future, who represents the absolute Dharma-world (*dharmadhātu*), or the cosmic Buddha-body. According to the explanation of the sutra, in this tower "the objects are arrayed in such a way that their mutual separateness no more exists, as they are all fused, but each object thereby never loses its individuality, for the image of the Maitreya devotee is reflected in each one of the objects, and this not only in specific quarters, but everywhere all over the Tower, so that there is a thoroughgoing mutual interreflection of images." [19] The final goal of the efforts of all sentient beings is entrance into the Tower of Maitreya, which signifies the attainment of perfect enlightenment, or entrance into the light of the Dharma-world, in which there will be no more spatial juxtaposition, since all things, illumined by one light, interpenetrate one another in the unity of Buddha. The enlightened one abides nowhere and everywhere; he is infinite light. As he possesses Buddha in every particle of dust, he grasps eternity in every moment. The boundaries of space and time have melted away. The Buddha-reality is pure spirit.

The doctrine of the *Avatamsaka* is a religious cosmotheism. The sutra which tells of the pilgrimage of Sudana to the Tower of Maitreya, and of the glories of this miraculous tower, brings home to the believer, in trembling awe, the total reality and unlimited power of Buddha. But the supreme mystery revealed to him is that this world of appearances, and every manifestation in it, as well as the Tower of Maitreya itself, are nothing other than the Buddha.

While the *Avatamsaka Sutras* proclaim the oneness of the Buddha-reality as a religious revelation, the Chinese school of

Hua-yen formulated the daring symbolism of the *Avatamsaka* in philosophical concepts. Thus there arose the highly speculative monistic metaphysics of Hua-yen (Jap.: Kegon). The Fifth Patriarch of the Hua-yen school, Kuei-feng Tsung-mi (779-841), one of the most important figures in Chinese Buddhism, appears in Zen genealogy as the head of one of the flourishing Zen schools of his time.[20] This learned monk, as a Zen disciple devoted to the mystic way of illumination, regarded the Kegon doctrine as the highest expression of the Buddhatruth. This is evident in his many writings, especially in the *Treatise on the Origin of Man,* which is still used as an introduction to Buddhist thought and studied eagerly in temples today. In his interpretation of Buddhist doctrine, Fa-yen, the founder of one of the "Five Houses" in Chinese Zen (see Chapter 7), emphasizes the basic principle of Kegon metaphysics, which is sameness in difference and difference in sameness.[21] During the Sung era the inner affinity of Zen to Kegon led to a complete assimilation of the latter by the Chinese Zen masters. The preference for the *Avatamsaka Sutras* and for Kegon metaphysics persists undiminished in Japan today.

The attitude toward nature peculiar to Zen disciples draws its nourishment from the cosmotheistic world-view set forth so magnificently in the *Avatamsaka Sutras.* The religiously rooted conviction of the divine unity of the universe permits the search for the fulfillment of one's own deepest being by fusion with nature. Life in the Zen monastery is immersed in nature. The natural phenomena in the flow of changing seasons determine the rhythm of psychic life. With loving devotion, the novice watches the hawk as it circles the mountain peak on whose slope the monastery rests. Every living being and every minute thing is significant, since even the tiniest thing contains the whole mystery. Reverence for the sanctity of the universe vibrates through Zen art, and permeates the whole of ancient Japanese culture. It is from this religious mooring that the

Japanese appreciation of nature must be understood. To be sure, its inadequacies and limitations derive in the last analysis from an inevitable subsidence into a pessimistic and depersonalizing naturalism.

A further relationship between Kegon and Zen remains to be traced. Kegon metaphysics is idealistic, as is the mainstream of Mahayanist philosophy. The Absolute Being, Buddha, is spirit. The corporeal world possesses no nature of its own. Things derive all reality from the idea, from the spirit (*cittamātram*). Zen was able to achieve a high degree of spiritualization, which it passed on to Japanese art and culture. Zen painters never paint material things in their materiality. Their delicate ink sketches disclose the spiritual substance without sacrificing the objectivity of their themes. The things thus depicted are illuminated and permit their substance, the spirit, to be seen. For true reality is spirit and the spirit is embodied in material things. The Eastern mind transcends, by spiritual insight, "objectivity and abstraction, which for us are mutually exclusive opposites or poles of tension." "Thus even in a picture which is detached from the empirical, phenomenal world, there can be an abundance of concrete reality." [22]

The Vimalikīrti Sutra—
The Way of Enlightenment for All

Nowhere are the spirit and doctrine of Mahāyāna expressed more attractively than in the *Vimalikīrti Sutra*. This sutra was explained by many Chinese and Japanese commentators, the most famous of whom was the Japanese prince regent and devout promoter of Buddhism, Shōtoku Taishi (574-622). The entire sutra has been translated into English and German,[23] and provides even the common reader with an easily readable and stimulating text.

The central figure is the pious householder (*grhapati*), Vimalikīrti, who, without having been ordained a monk, attained a high degree of enlightenment as a layman, and throughout his career consistently lived the Bodhisattva life. Whether his personality is historical or only fictitious we do not know. This sutra ministers to lay Buddhism as developed in Mahāyāna and demonstrates the universal character of the Buddhist way of salvation. In doctrinal content it differs little from the other Mahāyāna sutras. Because of its strong emphasis on enlightenment, Zen devotees have always been attracted by it. We shall mention only some of its characteristics most akin to Zen.

Vimalikīrti teaches right meditation. Right meditation is concentration of the spirit even while one is engaged in worldly activities. Such meditation preserves inner tranquillity and consists in permitting "the mind to dwell neither within nor without [the self]. . . . To sit thus is not necessarily a quiet sitting." [24]

Vimalikīrti teaches the right kind of begging. "The begging of alms should be done not for the sake of eating. Thou shouldst accept food not cherishing the thought of acceptance. . . . One who eats in such a manner, neither with passions nor without them, is neither engaged in meditation nor awakened from it, abides neither in this world nor in *nirvāna*." [25]

Vimalikīrti shows the right way to preach the law to the novices. "Thou shouldst enter into meditation and examine the minds of those people before thou wouldst preach. Filthy food should never be put into a jewelled bowl. . . . A beryl should not be taken for a crystal. . . . A great ocean can never be put into the footprints of a cow." [26]

Vimalikīrti bases these and similar instructions on his knowledge of the emptiness of all things. All earthly entanglements, all human states of being such as sickness and pain, or desire and guilt, are unreal and empty. The body of the Tathāgata knows neither sickness nor pain, neither desire nor passion. It is unconditioned. But, counseled Vimalikīrti, "Go, never be ashamed of begging for milk. . . . The Buddha . . . has brought illness on himself only in order to awaken all beings to enlightenment." [27] His illness is an empty appearance. So likewise his compassion is not compassion of a human kind.

The language of this sutra is concrete and impressive. Spiced with analogies and examples, it is particularly attractive to the layman, who learns that the way of enlightenment can be pursued in ordinary, everyday life. Everything depends on the proper spiritual state. Without destruction of the body, the enlightened one lives as in *nirvāna*. It is the "state of being neither released nor bound." [28] The sutra sharply delineates this suspended state of being in which one "ought neither to abandon the created nor to attach himself to the uncreated." [29] It is the paradox of the Bodhisattva existence which beckons on the way to enlightenment.

At the climax of the sutra, Zen appears unmistakably as ultimate Wisdom. Thirty-two Bodhisattvas sought to explain in words the doctrine of nonduality (*advaya*), each one setting forth the solution of a pair of opposites, such as becoming and dissolving, purity and impurity, ego and outer world, *samsāra* and *nirvāna*. Finally Manjuśrī, the Bodhisattva of Wisdom, spoke: "According to my view, with regard to all things there is nothing to be said nor to be expressed, nor to be thought about them; they transcend all questioning and answering. This is to enter into the doctrine of nonduality. Thereupon he requested Vimalikīrti to state his view. "Vimalikīrti remained silent and said not a word." For this the Bodhisattva of Wisdom praised him, saying, "Well done, well done, ultimately not to have any letters or words, this is indeed to enter the doctrine of nonduality. [30] This is precisely the viewpoint of Zen. The unity which transcends all contradictions is unutterable.

For this reason, all the masters of Zen show a reticence about words similar to that of Vimalikīrti. "An intelligent man never adheres. The letter is far from the substance of the matter, and in the substance the letter does not exist." [31] One wonders whether the disciples of Zen also recognized their ideal in the Buddha-land described by the sutra. "There is a pure land of Buddha where one performs Buddha work by means of solitude, silence, wordlessness, and uncreatedness." [32] As he who has attained enlightenment knows, out of the non-acting of silence flows pure activity.

The Psychological View of the Process of Enlightenment in the Lankāvatāra Sutra

For our knowledge of the *Lankāvatāra Sutra* we likewise owe much to Suzuki's comprehensive volume of studies on this difficult but most interesting sutra. Of all the sacred scriptures of Buddhism, this sutra comes closest to Zen. According to Zen tradition Bodhidharma, the founder of the Zen school in China, once gave a copy of the four-volume translation of the *Lankāvatāra Sutra* in Chinese to his disciple Hui-k'o, saying: "As I observe, there are no other sutras in China but this; you take it for your guidance, and you will naturally save the world." [33]

Bodhidharma, and even more so his disciple Hui-k'o, are said to have based their "way of enlightenment" on this sutra, which for a long time continued to be held in high esteem among the Chinese Zen masters. But because of its obscure style and enigmatic phrasing, it could not maintain its preferred position indefinitely. The Fifth Patriarch, Hung-jên, recommended to his disciple Hui-nêng the *Diamond Sutra,* which belongs to the sutras of Transcendental Wisdom. From then on, it was this sutra that played the leading role.

The rejection of all sutras by Zen masters is of much later date. Those members of the Zen school who, during the Sung era, repudiated all sutra teachings, mistakenly justified their extremism by basing it on Bodhidharma. Even Suzuki has to admit that in their attempt to deny a relationship between

Bodhidharma and the *Lankāvatāra Sutra* they went too far. According to Suzuki, "the teaching of Zen is not derived from the *Lankāvatāra*, but is only confirmed by it." [34]

The text of the sutra consists primarily of a dialogue between the Buddha and the Bodhisattva Mahāmati. The Bodhisattva asks the Buddha to throw light on one hundred and eight questions. The questions, and Buddha's answers as well, are a singular mixture of profound philosophy and trite, often contradictory, platitudes. They are followed by a long series of negations, quite unrelated to the hundred and eight questions, but nonetheless accepted as answers. The conspicuously irrational character of this sutra demonstrates its close relationship to Zen. Possibly the obscure allusions and the odd replies may have a function similar to that of the *kōan* in Zen, namely, to unmask the inadequacy of reason and hence point to the way of pure experience. This sutra—in contrast to other writings—has a strongly subjective bias, stressing the psychological conditions of the process of enlightenment. For this reason, as Suzuki believes, Bodhidharma treasured it above all others. In dating this sutra, one must note the highly evolved understanding of psychic structures.[35]

All Mahāyāna sutras agree in the basic thesis that the supreme liberating knowledge of the ultimate truth cannot be acquired without inner enlightenment. There is also considerable agreement among them regarding the metaphysical implications of the enlightened view. The *Lankāvatāra Sutra* at no point runs counter to the general tendency of the monistic and idealistic teaching of the Great Vehicle. The special interest of this sutra in the psychic aspects of the process of enlightenment is evident in its preference for expressions which describe states and changes of the soul of the subject. In an exhaustive study of this terminology, Suzuki finds this emphasis on practical inner experience, in preference to philosophical, metaphysical insights, expressed in such Sanskrit terms as *gocara, lakshana, gati, gatigama,* and *adhigama.*[36]

The Supreme Knowledge comprehends the emptiness (*śūn-yatā*) of all things; it grasps reality in its thusness (*yathābhū-tam*) and touches the unborn (*anutpāda*) essence of the Buddha. The enlightened view is acquired through a unique and sudden turning (*parāvritti*) which takes place at the very base of consciousness after the negation of all individuality and particularity. The mind comprehends that the outer world is but a manifestation of one's own spirit, and at the root of the faculty of discrimination occurs an upheaval which is libera-tion and not destruction.[37]

The psychology of the sutra is based on the theory of the "store-consciousness" (*ālayavijñāna*). This is regarded as a su-perindividual, universal consciousness, from which issue the seven other consciousnesses—together accounting for the total conscious life of man, from ego-consciousness to cosmic-consciousness. The store-consciousness is identical with the im-personal womb of the Perfected One (*tathāgatagarbha*), which is the source of all emanations in the transitory world of re-births, and in which the seeds (*bīja*) of all things are preserved. When, for reasons that elude explanation, the seeds are set in motion, the unconscious recollection of all activities, which re-sides in the store-consciousness, acts as a delicate fragrance (*vāsanā*) and stimulates the developing psychic processes. The narcotic effect of this deceptive "fragrance," which propels sentient beings in ignorance and desire through the realm of reincarnations, is broken through by the spiritual upheaval that leads to enlightenment. The impulse for this experience comes ultimately from wisdom (*prajñā*) which makes possible the re-turn from the multiplicity of appearances to unity.

In enlightenment the eye of wisdom is opened to an intui-tive view of being which, in the religious language of Mahāyāna, is identical with entrance into the cosmic Buddha-body or *nirvāna*. In an approximation to depth psychology, Suzuki, referring to the Sanskrit term *parinishpanna*, which signifies the perfection of knowledge, interprets this perfect knowledge transcending all duality as the self-realization of man.[38] Similarly the Sixth Patriarch, Hui-nêng, speaks of the "seeing into one's own nature" or of "beholding one's original countenance before birth" as the way to realization of the Buddha-nature which exists in all living beings. Later we will discuss the place of Hui-nêng in the history of Buddhist thought; his doctrine of enlightenment combines the basic concepts of Mahāyāna with Taoist influence. Hui-nêng stands outside the tradition of the *Lankāvatāra Sutra*. Rather, he approximates the school of Transcendental Wisdom, which regards "the primordial purity of the mind"—a concept first formulated by the Mahāsāmghikas —as a prerequisite to the attainment of Buddhahood.[39]

With regard to the relationship between the *Lankāvatāra Sutra* and Zen, the doctrine of instantaneous enlightenment is important. Among the questions which the Bodhisattva Mahāmati addresses to the Buddha is this one: "Is the cleansing which is effected by the Buddha instantaneous or by degrees . . . ?" Unfortunately, the text is not clear in the answer. The Chinese translations disagree, while the Sanskrit original is garbled. According to Suzuki, the answer of the sutra is, "Sometimes instantaneously, sometimes by degrees." And he explains further that in any case, even in gradual purification, the initiate experiences the inner change suddenly in his consciousness. "The process needed by the Buddha for the cleansing is sometimes gradual and sometimes abrupt. But the notion of revulsion or up-turning (*parāvritti*) leads us to imagine the process to be abrupt rather than gradual, while in our actual experience of life what the psychologist calls conversion takes place in either way, gradual or abrupt. . . . Psychologically this is a phenomenon suddenly happening in the consciousness. When a man was walking in a certain direction all the time, his steps are all of a sudden made to turn back; he faces now the North instead of the South. This abrupt shift of the vista is a revolution, revulsion; he is sure to be strongly conscious of the transformation." [40]

Just as the ineffability of inner experience is a common characteristic of all mystical doctrines, so in Mahāyāna the immediate view of truth achieved in enlightenment is regarded as inexpressible in human concepts and words. But the *Lankāvatāra Sutra* advances beyond this point in the repudiation of words as the vehicle of expression, and in so doing serves as a model to Zen, for it speaks of some Buddha-lands where "the Buddha-teaching is carried out by mere gazing, or by the contraction of the facial muscles, or by the raising of the eyebrows, by frowning or smiling, by clearing the throat, by the twinkling of an eye, by merely thinking, or by a motion of some kind." [41] Zen is well known to have invented a motley abundance of such expressions of enlightenment. We read of Zen masters who grimaced or lifted a finger or uttered a cry to indicate supreme enlightenment. In this they found themselves following the Buddha, who "in his sermon on the Vulture Peak once held up a flower and displayed it to the assembled multitude." Master Wu-mên celebrates this episode, in which the transmission of supreme truth "apart from written signs and words" is said to have begun, in the following lines of verse:

The Great Serpent comes, turns the flower
And shows it.
Kāshyapa distorts his countenance.
Men and heaven remain dark. [42]

According to Japanese exegetes, the final line signifies unutterable enlightenment. While the disciple Kāshyapa, touched by the spirit of Buddha, merely distorts his face, heaven and earth remain mute.

The rejection of words is not without danger. He who rejects the word, the loftiest revelation of the human spirit, sinks readily to a subhuman level. The Zen masters, in resorting to gestures, grimaces, and all possible signs, not infrequently end in the grotesque. One cannot unconditionally approve their attitude toward language. The basic error is apparent already in the *Lankāvatāra Sutra*: it regards the relationship between syllables (*akshara*) and reality (*tattvam*), word (*ruta*) and meaning (*artha*), and doctrine (*deśanā*) and truth (*siddhānta*) as merely external, similar to the finger with which one points to the moon.[43] Fingertip and moon remain infinitely separate.

The words of Master Wu-mên are similar: "It is as one striking at the moon with his staff, or as one scratching an itching foot separated from him by his shoe." [44] Analogies should not be forced. True, all mystics speak in lofty tones of the inadequacy of words. But the doctrine of enlightenment in Mahāyāna seems to deny the inner relationship between word and reality. Language, it says, remains fundamentally in the realm of false discriminations and attachments, and is basically subject to error. Therefore meditation must avoid language, since only thus can contact with truth be achieved. The only way to reality is to turn inward, where alone truth can be experienced. "The truth has indeed never been preached by the Buddha, seeing that one has to realize it within oneself." [45] Thus not only is the ineffability of enlightenment conditioned by the mystical character of the experience, but it corresponds to the monistic and immanentist metaphysics of Mahāyāna.

The Buddhist doctrine on enlightenment is to be found in all of the Mahāyāna sutras. Limiting our inquiry into the relationship of the Mahāyāna sutras and Zen to the few sutras whose strong influence on Zen has been historically established, we have been able to demonstrate practically all the basic characteristics of Zen. This result is important for our understanding of the historical background of Zen, and must likewise guide us in our attempt to interpret Zen experience. For "no religious experience can stand outside a more or less intellectual interpretation of it." [46] In the case of Zen, the philosophic background which all religion requires is provided by the Mahāyāna sutras. This is not to deny the Chinese spirit all originality in the creation of Zen. But it is of great importance to delineate properly the contribution of China and Japan to this peculiar fruit on the copiously branched tree of Buddhism. The Mahāyāna sutras are, without doubt, the mother soil from which Zen sprang.

4   The Anticipation of Zen in Chinese Buddhism

The Historical Understanding of Zen

Zen is the school of enlightenment born from the mystical stream in Buddhism. Even though the experience of Zen lies beyond rational categories, this fact does not obviate the necessity of a careful historical analysis. D. T. Suzuki, the Japanese interpreter of Zen to the Occident, was accused by his Chinese colleague, Hu Shih, of not recognizing adequately the historical conditions out of which Zen arose. Hu Shih writes:

> It is this denial of the capability of the human intelligence to understand and evaluate Zen that I emphatically refuse to accept. . . . The Ch'an (Zen) movement is an integral part of the history of Chinese Buddhism, and the history of Chinese Buddhism is an integral part of the general history of Chinese thought. Ch'an can be properly understood only in its historical setting just as any other Chinese philosophical school must be studied and understood in its historical setting.[1]

In his reply, Suzuki emphasizes the time- and space-transcending character of the Zen experience to which no historical research can have access. But when in the course of his reply, as in all his works, he cites copiously the words and anecdotes of the early Chinese Zen masters, he nonetheless places his reader in a definite intellectual milieu. It is therefore not a matter of indifference in our interpretation of Zen to become acquainted with the Chinese heroes of the T'ang and Sung periods who figure in these anecdotes, and to gain some knowledge of their education and their view of life, together with their customs and ancestral faith. We are thus driven to historical inquiry.

The historical study of Zen, however, is rendered difficult because of the particular character of the sources. The chronicles regarding the early stages of Zen in China, which have been greatly esteemed by Zen adherents since the earliest times, are not wholly reliable from a historical viewpoint.[2] They are religious literature, written without accurate historical intention, but designed rather to convey the Zen spirit. The past is glorified and tailored to fit the ideal to which the writers of the Sung period (960-1279) subscribed. The historical image which was based on the chronicles was long doubted by scholars, but it could be improved only after a number of important texts, among them manuscripts found in Tun-huang by A. Stein and P. Pelliot, shed new light on the early Zen era.[3] Thereupon Japanese Zen Buddhologists, above all Ui Hakujū and Masunaga Reihō, sought to set forth the true course of events.[4] They also took into consideration the predecessors of Zen in China before the time of Bodhidharma, as well as the Indian background of the Zen movement, with which we dealt in the first chapters of the present book. In the following pages we shall seek to trace the ideological stages of early Zen history in China.

The Introduction of Buddhist Meditation into China

The spread of Buddhism from India to China ranks as one of the major events in the history of religion. It meant the transplanting of a higher religion with its authoritative dogma and cult into a land of ancient culture. The influx of Buddhism to

China began in the first century of the Christian era, and by the fourth century the movement had reached a high state of development. The enormous task of translating the hundreds of volumes of the Buddhist Canon from Pali and Sanskrit into Chinese testifies to the tremendous diligence of the monks as well as to their rare ability to feel their way into a foreign culture.

The rapid success of the Buddhist mission in China points to a certain superiority of Buddhism as a religion over the Taoist folk religion, encrusted as it was with magic and superstition. On the other hand, its persistent force among all classes of Chinese people and especially its penetration of the whole of Chinese culture can be explained only on the basis of an inner kinship between ancient Chinese thought and Buddhism.

The relationship of Chinese to Indian Buddhism has been variously interpreted. In contrast to the European scholars who, approaching the matter from their studies of India, attributed little originality to Chinese Buddhism, educated Chinese of the early centuries found in Buddhism, as in Taoism and Confucianism, so full an expression of their own genius that these three teachings together came to be regarded as representative of the religious mind of China.[5] Thus for the Buddhist terms they coined Chinese equivalents. The Primal Nothingness (*pên-wu*) of Taoism prepared the way for the understanding of the Buddhist negativism of the Nonego, the Void, and *nirvāna*. The Middle Way of Mahayanist philosophy was prefigured in the teaching of Nonacting (*wu-wei*). In their enlightenment (*sambodhi*) Buddhists grasped the Absolute, which classic Chinese thinkers had conceived as the Great One (*t'ai-yi*).

Admittedly, there are important differences between Indian and Chinese patterns of thought. Especially the mood associated with related and corresponding concepts is not identical. Cosmic oneness with the All is felt differently by the Chinese, who live harmoniously with nature, than by the Indians, who are inclined to flee the world. But since Buddhism displayed broad tolerance in the interpretation of its doctrines, it was possible to overlook such differences. Conflict did develop, however, with the Taoists, who sought comfort in the incredible but significant tale that Lao-tzŭ, "disappointed by the lack of understanding among his countrymen, went to India to preach Buddhism there." [6] The root for the striking inner kinship between the basic ideas of Buddhism and Taoism lies in the naturalistic apprehension of the world and of life which inspires the Mahāyāna sutras as well as Chinese thinkers such as Chuang-tzŭ and Lao-tzŭ. The naturalistic germ of Mahāyāna Buddhism found more congenial possibilities for development in the spiritual climate of China than in the country of its origin, India. Whereas the Indians were inhibited by their agonizing struggle for salvation, the Chinese, who desired nothing so much as to penetrate the secrets of nature, abandoned themselves completely to the Taoist-Buddhist naturalism.

Similarly, the new experience which Buddhism offered in meditation was not foreign to the Chinese. [7] In the great works of their own antiquity they read of superhuman wisdom, of ecstasies, and of miraculous powers. Taoism likewise teaches ways of meditation, and recommends the mastery of breathing as a means to spiritual concentration and longevity. Among the earliest translations of Buddhist sutras are to be found texts that deal with Buddhist meditation and describe the various stages of concentration along the way to liberating knowledge.

We do not know how earnestly the first Chinese Buddhists practiced these Indian instructions. But in any event the Chinese received, along with the doctrine and cult of Buddhism, the knowledge of Buddhist meditation. They rendered the Sanskrit term *dhyāna* as *ch'an* (archaic: *ḍian*), which in Japanese became *zen*—a term denoting ceremonial renunciation or release. [8] Thus the meditation taught in the Hīnayāna Canon was called "the Zen of the Lesser Vehicle," and in the Mahāyāna Canon, "the Zen of the Great Vehicle." Originally the same methods were employed, but, depending on the viewpoint held, the substance of concentration was interpreted either as Hina-yanist or as Mahayanist. This is an illustration of our general observation that the metaphysical content conditions the mystical experience and gives it its peculiar character.

The two earliest forms of Mahayanist meditation in China are the Amida vision and the concentration of Transcendental Wisdom (*prajñāpāramitā-samādhi*). The cult of the Buddha Amitābha (Jap.: Amida) early penetrated deep into the Chinese soul. Tao-an (312-385), who as a Chinese accepted the Buddhist teachings wholeheartedly and combined them with the Chinese attitude toward life, fervently studied the *Prajñā-pāramitā Sutras* and at the same time placed great emphasis on practice and meditation. He is regarded as the first important Chinese representative of the Great Vehicle. His disciple, Hui-yüan (334-416), though a monk, remained with the nobility and introduced Buddhism to Chinese intellectuals. He is famous as the founder of the Pure Land sect and as the first Chinese monk to create a Buddhist community in China.[9] It was through him that Mount Lu on the Yangtze River became an important center in the Buddhist movement. In this circle meditation was cultivated assiduously in order to catch, through visions and ecstasies, a glimpse of the glory of Amida's Western Paradise and the otherworldly Buddha-lands. Beyond this, through meditation, Hui-yüan sought unity with the Absolute or the source of all things, whether this be called Nature or World-soul or Buddha. "Meditation cannot reach full quiescence without insight. Insight cannot reflect the depth without meditation."[10] Buddhist and Taoist elements are combined in the meditation of Hui-yüan. In Taoism the depth of reality is called Primal Nothingness, which is comprehended in the *prajñā*-wisdom which sees through the emptiness of all things.

Many of the philosophical mystics among the Chinese Buddhists, in the same manner as Hui-yüan, repeated the name of Buddha (Jap.: *nembutsu*) on all stages of their spiritual ascent, without sensing any contradiction between metaphysical immersion in the complete Void and the highly imaginative Amida vision which leads to blessedness.

Kumarajīva and Buddhabhadra

The central personality in early Chinese Buddhism was the Indian teacher Kumarajīva (d. 413), who went to Ch'ang-an in 403, and during a brief span of about ten years established a brilliant career there. In the translation institute which he founded and headed, many Hīnayāna and Mahāyāna works were rendered into Chinese.[11] Kumarajīva was a convinced Mahayanist, an adherent of the Middle Way of Nāgārjuna, and an ardent champion of the Great Vehicle, which he helped to victory in China by his energetic activity. He himself was not actually skilled in meditation but promoted it among his numerous Chinese disciples, many of whom became accomplished in distinctly Mahayanist concentration methods.

For the standard authority on Buddhist meditation we must turn to another great Indian master, in character and inclination the opposite of Kumarajīva, namely, Buddhabhadra. Though fifteen years younger, he surpassed Kumarajīva in virtue and insight, enjoying among his Chinese contemporaries the highest esteem because of his miraculous powers.[12] Less of a scholar than Kumarajīva, he loved solitude and stayed aloof from the royal court, devoting his best energies to meditation. Upon his arrival in China he lived with Kumarajīva in Ch'ang-an until he was driven by hostility from the quarrelsome temple community. In the company of more than forty monks, he sought refuge on Mount Lu, where the ever-hospitable Hui-yüan received him.

Buddhabhadra actually stood halfway between Hīnayāna and Mahāyāna. In background and upbringing he was a Hinayanist. In his method of concentration he followed the *Dharmatrāta-dhyāna Sutra*, which teaches the Hinayanist mode of breath regulation, contemplation of the impurities, concentration on the Four Immeasurables, and fixation on the Five Elements (*skandha*), the six sense organs (*indrīya*), and the twelvefold chain of causality. During his sojourn at Mount Lu he translated this sutra into Chinese and discoursed upon it. But the distinction between Hīnayāna and Mahāyāna was so vague in the minds of his disciples that in a letter dating from this time he was called a "master of Mahāyāna meditation." [13] The sutra which he translated was mistakenly regarded as Mahayanist. This confusion shows the uncertainty of the transitional period.

From Mount Lu Buddhabhadra turned south to the capital city of Chien-k'ang, where he was effectively active as a teacher and master in meditation, and as a translator as well. His greatest service to Chinese Buddhism was his translation of the voluminous *Buddhāvatamsaka-mahāvaipulya Sutra*, which became the basic text of the Kegon school. He died in Chien-k'ang in the year 429. His pupil Hsüan-kao (d. 444) was in sharp opposition to the new ideas of Tao-sheng regarding instantaneous enlightenment. The progressive movement arose from the circle around Kumarajīva, but later on there also arose a generation of proponents of pure Mahayanist meditation among the followers of Buddhabhadra. [14]

"Wisdom Not Being Knowledge"

During the first great period of Chinese Buddhism, at the turn of the fifth century, the most brilliant representative was Seng-chao (384-414), Kumarajīva's highly gifted disciple, who died an untimely death. Of humble origin, he entered the school of that celebrated master, fervently embraced the Buddhist path of salvation, mastered the metaphysical speculations of the Middle Way doctrine, and was able to combine the wisdom of Chuang-tzŭ, Lao-tzŭ, and the Neo-Taoists, with which he had been familiar from childhood, with the Buddhist doctrine of the Great Vehicle. His mystical nature inclined to meditation and concentration. He pursued the supreme truth. "This truth is a vision; it is not in the words of the textbooks themselves but lies behind the words. It cannot be learned but must be experienced. It is discovered in moments of 'ecstatic acceptance' of life. . . ." [15]

At the age of twenty-three this thoughtful youth succeeded in producing a masterpiece of philosophical mysticism. His treatise *On Prajñā Not Being Knowledge* strikes at the heart of the paradox of the metaphysics of Nāgārjuna. *Prajñā*, he says, is "the illuminating power of not-knowledge" which reveals true reality. "Hence the sage is like an empty hollow. He cherishes no knowledge. He dwells in the world of change and utility, yet holds himself to the realm of nonactivity (*wu-wei*). He rests within the walls of the nameable, yet lives in the open country of that which transcends speech. He is silent and alone, void and open, where his state of being cannot be clothed in language. Nothing more can be said of him." [16]

The transcendental wisdom of Buddhism sacrificed none of its dialectical acuteness in assuming a Chinese garb but rather gained in figurative power. Seng-chao shows how the truth, mirrorlike, reflects the ten thousand things. The image of the mirror had, of course, already been employed in the Mahāyāna sutras. But Seng-chao may have recalled Chuang-tzŭ's saying: "The Perfect Man employs his mind as a mirror." [17] The likening of the human mind to a mirror became one of the best-loved motifs in Zen literature. A Chinese Zen master of a later period, Tê-ching (1546-1623), read in the writings of Seng-chao paradoxical sentences which, in the same way as a *kōan*, stimulated his experience of enlightenment. In a blinding flash of illumination, the meaning of Seng-chao's words became clear to him: "The raging storm which uproots mountains actually is calm; the rushing streams do not flow; the hot air which can be seen in springtime rising from the surface of a lake is motionless; sun and moon, though revolving in their orbits, do not turn round." [18] The relationship of Seng-chao to Zen is to be found in his orientation toward the immediate and experiential perception of absolute truth, and reveals itself in his preference for the paradox as the means of expressing the inexpressible. "The Inscrutable is found in an intuitive experience, which opens insight into the Oneness of Illusion and Reality." [19] This experience is final, and hence the goal where all ways meet.

Basing itself on the canonical texts of Buddhist scripture, the *Book of Chao* regards the way of enlightenment as one of gradual progress. "A Sutra says: 'Three arrows hit the target; three animals cross the river. The hitting and the crossing is the same, but the arrows penetrate more or less deeply and the animals are submerged to different depths because they differ in strength.'" [20] However, not on the way only, but also in the actual comprehension of truth there are variations as well as gradual progression. Seeing that the knowledge of all earthly things is impossible, "how much less will it be possible to comprehend at once the infinity of supramundane Emptiness?" [21]

Of his own inner experience, Seng-chao has left no record. His treatises and letters, however, reveal a rare wealth and loftiness of spirit. With the intransigence of the mystic he demands the surrender of everything for the sake of the One—a postulate revealed to him in the Buddha's message of salvation and one that accords with the wisdom of the Chinese fathers, known as Tao and the Great Doctrine. In the work of Seng-chao the synthesis of Buddhism and the Chinese view of life was stated convincingly for the first time.

The Suddenness of Enlightenment

Because of his doctrine of instantaneous enlightenment, Tao-sheng (ca. A.D. 360-434), likewise one of the followers of Kumarajīva, has been called "the actual founder of Zen." [22] Fung Yu-lan, however, modifies this claim when he traces, "ideologically speaking, the origin of the Ch'an school . . . back to Tao-sheng." [23] It is certain that Tao-sheng, with his "new doctrine," is of major importance to an understanding of Zen. He, too, belongs to the early generation of Chinese Buddhists who combined the Law of Buddha with Chinese thought and thus planted it in Chinese soil.

From early youth, Tao-sheng was reared in a monastery. His first teacher was a monk of insignificant intellect but genuine devoutness, Fa-t'ai, in Chien-k'ang. Tao-sheng embraced the Buddhist teaching with fervent conviction, but his views of life were formed by Chinese and, above all, Taoist thought. The Buddha is the Tao, the cosmic Law (*li*), or Nature, i.e., the impersonal absolute Law which determines human life. Since all sentient beings participate in the Buddha-nature, all men, including the "heathen" or non-Buddhists (*icchantika*), whose lot was much disputed by Buddhist theologians, were destined to attain Buddhahood eventually. Tao-sheng regarded this teaching of the Buddha-nature of all sentient beings as the core of the Buddhist creed. This position he maintained unflinchingly through many disputes, until the appearance of the *Nirvāna Sutra*, which states this doctrine unequivocally, settled the controversy in his favor.[24]

Surrounded by friends and monks, Tao-sheng retained the independence of a free and strong spirit. At a mature age he visited the two main centers of Chinese Buddhism of that period, Mount Lu on the Yangtze River and the northern capital Ch'ang-an. Near Hui-yüan on Mount Lu he met Sangha-deva, an Indian Hīnayāna scholar of the Sarvāstivādin school, with whom he discussed the problems of Buddhist philosophy. He did not share the belief of his friends in the Western Paradise of Amida. There is no trace in his writings of the exuberantly imaginative mysticism of the Amida devotees. "The fish trap must be forgotten when the fish is caught." [25] These words of Chuang-tzǔ he applied to Buddhist meditation. The fish, reality, is the Buddha who cannot be caught definitively in human words. And yet Tao-sheng treasured and esteemed the sutras in which everything has its meaning. "The Buddha does not lie." He did not lie "when he substituted the sutras for himself." [26]

Tao-sheng's short stay at Ch'ang-an (405-408), where the life of the monks was devoted entirely to the work of translating and interpreting the sutras, confirmed his high regard for these scriptures. Three years were enough to make of him one of the four chief disciples of Kumarajīva. His sudden return to Mount Lu, and from there to Chien-k'ang, seems to have been caused by the strained atmosphere of the monastic community of Ch'ang-an. What he had attained there bore immediate fruit in the tireless activity of his later years. In the literary realm, his commentaries on the Mahāyāna sutras occupy the principal place. His chief fame rests on two treatises, one on retribution ("A good action entails no retribution") and one on instantaneous enlightenment. With the latter we are acquainted only indirectly through the work of Hsieh Ling-yün (385-433).[27] This text guarantees Tao-sheng an important place in the history of Buddhist mysticism.

It is unlikely that Hsieh Ling-yün, being a layman, understood all the subtleties of Buddhist mystic teaching. Even more than that of the monks, his Buddhism was immersed in the syncretism of the time. However, on the whole, his presentation was approved by Tao-sheng. Hsieh Ling-yün contrasts the viewpoint of his friend with the teaching of Buddha on the one hand, according to which enlightenment is attained at the end of a long and difficult road, and on the other, with a saying of Kung-tzǔ about his disciple Yen Hui which, in true Neo-Taoist manner, he misinterprets in a mystical sense. Over against these highest authorities he presents his friend Tao-sheng as "a Buddhist with a new doctrine, which is to be regarded as true, final, and superior both to the wearisome doctrine of Buddha and to the wisdom of Kung-tzǔ, who did not penetrate the Void." [28]

What is this "new doctrine"? Or first of all, in what sense can the doctrine of sudden enlightenment be regarded as new? A clarification of this concept is all the more called for since at a later date it was interpreted variously and often ambiguously. From its beginnings, Buddhism has been a way of enlightenment. In common usage as well as in early Buddhist writings, enlightenment is regarded as a new insight or vision which breaks suddenly upon the inner eye and is taken up in the consciousness. The early Buddhist writings have much to say about enlightenment. As Shākyamuni under the pipal tree experienced the joy of enlightenment, so, in manifold ways, did his disciples, especially the monks and nuns whose songs were included in the canon. The Mahāyāna sutras, also, present a doctrine of enlightenment which takes into consideration the experiential character of the comprehension of truth. One can therefore say that instantaneous enlightenment is by no means as foreign to Indian Buddhism as Hsieh Ling-yün presumed when he wrote that because of their bent for intuitive comprehension the Chinese gave preference to sudden illumination, while the Indians, with their more strongly developed scientific inclination, chose the gradual way. [29]

It is correct, however, that the canon of Indian Buddhism describes the way to final realization—namely, to enlightenment and *nirvāna*—in the form of a gradually ascending path. Later, especially in Hīnayāna, method and system, scheme and analysis tended to supplant the spirit, though hardly ever was the uniqueness of the experience of enlightenment actually denied. The stages and gradations refer to the way and not to the goal of enlightenment, to the process and not to the liberating insight itself. It is important to note that, conceptually, instantaneous enlightenment applies first of all to the goal. The attainment of the goal happens suddenly, in the instant of arrival after the ardors of the way. A further distinction concerns the objective and the subjective aspects of the apprehension of the goal. The goal of the mystic way of salvation is the Absolute, which by its very nature must be conceived as a simple reality and an indivisible whole. In terms of the object, gradual stages of perception are impossible. And yet, from the subjective viewpoint, there is the possibility of gradations in comprehension. In the *Lotus Sutra*, the moment of enlightenment is divided into four parts. Tao-sheng rejects this concept. From the Mahayanist viewpoint one must say "that these four steps are taken by the believer in one single act of Illumination." [30]

Tao-sheng's doctrine of sudden enlightenment applies to the attainment of the goal in both its objective and its subjective aspects. Absolute Being by its very nature is simple, indivisible, and empty, and can be comprehended only *in toto*. Gradual enlightenment is a metaphysical absurdity. But likewise the subjective perception of truth occurs in a single indivisible act. "The fruit drops when it is ripe." "The woodcutter halts when only empty space is left." "When the mountain is climbed, the landscape of the goal appears all at once." [31] This change in view effects a spiritual transformation. The eye of wisdom is opened to final knowledge. All effort along the way is like standing before a wall, for the breakthrough occurs suddenly. There is no "more or less" in penetration.[32]

All illustrations serve the same purpose of showing clearly the radical distinction between way and goal. The grasping of the goal lies beyond the categories that are valid along the way, such as those applied, for example, by the *Daśabhūmika Sutra* in describing the career of a Bodhisattva. Tao-sheng does not seek to solve the difficulties confronting his doctrine which arise out of the sutra texts. He accepts their authority in humble faith. The study of the sacred writings, like every other form of devout exercise, is useful on the way. For the Buddhagerm must grow in every being and the *karma* must ripen until the decisive instant in which time ends and the new mode of being begins.

Tao-sheng's doctrine encountered vigorous opposition among his contemporaries. It was felt that these "new" assertions could not be squared with the accepted teachings of the sutras. But Tao-sheng had the Mahāyāna sutras on his side. As authority for his doctrine of sudden enlightenment he cites the commentaries of his teacher, Kumarajīva, on the *Vimalikīrti Sutra.*[33] In no sense did he feel himself to be an innovator; rather, he was convinced that he was defending the true Buddhist teaching in accordance with Buddhist tradition. The introduction of Buddhist meditation into the realm of Chinese culture became part of the organic development of the spiritual heritage. There is no justification to assume a break with the past.

The greatest opponent to the doctrine of sudden enlightenment at the time was another disciple of Kumarajīva, Hui-kuan (d. 443 or, at the latest, 447). His treatise on gradual enlightenment, in which five periods and seven stages are distinguished, represents an early attempt to assign the Hīnayāna and Mahāyāna sutras to different stages of the teaching of Buddha.

The controversy regarding sudden enlightenment continued after Tao-sheng's death. Fa-yüan (d. 489), a disciple of Hui-kuan, who shared the views of Tao-sheng, explained his doctrine before the Emperor Wên-ti (436). We also learn of a disputation between Tao-yu, a disciple of Tao-sheng, and Fa-yao at the court of Hsiao-wen Ti (460). This controversy continued throughout practically all of the fifth century, until interest in it gradually waned. However, no actual school of Tao-sheng subsisted throughout several generations. Nor has it been possible up to now to find a bridge of doctrinal influence linking Tao-sheng to the Zen of Bodhidharma.[34] Hence, Tao-sheng cannot rightfully be proclaimed as founder of the Zen school.

The early history of Chinese Buddhism affords important insight into the origins of Zen. With the Buddhist teachings, a broad stream of Indian mysticism, including ancient Yoga traditions, entered China. Hīnayāna and Mahāyāna were welcomed eagerly and indiscriminately. The fusion of Mahayanist metaphysics with the Chinese view of life was so complete that the borderline between original thought and subsequent influence can no longer be clearly traced. In the wake of the great Indian teachers and translators there followed a generation of independent thinkers who were also masters in meditation. From the school of Kumarajīva came eminent men like Seng-chao, whose influence on later Zen masters was probably stronger than any other, and Tao-sheng, of whom the Japanese Zen Buddhologist Ui says, "His teaching was to a large degree Zen-like and his influence was very great." [35] Thus we can penetrate chronologically and ideologically closer to the true sources of Zen, in compensation for the darkness with which myth has covered the original spring.

5 *Zen Patriarchs of the Early Period*

Bodhidharma

It is of great fascination to both the adherents and the students of a religious movement to probe its origins, though most often these are enshrouded in darkness. Legend frequently distorts the figure of the founder, while his teachings are lifted from their context in the past to accentuate the originality of their genius. Both tendencies have colored the figure of Bodhidharma and his school of meditation. This is expressed in the famous four-line stanza which is attributed to Bodhidharma but was actually formulated much later, during the T'ang period, when Zen had reached its apogee:

A special tradition outside the scriptures;
No dependence upon words and letters;
Direct pointing at the soul of man;
Seeing into one's own nature, and the attainment of
  Buddhahood.[1]

Later generations saw in these lines the essence of Zen, which for them was embodied in the figure of Bodhidharma. In Zen literature the question of Bodhidharma's coming from the West became the question of the meaning of Zen as such, in the same way that the question of "Buddha" signifies the question of ultimate reality. In the consciousness of his believers, Bodhidharma stands alongside the Buddha.

In this verse Bodhidharma appears as mediator of a new and immediate spiritual tradition which professedly goes back to Shākyamuni himself. Once Buddha turned a flower in his fingers while his face "broke into laughter." Among all his disciples, only Kāshyapa understood the deep meaning of this laughter. He was entrusted with "the seal of the Buddha-mind" on which the Zen tradition rests.[2] It is in this manner that the later Zen writings, at the moment of the school's full flowering in China, presented the origin of the Zen patriarchate, which handed on the spirit of Zen from master to disciple. The tale of the patriarchate and of its insignia, namely, the robe and the alms bowl, comprises the core of the Bodhidharma legend. As the last in a line of twenty-eight Indian patriarchs, whose names do not exactly agree in the various chronicles, Bodhidharma is said to have gone to China to found there, as the First Patriarch, the tradition of Chinese Zen.[3]

As time went on, many resplendent and miraculous features were attributed to him.[4] He is said to have stemmed from South Indian Brahmans, or even to have been of royal descent. He left his home and, after long and toilsome travel, came to South China. In an encounter with the Emperor Wu-ti (502-550), the founder of the Liang dynasty there, he fearlessly asserted the futility of building Buddhist temples and of the recitation of the sutras. Thereupon he crossed the wide Yangtze River on a reed and for nine years remained seated before the wall of a monastery until his legs withered away; his mind he bequeathed to his disciple Hui-k'o. The chronicles report further that his doctrine of a new way to enlightenment aroused strong opposition. Six times he is said to have miraculously foiled his enemies' attempts to poison him, and three times to have refused the invitation of the Emperor Hsiao-ming to the court of the northern kingdom. Dramatic episodes such as attempts on his life and invitations to the imperial court were probably meant to stress the strong impression he made on his contemporaries, something not adequately recognized in the simple biography of the historian Tao-hsüan (d. 667). A late embellishment is the tale of a monk, Sung-yün, according to which he met Bodhidharma three years after his death in Central Asia, carrying a sandal in one hand, the other sandal being found at the opening of the grave. Other traditions speak of the return of the patriarch to India or of his crossing over to Japan.

Many of the legendary details reflect the tendency of disciples to concentrate all possible honors on their dead master. Equally fictitious conversations on enlightenment between Bodhidharma and his disciples, couched in the style of the later *kōan*, illustrate the Zen way to enlightenment as it was taught by the classic masters of the T'ang and Sung periods. The chief motive behind the inventions of the Bodhidharma legend was the attempt of the Zen school to present against its enemies a sacred line of tradition which would safeguard its doctrine and spirit.

Reliable facts about the life of Bodhidharma are extremely few. That he existed and was a native of India can be regarded as definitely established. He remained in South China only briefly and then turned north, where he apparently devoted more than forty years to the establishment of his doctrine of enlightenment. As an Indian *dhyāna* master, he enjoyed great esteem and won many disciples. Between 516 and 526 he appeared in the Yung-ning-ssŭ temple near Lo-yang. Another monastery, Shao-lin-ssŭ on nearby Mount Sung, is traditionally associated with his name. There he is said to have been seated for nine years without interruption, gazing at a wall, and to have transmitted the Dharma to his disciple Hui-k'o.[5] He died (before 534) at a ripe age. Tao-hsüan ends his biography with the words, "He made peregrination and teaching his task. Where he died is not known."

The scant reliable information we possess of the life and work of Bodhidharma is insufficient to explain his position in the Zen school and in Chinese Buddhism. We know the names of a goodly number of other masters in meditation from this same period.[6] It was at this time that followers of Buddhabhadra in North China, together with other teachers of enlightenment, consummated the final transition from Hīnayāna to Mahāyāna, while in the South the followers of the "School of the Three Treatises" (*Shan-lun*; Jap.: *Sanron*) were inspired in their practice of meditation by the philosophy of Nāgārjuna and the doctrine of Supreme Wisdom (*prajñāpāramitā*). Mahayanist metaphysics provided the basis for a doctrine of enlightenment, the clarification of which was attempted in heated discussions as to whether enlightenment comes suddenly or gradually. This background for the evaluation of Bodhidharma's achievement is more clear than his doctrine, which is preserved for us in only one writing, indeed, only in a single word, and even this word seems to be spurious.[7]

In the text of *Two Entrances and Four Acts*, which, with a preface by T'an-lin, is to be found in the chronicles of the Sung period and in abbreviated form in Tao-hsüan's biography of Bodhidharma, the doctrine of the master may be recorded by one of his disciples. The passage deals with two Entrances upon the Way (*tao*), namely the Entrance by Reason and the Entrance by Conduct. The content and structure of this text scarcely differ from a passage in the *Vajrasamādhi Sutra*.[8] In the Entrance by Reason, the unity of all living beings in the one true nature is grasped, a nature which cannot fully disclose itself because it is hidden by the dust of external things and by confusing ideas. "When one, abandoning the false and embracing the true, in simplicity of thought abides in *pi-kuan*, one finds that there is neither selfhood nor otherness, that the masses and the worthies are of one essence." The sutra names the knowledge of true being which transcends all differentiation the "vision of enlightenment" (*chüeh-kuan*), an expression which occurs also in Zen literature. In the text of Bodhidharma quoted above, the term *pi-kuan*, literally "wall-gazing," is something new. Tao-hsüan praises, as Bodhidharma's greatest achievement, his teaching of "Mahayanist wall-contemplation." Undoubtedly this term not merely refers to physically staring at a wall,[9] but may be regarded as an allusion to the steepness and suddenness of the vision of enlightenment. At a later period this idea was linked to the legend of Bodhidharma's nine years of gazing at a wall in the monastery of Shao-lin-ssŭ, and *pi-kuan* came to be regarded as the appropriate expression for the way to enlightenment peculiar to Zen. In common usage Bodhidharma was called the "wall-gazing Brahman."

The calming of the spirit through sudden enlightenment and the understanding of the true Buddha-nature is designated in the text as the "Entrance by Reason" (Chin.: *li*), while the goal which is attained is called *tao*. This terminology brings the doctrine of Bodhidharma close to the Sino-Buddhist ideology of Tao-sheng, as Ui has already pointed out.[10] Ui, however, denies any interdependence between them. Rather, he seeks to weaken the suggestion of dependence by arguing that the learned commentator of the sutras, Tao-sheng, lacked the practical experience which is postulated by *pi-kuan*. Beyond the concept of the Mahayanist wall-gazing of Bodhidharma, this text presents nothing original.

In the Entrance by the Four Acts, the general Mahayanist attitudes, based on various passages in the *Vimalikīrti* and the *Nirvāna Sutras* and issuing from the doctrines of the Perfect Virtues (*pāramitā*), *karma*, and the emptiness of all things, are set forth. Thus the line, "No dependence upon words and letters" does not apply to Bodhidharma. The First Patriarch does not seem to have rejected the sutras, but rather to have treasured them highly.

The Zen of Bodhidharma, even though it fails to afford historical certainty, seems to lead a step further in the direction indicated by the pioneers of Chinese Buddhism, namely, Tao-an, Hui-yüan, Seng-chao, and, above all, Tao-sheng. The Chinese touch, which stems especially from Taoism, is clearly recognizable also in Bodhidharma, but in terms of basic doctrine he deviates at no point from the great Mahāyāna sutras.[11]

The fusion of the Indian and the Chinese spirit in Zen is unmistakably evident from the very first days of Zen history. According to the tradition, the twenty-eighth Indian and first Chinese patriarch represents the bridge between the two countries. Nonetheless, the actual historical role of Bodhidharma in this process remains obscure. In the concept of wall-gazing, the suddenness of enlightenment receives a sharp delineation. Yet here, too, the single word *pi-kuan* does not suffice to determine the scope and degree of suddenness of enlightenment taught and attained by Bodhidharma in distinction to other approaches.

Disciples and Followers

The life of Hui-k'o, Bodhidharma's successor, is closely interwoven with that of the First Patriarch.[12] The two most important episodes at the beginning of his Zen career, namely, his admission as a disciple and his investiture as a patriarch, are especially embellished by the inventive genius of the chroniclers. The master-disciple relationship is said to have been initiated in a most dramatic scene. Hui-k'o waited in the snow before the monastery of Shao-lin-ssŭ, incessantly pleading for admission to discipleship. His pleas, however, were ignored. So he cut off his arm and presented it to the master. Impressed with the earnestness of his desire, Bodhidharma admitted him to discipleship. Tao-hsüan gives the lie to this anecdote when he relates that it was robbers who struck off Hui-k'o's arm.

Bodhidharma's equally famous last conversation with his disciples which, similarly to the story of Hui-k'o's arm, was used by later generations as a *kōan* exercise, obviously did not happen as described. The chronicle from the Sung period reports this event as follows:

Nine years had passed and he [Bodhidharma] now wished to return westward to India. He called his disciples and said: "The time has now come. Why does not each of you say what you have attained?"

The disciple Tao-fu replied: "As I see it [the truth] neither adheres to words or letters nor is it separate from them. Yet it functions as the Way."

The Master said: "You have attained my skin."

Then a nun, Tsung-chih, spoke: "As I understand it, [the truth] is like the auspicious glimpse of the Buddha Land of Akshobya; it is seen once, but not a second time."

The Master replied: "You have attained my flesh."

Tao-yü said: "The four great elements are originally empty; the five *skandhas* have no existence. According to my belief, there is no *dharma* to be grasped."

To him the Master replied: "You have attained my bones."

Finally there was Hui-k'o. He bowed respectfully and stood silent.

The Master said: "You have attained my marrow." [13]

This story is significant as a typical expression of Zen which affirms the basic tenets of Mahāyāna philosophy, namely, Nāgārjuna's speculation regarding the indeterminate character of reality, and the *prajñāpāramitā* doctrine, but which sees the Supreme Wisdom in silence. Following this conversation, the chronicle reports the transmission of the office of the patriarch and the insignia pertaining to it. Hui-k'o was charged to preserve and transmit unadulterated the Dharma first entrusted to

Kāshyapa by the Buddha. Then follows the stanza, likewise spurious, in which Bodhidharma foretells the future of Zen in China:

> Originally I came to this land
> To transmit the Dharma and to save from error.
> A flower with five petals opens;
> Of itself the fruit will ripen.

After the subtraction of legendary accretions, the life of Hui-k'o shrinks to a few fairly certain facts. His life span extended from A.D. 484 to 590 or, more likely, from 487 to 593 —depending on whether one fixes his apprenticeship under Bodhidharma at nine years or, according to the biography by Tao-hsüan, at six years. At the time of his encounter with Bodhidharma, Hui-k'o was in the prime of life and possessed a broad education. During his youth he had studied Taoism, and he was familiar with the Chinese classics and the philosophical literature of Buddhism. After the death of Bodhidharma he led a difficult itinerant life. Tao-hsüan tells of enmity and persecution which he underwent in Yeh-tu, the capital of the eastern half of the Wei Kingdom after its division (534), through the intrigues of a *dhyāna* master named Tao-hêng. During the general Buddhist persecution in the northern kingdom (574) Hui-k'o fled and hid himself in the mountains near the Yangtze River. But this storm did not last long. Soon it was possible for him to return to the capital, where he lived another decade and then died at a great age.

Hui-k'o's relationship to Bodhidharma is thus reduced to that of master and disciple, which occasioned a strong influence on the former's teachings. According to the historical work of Tao-Hsüan it culminated in the transmission of the four volumes of the *Lankāvatāra Sutra* from Bodhidharma to his successor. More daring and direct of expression than his master, Hui-k'o shapes the idealist monism of this sutra in strong and positive formulations which repeat the basic thought that all the *dharmas* are one mind. It is from this unity of all things that he deduces the foolishness of attachment and of choice. Once the mind has attained full liberty, it manifests its true nature and realizes the unity which transcends all differentiation. The following extract, transmitted by his biographer, Tao-Hsüan, is characteristic of Hui-k'o's doctrine:

> The deepest truth lies in the principle of identity. It is due to one's ignorance that the mani-jewel is taken for a piece of brick, but lo! when one is suddenly awakened to self-enlightenment, it is realised that one is in possession of the real jewel. The ignorant and the enlightened are of one essence, they are not really to be separated. We should know that all things are such as they are. . . . When we know that between this body and the Buddha there is nothing to separate one from the other, what is the use of seeking *nirvāna* [as something external to ourselves]? [14]

Hui-k'o knows that entrance upon the Way can be gained only by immediate experience. To him who has thus experienced enlightenment, there remains nothing further for which to strive. What Hui-k'o says philosophically regarding the enlightenment and manifestation of one's own spirit, Hui-nêng and his disciples realize in sudden experience.

Seng-ts'an, the Third Patriarch in the line of Chinese Zen, is not accorded a separate biography in the great historical work of Tao-hsüan. Facts about his life are so scant that his historicity has at times been questioned. Nevertheless his name is certified in the later traditional lists of both the northern and the southern Zen movement. He is also mentioned by Tao-hsüan.[15] We know nothing of his background and youth. Owing to his great detachment from this world—the epitaph on his tombstone compares him for this reason to the Bodhisattva Vimalikīrti—he apparently never spoke of his own affairs. For six years he studied with Hui-k'o and received from him the seal of the Dharma. His first encounter with the master is described as a conversation in the *kōan* manner, obviously an addition of later times. Like Hui-k'o, he led the itinerant life of a mendicant monk equipped with "one robe and one alms bowl." He was praised especially for his friendliness and moderation, his magnanimity and gentleness. During the Buddhist persecution (574) he fled with Hui-k'o to the mountains, but parted from him when the latter went to the capital city, Yeh-tu. The accounts of his final destiny do not agree in detail, but according to fairly reliable information he died in the year 606.

Traditionally, the poem of *The Seal of the Believing Mind* is attributed to Seng-ts'an; if he did not write it, he is at least said to have recited it before his disciples.[16] It is a hymn addressed to the Tao in which Chinese speculation and the religious inspiration of Buddhism combine to praise the Unfathomable. The Taoist coloring becomes evident in the naturalistic lyricism of the verses. The metaphysical ideas of emptiness and of the ultimate unity beyond all opposites in the thusness of existence have been the common property of Mahāyāna since the rise of the doctrine of Transcendental Wisdom (*prajñā-pāramitā*) and the philosophical teaching of Nāgārjuna. In many passages the composition is akin to the *Avatamsaka* (*Kegon*) *Sutras*, especially in the animated closing verses, which follow here:

> In the higher realm of true Suchness
> There is neither "self" nor "other":
> When direct identification is sought,
> We can only say, "not two."
>
> In being "not two" all is the same,
> All that is comprehended in it;
> The wise in the ten quarters,
> They all enter into this Absolute Reason.
>
> This Absolute Reason is beyond quickening (time) and
>   extending (space),

For it, one instant is ten thousand years;
Whether we see it or not,
It is manifest everywhere in all the ten quarters.

Infinitely small things are as large as large things can be,
For here no external conditions obtain;
Infinitely large things are as small as small things can be,
For objective limits are here of no consideration.

What is is the same as what is not,
What is not is the same as what is;
Where this state of things fails to obtain,
Indeed, no tarrying there.

One in All,
All in One—
If only this is realised,
No more worry about your not being perfect!

Where Mind and each believing mind are not divided,
And undivided are each believing mind and Mind,
This is where words fail;
For it is not of the past, present, and future.

In the following generation under Tao-hsin (580-651), whom the chronicles name as the Fourth Patriarch, a transformation occurred in the mode of living which did much to enable Zen to strike roots in Chinese society.[17] This change, which later was to lead to ordered communal life in the monasteries during the T'ang and Sung periods, was initiated when Tao-hsin gave up the itinerant life of the mendicant which his predecessors had preferred, in favor of a fixed abode. After his separation from his master, Seng-ts'an (602), whom he had followed for ten years, Tao-hsin lived for another ten years in a monastery on Mount Lu. He moved finally to nearby Shuan-fêng Mountain, where he labored fruitfully for more than thirty years and led more than five hundred disciples on the way to enlightenment.

Tao-hsin was a strong personality who, by his scholarly training and ascetic bent, attracted distinguished men who entrusted themselves for a time to his guidance. With many people engaged in the common life, definite forms of community living were bound to arise. As numbers increased, the spontaneous alms of the faithful could no longer suffice. Begging excursions in the vicinity were of little use and public funds were not available. Nothing remained for the monks but to go to work themselves. They now not only undertook household tasks but tilled gardens and fields to provide the necessities of life. Whether there was specialization from the beginning as in later times, which permitted some to devote themselves to meditation while others engaged in administration or manual labor, cannot be determined from the sources. In any event, the preservation of the inner attitude, the spirit of Zen, in the midst of daily activities was extremely important in the new way of life. Now, not only were the sitting in the meditation hall and the recitation of the sutras performed in the Zen spirit, but also the daily duties in house and field. "Working, dwelling, sitting, resting," as four Chinese ideographs express it pregnantly, are all alike Zen. Thus we have here an impact of the social structure and the economic conditions of life on the ideological basis of the movement similar to what occurred in Western monasticism during the Middle Ages. This broadening of Zen opened possibilities for laymen, who in the course of further development were thus enabled to create a comprehensive Zen culture.

Tao-hsin, who was akin to Dōgen in his esteem of the practice of *zazen*, sat in meditation day and night. It is said of him that for sixty years he did not recline once. Repeatedly he admonished his disciples:

> Sit earnestly in meditation! The sitting in meditation is basic to all else. By the time you have done this for three to five years, you will be able to ward off starvation with a bit of meal. Close

the door and sit! Do not read the sutras, and speak to no man! If you will so exercise yourself and persist in it for a long time, the fruit will be sweet like the meat which a monkey takes from the nutshell. But such people are very rare.[18]

Tradition also tells of a special method of concentration which Tao-hsin is said to have commended to his disciples.[19] He put the emphasis on spiritual realization. Well versed in the sutras, he loved to interpret them in a free and original manner. The unity of all *dharmas* and the spirituality of all reality are the quintessence of his teaching.

The successor of Tao-hsin in the line of patriarchs was his disciple Hung-jên (601-674). As in the case of his predecessors, he too is said to have been introduced to his office by a typical *kōan* conversation. The episode, however, is hardly authentic, since his admission to the school of Tao-hsin reportedly took place at the age of six. The biographers praise his zeal, claiming that he worked throughout the day, and then sat in meditation during the night until dawn. The later chronicles speak of two invitations to the imperial court, both of which he declined. On the second occasion he is said to have told the envoy that he would refuse even if he should be executed. Thereupon the Emperor praised him, the story concludes, in typical legendary fashion.

Under Hung-jên, communal life developed further, though after the death of his master he moved his residence to nearby Mount P'ing-jung. The number of disciples increased apace.[20] Much like his predecessor, he sought to perfect the practice of meditation, and developed his own special method in accordance with the *Avatamsaka Sutras*. Among the Tun-huang manuscripts there is a text attributed to him, though its authorship remains doubtful.[21] The accounts differ on the date of his death, but the year 674 seems the most nearly correct.

The final step beyond the Indian *dhyāna* meditation was the most important fact in the early development of Zen in China.

At this time the central aim of master and disciple alike was the realization of the absolute Buddha-reality by means of enlightenment. Though the sutras were highly esteemed and diligently studied and recited, illumination was expected from meditation rather than from intellectual endeavor. The apparently genuine texts from this period give evidence of logical thought schooled in the canonical writings. Paradoxical twists of language are rare, and there is as yet no trace of artificial devices such as the *kōan*, shouting, beating with a rod, grimaces, and the like. During the sixty years of communal life in the solitude of those eastern mountains a widening of life into social patterns came into being. The Zen congregation which formed around the two enlightened patriarchs, Tao-hsin and Hung-jên, became known under the name of "The Dharma Gate of the East Mountain" or "The Pure Gate of the East Mountain," and aroused great admiration. Zen revealed itself increasingly as a creative cultural force.

Schisms and Oppositions

Despite lack of clarity in detail, one can trace the spread of the meditation movement generally during the early history of Chinese Zen. Obviously, the transmission of this tradition did not occur merely in the direct line of patriarchal descent, as is claimed in the later chronicles. Chinese historical sources record numerous names of masters in meditation. After Bodhidharma two distinct types appeared. In addition to the mendicant monks who, in total renunciation of the world, lived in solitude and exclusively for the sake of enlightenment, there were teaching monks who settled down in communities and combined teaching with meditation. Only those men given exclusively to the practice of meditation were regarded as the true representatives of Zen, but there were groups of disciples which overlapped one another, and which did not necessarily segregate themselves from other Buddhist schools.[22]

The first important split to occur in Bodhidharma's Zen was the movement founded by a disciple of the Fourth Patriarch (Tao-hsin) named Fa-yung (594-657), which was taken to Japan during the Heian period by Dengyō Daishi (767-822).[23] In China, this sect claimed many adherents as late as the eighth generation. It was close in spirit to the "School of the Three Treatises," which cultivated the philosophy of Nāgārjuna,[24] and taught that illumination is achieved through contemplation of the Void.

The next split, of extreme importance in the development of Zen thought, was the division of Zen into a northern and a southern sect after the Fifth Patriarch, Hung-jên. For the historical study of Zen, the development of this schism constitutes the second hopeless entanglement of complex questions. As in the life of Bodhidharma, the later Zen chronicles report dramatic events which shed light on the Zen experience, and which present the exclusive claims of the victorious southern sect. According to the *Sutra Spoken by the Sixth Patriarch from the High Seat of the Gem of the Law*, Hung-jên ordered all the disciples to compose a *gāthā* (stanza or verse) in order to reveal to the master their degree of enlightenment.[25] In this way he planned to discover a successor to whom he could entrust the patriarchal insignia.

Foremost among the disciples at this time was Shên-hsiu (606-706), who, in the view of his peers, deserved the succession.[26] Shên-hsiu, however, though well versed in the sutras, was still far from enlightenment. The master's request cast him into a mood of deep apprehension. But finally he produced a *gāthā*, and at night wrote it on the wall of the pillared hall of the monastery:

The body is the Bodhi tree [enlightenment],
The mind is like a clear mirror standing.

Take care to wipe it all the time,
Allow no grain of dust to cling.

The following morning the other disciples read the lines with admiration and secretly believed the question of the succession settled. In the presence of all, Hung-jên praised this composition, but privately he told Shên-hsiu that the poem showed no sign of enlightenment and suggested that he write another. These lines were devoid of logical contradiction and could be interpreted readily by resolving the two allegories; they were therefore not acceptable as an expression of true enlightenment.

At this time a young boy of little or no education named Hui-nêng (638-713) was living in the monastery. He had come from South China eight months earlier and had begged the master for admission to the circle of disciples, but had been set, instead, to splitting wood and grinding rice, although the master had immediately recognized his extraordinary intuitive and intellectual capacities. This boy heard of the *gāthā*, and since he could neither read nor write, he had it read to him twice. Thereupon he formulated a second stanza and requested that this, too, be written on the wall. These were his lines:

The Bodhi is not like a tree,
The clear mirror is nowhere standing.
Fundamentally not one thing exists;
Where, then, is a grain of dust to cling?

The admiration of all the disciples over the verse of the illiterate peasant knew no bounds. And yet the master was reserved in his praise. He erased the lines, saying that Hui-nêng also had not yet attained enlightenment. But secretly he summoned Hui-nêng to his room by night and conferred the patriarchal insignia upon him. Thereupon he ordered the young man to flee south across the Yangtze, since he feared the envy of Shên-hsiu and the other disciples.[27]

This legend, which traces the origin of the schism between

the northern and southern sects of Chinese Zen to the *gāthā* contest between the two unequal disciples, stems from the southern sect of Shên-hui (668-760), a disciple of Hui-nêng. Thanks to the failure of the northern movement to develop after the death of the disciples of Shên-hsiu, and to the wide dissemination of the chronicles and *kōan* collections of the southern group, this account of the rise of the schism carried the day. Actually, there is no certain knowledge about the enmity between Shên-hsiu and Hui-nêng. If there was disagreement as to the Way of Enlightenment, it was not serious enough to prevent Shên-hsiu from commending his erstwhile colleague Hui-nêng to the royal court, whose high esteem he himself enjoyed.[28] Shên-hsiu's last years in the northern capital of Lo-yang were crowned with the glory of imperial recognition, which brought him decorations and honor. The reputation of his school continued under his two outstanding disciples, P'u-chi (651-739) and I-fu (658-736).

According to one account, Shên-hui maintained personal contact with Shên-hsiu. He is said to have spent three years of his youth in the school of the head of the northern movement, and later to have turned to Hui-nêng, who admitted him to the circle of his followers. This period of apprenticeship was reportedly interrupted by a trip through North China.[29] Such a course of events would explain his knowledge of the northern sect, but all the same appears unlikely. It is certain that Shên-hui did spend several years with Hui-nêng, perhaps until the latter's death. In the year 720 we find him not far from Lo-yang in Nan-yang, where he taught meditation. At that time the northern sect flourished there under the two brilliant disciples of Shên-hsiu, and enjoyed the favor of the court. By comparison, Shên-hui's fame is not worthy of mention. Only much later, after the rise of enmity against the northern sect, does he seem to have gained a degree of prominence.

A detailed account of the final break between the northern

and southern groups is contained in the *Words of Shên-hui,* a text found among the Tun-huang manuscripts.[30] The first serious attack occurred in a large assembly convened by Shên-hui in the monastery of Ta-yün-ssŭ at Hua-t'ai, which was "open to all" and attended by adherents of various sects. The purpose of the proceedings was "to determine the true and the false with regard to [the succession of] the southern sect of Bodhidharma." The criticisms directed against the northern sect can be summarized in two groups: first, this sect was said to have deviated from the true line of tradition and to have usurped the patriarchate for itself; and second, it was said to have held an erroneous view of enlightenment and ascetic exercise. It has been pointed out that Shên-hui, who at the age of sixty-six staked his life on the eradication of the other sect, must have been a man "of extraordinary moral and physical vigor." [31] His biographer, Tsung-mi (780-841), emphasizes the danger of attacking so powerful an opponent as P'u-chi, and tells of repeated attempts on Shên-hui's life. Shên-hui at that time stood at the height of his fame. He had many followers, and outstanding contemporaries praised his knowledge and acuity of mind. A fearless fighter, he struck out at his opponents relentlessly, directing his blows from the headquarters of his sect in the Ho-tse-ssŭ monastery at Lo-yang, especially in his monthly doctrinal lectures. The decline of the northern sect after the death of the two important disciples of Shên-hsiu, P'u-chi and I-fu, was no doubt mainly the result of his violent attacks. The last years of Shên-hui's life were darkened by slander and political confusion. He fell into disgrace at the court, and had to move his residence repeatedly, until shortly before his death he was restored to honor. All in all, Shên-hui was an unusual man, of extraordinary energy and intellectual vigor to the last. What were the motives that impelled him?

Shên-hui and his disciples justified their attack on their opponents by the latter's acts of hostility. In the writings of the southern sect, the adherents of the northern group are accused of plots such as the theft of the patriarchal robe and the alteration of the inscription on Hui-nêng's tomb. Undoubtedly this was unfounded. The reliable accounts give no basis for such accusations. Though P'u-chi regarded himself as "the seventh page in the Zen book," he did not contest the succession of Hui-nêng. Neither Shên-hsiu nor his disciples gave rise to the quarrel by making their secondary line into the main line of descent, as the accusers claimed. The northern wing was flourishing vigorously in Lo-yang when Shên-hui arrived in the territory. But this fact in itself, while it hindered the rise of the southern movement, did not call for persecution provided Shên-hui was not activated by ambition and thirst for power. One need not brand him an intriguer, yet even Ui, in examining the presentation of Hu Shih, acknowledges in Shên-hui "traits which deserve moral censure and the reproach of intolerance." [32] The list of succession of the Zen patriarchate which he fabricated in the Ho-tse monastery at Lo-yang may not have been a conscious deception. The idea of the transmission of the Dharma is found throughout the whole of Chinese Buddhism and was familiar to Shên-hui. The succession of names as he lists them corresponded to his historical knowledge. Passionately he promotes the recognition of Hui-nêng as the Sixth Patriarch, in whose line of succession he stands and whose tradition he feels called upon to pass on to others. No doubt personal ambition played a role in his rivalry against his opponents, yet his battle against the northern sect was no mere struggle for power. Mixed with less honorable motives was the conviction that he had inherited from his master the sole truth concerning the Way of Enlightenment. The opposition of ideas between the northern and southern sects is usually characterized by the terms "gradual" and "instantaneous."

For our knowledge of the doctrines of the northern sect we are forced to rely almost exclusively on the writings of its opponents, which present no objective picture. It must be made clear at the outset that the northern sect also belonged to Bodhidharma's Zen and represented the basic Mahayanist ideas. The "original mind" is to be experienced in enlightenment, which is regarded as the sudden awakening to the realization of one's own Buddha-nature. Basing their views on the *Lankā-vatāra Sutra*, which taught gradual exercises and sudden realization, Shên-hsiu and his disciples attached great importance to the preparatory practices. Through these, all obscurities, all dust, were to be wiped from the mirror of the pure original mind. Obscurities and passions (*kleśa*) they regarded as something actually existing, the removal of which requires great effort and can be achieved only gradually, step by step. The instantaneous character of the experience of enlightenment was not denied, but because of the shift of emphasis to the gradual process, their opponents were able to accuse them of gradualism.

The point of deviation lay not only in overemphasis, however, but also in a misunderstanding of the ascetic exercise. According to orthodox Zen doctrine, which Shên-hui led to victory, the passions are empty and unreal, as is the self. This is implied in the verses of Hui-nêng: "The clear mirror is nowhere standing. . . . Where, then, is a grain of dust to cling?" The two *gāthā* express the difference between the two sects in a striking way. Where Shên-hsiu advises the cleansing of the mirror, the paradoxical verse of Hui-nêng points to the nothingness of all things, including the exercise itself. As long as passions are taken seriously the mind is inclined to differentiate. But to him who has understood the doctrine, all things are equal. Passions are equated with enlightenment; avarice and the Way are the same. There are no hindrances. The metaphysics of orthodox Zen is a radical and absolute monism of identity.

It is this divergent view concerning the passions that constitutes the metaphysical core of the contest between the two sects in Chinese Zen. The concepts of suddenness and gradual- ism are fluid and thus demand definition in each case. The North also knew sudden enlightenment; but Shên-hsiu took into consideration the varying dispositions and abilities of his disciples and did not conduct them all along the same way. Furthermore, as a scholar he directed his attention to the meta- physical doctrine of the sutras. But the sect of Shên-hui, the Ho-tse, likewise did not postulate the most radical view of instantaneousness. In contrast to the classic masters of the southern sect—those highly original thinkers who followed Hui- nêng and led Chinese Zen to its full flowering—the followers of Shên-hui remained attached to the learned study of the sutras. Shên-hui himself, who obtained the Dharma seal of the succession only after a long trial, recognized a gradual way for persons of minor gifts.[33] His attack on the northern sect con- tributed decisively to the articulation of the proper character of Zen. The evaluation of his achievement will depend on the position of the critic. Shên-hsiu presented the Mahayanist tradition of meditation in all its amplitude, while the southern school made the single factor of instantaneous enlightenment the sole criterion of orthodoxy. Historical inquiry can trace both views to the way of the early patriarchs. Hung-jên, the fifth successor of Bodhidharma, had the highest regard for both disciples, Hui-nêng and Shên-hsiu. If it remains uncertain whether he designated Hui-nêng as his successor in the patri- archate, it has been established that he was full of praise for Shên-hsiu, who, according to his testimony, fully attained "the Dharma of the Eastern Mountain." [34] Hui-nêng and his dis- ciples brought about the decisive change in the development of Chinese Zen and gave the final cast to its character.

6   *The High Period of Chinese Zen*

The Sixth Patriarch

In Zen history, Hui-nêng, the fifth successor, is regarded, next to Bodhidharma, as the second and actual founder. The Sixth Patriarch is hallowed by the veneration of many generations of disciples. As with Shākyamuni and Bodhidharma, legends of miraculous powers enhance his authority as a transmitter of the Zen spirit. If in our assessment of historical personalities we may argue from effect to cause, Hui-nêng must have been an extraordinary man. Unfortunately, our knowledge of his life and work is uncertain, despite the fact that the numerous Zen texts from the T'ang and Sung periods contain an abundance of biographical material.[1]

In addition to the predilection of Chinese Zen for embellishing with legendary qualities the deeds and vicissitudes of the great masters, the sources are here beclouded by the quarrel between the southern and the northern sect. At the center of the biography of Hui-nêng stands the dramatic episode of his nocturnal accession to the patriarchate, which followed the *gāthā* contest between the two disciples of Hung-jên and led to Hui-nêng's sudden flight from Wang-mei, the abode of Hung-jên. The further accounts of persecution by his opponents and of other dangers are likewise tendentious inventions aimed at the detriment of the northern sect.

Hui-nêng had survived a poor and rigorous boyhood when he went to Hung-jên.² His father had died early—according to some sources, when the boy was but three years old. With his aging mother he eked out a meager existence. They lived from the sale of firewood, which the youth carried to market. One day he heard a customer read from a Buddhist sutra. This awakened his spirit to sudden enlightenment. When he asked for the name of the sacred text, he was told that it was the *Diamond Sutra* (one of the sutras of Transcendental Wisdom). The customer went on to tell him of Hung-jên's flourishing school of enlightenment on the East Mountain. Hui-nêng's decision was quickly made. That first, with the help of the customer, he made provision for his aged mother is a later invention. Equally implausible is his alleged illiteracy. The same sources which highlight the account with this assertion attest his knowledge of the Mahāyāna sutras. As early as his first conversation with the Fifth Patriarch, Hung-jên, he speaks of the Buddha-nature of all sentient beings in a manner reminiscent of the *Nirvāna Sutra*. His lectures reveal a knowledge of at least seven great sutras.³

As to Hui-nêng's early years, only his relationship with Hung-jên can be regarded as historically certain. Since, according to the chronicles, he arrived at Wang-mei at the age of twenty-four, the year of his eight months' stay with Hung-jên can be fixed at 661. He had quickly obtained enlightenment and status, and now he returned to South China as the Sixth Patriarch.⁴ The next sixteen years he spent in the seclusion of his native mountains. We should note that at this time he had not yet forsworn the world to become a monk but continued life as a layman, nor was he as yet engaged in teaching.

In the year 676 Hui-nêng was ordained a monk, and the following year he returned to the monastery of Pao-lin-ssŭ, at

Ts'ao-ch'i in Kuang-tung Province, where he had stayed earlier. He now lectured regularly in the great Brahman temple of that city. His words carried the note of a new proclamation, and disciples streamed in from all directions. He turned down an invitation to the imperial court (705) which had been obtained for him by his colleague and rival, Shên-hsiu. Surrounded by his disciples, he died in his nearby native place, where, thanks to the favor of the Emperor, his old dwelling had been transformed into a temple. The *Sutra Spoken by the Sixth Patriarch from the High Seat of the Gem of the Law* contains, in addition to the core of his lectures in the great Brahman temple, his final instructions to his disciples and an account of his death.

There is the same lack of immediate and reliable sources for the teachings of Hui-nêng. The authentic old fragments in the first half of the sutra, which literary criticism still has to extricate from the accompanying glosses, must be closest to his spirit.[5] His commentary on the *Diamond Sutra* and the conversations with his disciples likewise present fragments of his thoughts. The basic texts of the southern sect further include the lectures and the inspired sermon of Shên-hui, whose ideas are in full harmony with the Hui-nêng sutra. At every point Shên-hui bases himself on Hui-nêng, who is regarded by all representatives of the southern sect as founder and final authority. But just how much of the classical Zen metaphysics actually derives from Hui-nêng's own genius, and how much of it was added by later disciples or was taken over from precursors, is difficult to determine. In any event, these early basic texts of the southern sect contain the complete Zen doctrine of enlightenment.

"To See into One's Nature and Become a Buddha"

The title "Zen Master of the Great Mirror," which was bestowed on Hui-nêng after his death, is indeed an apt designation of his genius. He experienced in sudden enlightenment
and realized in daily life the mirror-nature of the mind and
the spiritual nature of reality, which are the basic concepts of his
metaphysics. All reality is Spirit (Mind). The mind is one and,
like a mirror, is in motionless repose and yet perpetually active,
for its brightness reflects continuously. To behold the mind, no
special exercises of concentration are necessary. It is enough,
rather, to be freed from all duality in order that the mind may
shine in primal purity. "The enlightenment is your own nature.
Originally it was entirely pure. Only avail yourselves of this
mind and you will immediately become a Buddha." [6] Original
nature is inherently enlightened, it is wisdom (*prajñā*) and "of
itself in contemplation" (*samādhi*).[7] "Contemplation is not
distinct from wisdom, and wisdom is not distinct from contemplation. They are related as the lamp is to its light; both are
inseparable." [8] Therefore it is not necessary first to engage in
contemplation in order to attain wisdom. Contemplation and
wisdom are one and the same.

The prerequisite for the realization of this identity is the absence of passions, images, and thoughts. Originally self-nature
is free from all duality. "It is like the Void—without limitation,
also without angular or circular [form]; without greatness or
smallness, neither blue nor yellow, red nor white; without an
above or a below, neither long nor short; also without vexation
or joy, without yes or no, good or evil, beginning or end. All
Buddha-regions are entirely like the Void." [9]

The resolving of all opposites in the Void is the basic metaphysical doctrine of the *Diamond Sutra of Transcendental
Wisdom*, on which Hui-nêng founds his teachings. The absence
of thoughts, which is achieved in the practice of contemplation

by the suppression of all concepts, is regarded as the primal state of the mind whose mirror-light clings to no concept. The mind readily falls into the subtle error of conceiving absolute reality in objective terms in order thereby to dwell in it. "If the mind seeks to secure itself in *nirvāna,* it is bound by [the concept of] *nirvāna.* If it seeks to cling to the Void, it is bound by [the concept of] the Void." [10] Conversely, the absence of all thoughts indicates that the mind adheres to no object but engages rather in pure mirror-activity. This absolute knowing constitutes the unlimited activity of inexhaustible motion in the motionlessness of the mind.

In contrast to intuitive knowledge, the enlightenment of *prajñā* is directed toward no object; indeed, it consists of no conscious mental activity whatsoever. All objects are cleared away by the contemplation of the Void, and personal consciousness is overcome. Enlightenment occurs in the contemplation of one's own nature, which, like the Buddha-nature, is absolute and universal. Therefore it is equated with the Dharma-world (*dharmadhātu*), namely, the totality of all things. This nature is not awakened through outer means, but awakening occurs spontaneously at the base of the mind which comprehends the entire world of Dharma.

The cosmic character of enlightenment is explained by comparison with space. "One's own nature is of the same order as space. Its substance is identical with the Dharma-world." [11] All distinctions are nullified, and there is no difference between good and evil. "Good and evil are indeed contradictory, but their original nature is not different. This nondual nature is to be regarded as true nature. In this true nature there is no infection of good and evil. . . ." [12]

The distinction between enlightenment and illusion is likewise not one of essence. The fool is potentially equal to the sage, since he too possesses the Buddha-nature. The passions which hinder enlightenment do not really exist. "The ordinary

man is [at the same time] Buddha. The beclouding [of knowl-
edge] is [at the same time] Bodhi [enlightenment]." [13] When
one sees into one's own nature the passions disappear. The enlightened person is Buddha. This is "true deliverance." "Everyone is to deliver himself in his own nature." [14] In place of taking refuge in Buddha one is to take refuge in one's own nature.
"I advise you, understanding ones, to take refuge in the triple-
jewel of your own nature. . . ." [15] "The Buddha with his three
bodies subsists in our own nature. All men possess him in common." [16] "To take refuge by the mind in one's own nature is to
take refuge in the true Buddha." [17] The doctrine of autosalva-
tion centers on the identity of one's own nature with the Buddha. It is Buddha who, in the mind of the enlightened one,
saves himself.

Since in Zen everything depends on realization by sudden
experience, nowhere in the lectures and conversations which
constitute the core of the texts of the southern sect does one
find developed a philosophical epistemology. And yet quite
obviously it presupposes the monistic view according to which
all duality implies imperfection. Since self-consciousness and
objective knowledge introduce duality into the spirit, these
are excluded from the state of enlightenment. This is the viewpoint of pantheistic metaphysics. For the same reason Plotinus,
who in his epistemology postulates the unity of mind, of cognition and its object, denies that the absolute "One" possesses
the power of knowledge and self-consciousness.[18] Absolute
thought, which in creative response radiates and reflects all
things, transcends objective knowledge. Hui-nêng and his school
derived their metaphysical views from the Mahayanist doctrine
of Transcendental Wisdom (*prajñāpāramitā*), the sutras of
which they cherished above all others. "Take and read the
Diamond Prajñā Sutra and you will arrive at seeing into your
own nature. You must know that the merits of this sutra are
unfathomable and unlimited. . . . When the followers of Ma-

hāyāna and of the Supreme Vehicle hear the preaching of the *Diamond Sutra,* their spirit is opened to awakening." [19]

The philosophy of Mahāyāna Buddhism must be regarded as the first source of the metaphysical conception of Hui-nêng. One can detect in the expression and development of his thought much of the legacy of China. When, for example, Hui-nêng employs the conceptual scheme of substance and function in order to elucidate the relationship of contemplation (*samādhi*) and wisdom (*prajñā*), he actually pours Buddhist content into Chinese molds.[20] Likewise, he speaks of the Dharma-world in much the same way that the Taoists speak of the universe.[21] Nonetheless his cosmology stays within the Buddhist framework. The combination of the concepts of self-nature (*svabhāva*), Buddha-nature, and Buddha-knowledge is anticipated in the great Mahāyāna sutras.[22] Therefore it is difficult to point to anything completely new in Hui-nêng's teaching. And yet, even though the various elements of his proclamation existed beforehand, we can recognize his originality, the originality not of a thinker but of a mystic. Just as Meister Eckhart drew his teachings from scholastic philosophy, the Fathers of the Church, and Neo-Platonism, and formulated them anew in his mysticism, so Hui-nêng assimilated in his personal experience the Mahayanist metaphysics, enriched by Taoist influence, and proclaimed this message with the fervor of an evangelist.

Hui-nêng and his sect have not the remotest interest in a philosophical elaboration of the contents of enlightenment. For them, everything depends on the liberating experience. If Neo-Platonism develops an ontological doctrine of the stages of reality and derives an optimistic world-view from the goodness of the Absolute which radiates throughout all regions of being, the significance of Buddhist enlightenment is salvation from the cycle of earthly things.

The realization of enlightenment brings final liberation. This liberation is experienced immediately, as "a person feels both warm and cold when he drinks water." [23] Words are of no avail. "Just as one's hunger is not stilled by talking about food, so by mere speaking one cannot, in ten thousand aeons, attain to a view of reality." [24] As a pure and immediate experience, enlightenment seems to exclude all metaphysics. This leads Suzuki to speculate on the absence of metaphysics in Zen. But being based on an absolute monism, the nonmetaphysical, non-conceptual, and nonobjective thought of enlightenment does involve metaphysical assumptions. Hui-nêng is inspired by the doctrine of Transcendental Wisdom (*prajñāpāramitā*), on which the mystical metaphysics of his Zen is based.

The distinguishing mark of Hui-nêng's school of enlightenment is suddenness. But it must be specified clearly what is meant by suddenness, and wherein lies the difference from other ways of meditation. The peculiarity of the Zen of Hui-nêng is to be sought not so much in its pure experiential character (other schools likewise aim at sudden mystical experience) as in the disappearance of all stages on the way to enlightenment. The doctrine of the endless peregrination of sentient beings through cosmic space and time, in gradual ascent, arose in India. But in denying such progression, Zen does away with the purging of passions as well as with all efforts at conscious concentration. Liberation is not the overcoming of passions but rather their nonproduction. Enlightenment comes first. It is unmediated and sudden. Thereupon follows a phase of development, just as a mother gives birth to a child instantaneously and then nourishes it, or as the sun appears suddenly and then ice and dew melt away.[25] The unfolding is achieved by the exercises of the enlightened one, which differ substantially from preparatory practices. Wisdom shines and reflects of itself, in the works of the enlightened one.

It is in this divergent view of the place held by the exercises, as pointed out in the previous chapter, that we find the chief doctrinal conflict between the northern and southern sects. The elimination of all preliminary stages and the renunciation of all preparatory exercises is the typical Chinese element in the Zen of Hui-nêng. Shên-hui associates this sort of instantaneousness with the Chinese character, which in affairs of state permits the rapid rise of the common man to the rank of prince or military general.[26] Instantaneous and complete liberation without preliminary practice is the genuinely new element in Hui-nêng's way of enlightenment. This awakening in a single instant makes all effort superfluous. To be sure, there are differences in the subjective faculties of comprehension between those who are "quick to understand" and those who are "slow to understand," [27] but Hui-nêng does not construct a method of gradual approach based upon the psychological differences between people.

Shên-hui, however, who in the contest with the northern group led the teaching of Hui-nêng to triumph, did not dare to draw the final conclusions from his doctrine. In his sect, the Ho-tse, the sutras retain their place and theory eventually carries the day. The genuine heirs of Hui-nêng are the original Zen masters of the T'ang era, who in South China developed the Golden Age of Zen. They make of the renunciation of all methods the supreme method, and cultivate the nonpreparation of the spirit, because the door to enlightenment opens of its own accord.

Zen Masters of the T'ang Period

The period from the death of Hui-nêng in 713 until the persecution of Buddhism under the Emperor Wu-tsung (845) was the Golden Age of Chinese Zen, on which the chronicles, sayings, and *kōan* collections of later times present almost unlimited materials.[28] It was the time of those original Zen masters who in spiritual exaltation expressed their inexpressible experiences in ever new ways and paradoxical twists. The originality of these utterances stands in striking contrast to the monotony of their content. These vigorous and exuberant men thrust away all methods so as to be carried freely by the storm of the spirit. Endowed with an amazing facility of speech, they enriched the religious-mystical vocabulary with new terms which mock at reason and defy translation. During this period as well, Zen exerted a growing influence on Chinese culture.

"Westward from the river" and "southward from the lake," i.e., in the provinces of Kiangsi and Hunan, lay the center of classical Zen during this period. Thus one of the chronicles reports: "Westward from the river is the great 'Solitary One' [namely, Ma-tsu], the Master; southward from the lake is Shih-t'ou (700-790), the Master. People gather there in crowds. He who has not seen the two great masters is regarded as an ignoramus." [29]

Ma-tsu (707-786) was the dominant figure during the third generation after Hui-nêng. [30] As a follower of Huai-jang (677-744) he stood in the mainstream of Chinese Zen out of which arose the powerful Rinzai sect. He was the first to use shouting, known as *katsu* (Chin.: *ho*; Jap.: *katsu*), as a means to bring the disciple to enlightenment, a means later made famous by Lin-chi (Jap.: Rinzai). In Ma-tsu, paradox was mixed with rudeness. On one occasion, at the conclusion of a paradoxical dialogue, he suddenly grabbed the nose of his disciple Pai-chang and twisted it so violently that the latter cried out in pain —and attained enlightenment. The chronicle describes this robust figure as follows: "His appearance was remarkable. He strode along like a bull and glared about him like a tiger. If he stretched out his tongue, it reached up over his nose; on the soles of his feet were imprinted two circular marks." [31]

The important thing is not the sitting in meditation but the enlightenment, which can express itself in everything. While Ma-tsu was still a student, this was impressed upon him very vividly by his master, Huai-jang. Ma-tsu was then residing in the monastery continuously absorbed in meditation. His master, aware of his outstanding ability for the Dharma, asked him, "For what purpose are you sitting in meditation?" Ma-tsu answered, "I wish to become a Buddha." Thereupon the master picked up a tile and started rubbing it on a stone. Ma-tsu asked, "What are you doing, Master?" "I am polishing this tile to make a mirror," Huai-jang replied. "How can you make a mirror by rubbing a tile?" exclaimed Ma-tsu. "How can one become a Buddha by sitting in meditation?" countered the master.[32]

When we recall that in Zen the mirror symbolizes the enlightened mind, the meaning of this parable becomes evident. No practices are necessary to attain enlightenment, since the mind already possesses enlightenment within itself. Accordingly, Ma-tsu, in the key words of his doctrine, expressed this conviction as follows: "Apart from the mind there is no Buddha, and apart from the Buddha there is no mind. Do not cling to the good; do not reject the evil! As for purity or defilement—do not depend upon either one. Thus you will come to know the emptiness of the nature of sin. At no moment can you grasp sin, since it possesses no self-nature. Therefore the Three Worlds are only mind. The universe and all things bear the seal of the one Dharma." [33]

Ma-tsu expresses the core of Hui-nêng's teaching of "seeing into one's nature and becoming a Buddha" in pregnant formulations such as: "This very mind, this is the Buddha" and "Neither mind nor Buddha." [34] The identity of the mind with the Buddha and the total transcendence of the absolute mind-Buddha-reality is also upheld by his disciple Nan-ch'üan (748-834): "This is not mind, this is not Buddha, this is not a thing." In a doctrinal lecture to the people, striking because of its Taoist tinge, Nan-ch'üan elaborates this teaching, putting the words into the mouth of his master, Ma-tsu: "During the cycle (*kalpa*) of the Void there are no names. Since the appearance of Buddha in the world there are names. On the basis of these names men grasp the external characteristics [of things]. . . . The Great Tao includes everything without [distinction between] the holy and the profane. Whatever has a name is subject to limitations. Therefore the Elder of Kiangsi [Ma-tsu] said: 'This is not mind, this is not Buddha, this is not a thing.' " [35]

For more than thirty years Nan-ch'üan remained in the monastery named after him. There many disciples sought enlightenment under his guidance. The story of the killing of the cat, in which his most original disciple, Chao-chou (778-897), appears also, has become celebrated. The *Wu-mên-kuan* relates the episode as follows:

> Once in the monastery of Master Nan-ch'üan, the disciples of the East Hall and of the West Hall had an argument about a cat. Nan-ch'üan grabbed the cat and, holding it aloft, said: "If any one of you assembled here can say the right thing, the cat will be saved; if not, it will be killed." No one was able to answer. Thereupon Nan-ch'üan killed the cat. In the evening Chao-chou, who had been away for the day, returned. Nan-ch'üan turned to him and asked, "What would you have said had you been here?" Chao-chou took off his straw sandals, put them on his head, and walked out. "If you had been here," commented Nan-ch'üan, "the cat would have been saved." [36]

The saving word lay in the seemingly senseless action, which transcended all affirmation and negation.

There is no logical solution to the "paradoxical words and strange actions" which were introduced into South Chinese Zen, especially through Ma-tsu. The paradox discloses itself in the pregnant meaning of meaninglessness, to be found in the concrete situation of enlightenment. Probably the Zen master with the richest record of paradoxical sayings and remarkable actions is Chao-chou. Some of his sayings lend themselves to interpretation, as when he answers a request for instruction about enlightenment by simply saying, "Go wash your bowl." [37] Enlightenment can be found in everyday life. But many of his utterances push incoherence and absurdity to the extreme. "A monk once asked Chao-chou, 'When the entire body decomposes, there remains one thing, the eternal soul. What becomes of it?' The Master replied, 'The wind is blowing again this morning.'" [38] Or, "A monk asked Chao-chou, 'The ten thousand *dharmas* return to the One; to where does the One return?' The Master replied, 'While I was staying at Ch'ing-chou I made a robe that weighed seven pounds.'" [39] Such answers to metaphysical questions are meant to manifest the inadequacy of all words to express reality. Another saying of Chao-chou reveals true profundity: "A monk asked Chao-chou, 'If a poor man comes, what should one give him?' The Master answered, 'He lacks nothing.'" [40]

A rich collection of Chao-chou's sayings has come down to us, filled with the quick repartee and paradox of the master, who up to the venerable age of 120 continued to invent new eccentricities. His teachings center on the transcending of all differentiation. Enlightened stillness and the agitation of the passions are all one, the "nondual great Tao."

Another typical figure among the Zen masters of the T'ang period is Tê-shan (780-865), who stands in the tradition of Hsing-ssu (d. 740), the first among the disciples of Hui-nêng. Tê-shan came from North China. He was well versed in Buddhist learning, above all in the doctrine of Supreme Wisdom and in the *Diamond Sutra*. Reports about the flourishing Zen life in the South aroused painful doubts in his mind. Was it not culpable presumption to eschew the study of the sutras and to aspire to Buddhahood simply by seeing into one's own nature? For to grasp the truth, even with the help of the sacred scriptures, was an arduous undertaking. So, in a hostile mood, he set out for the South to combat these frivolous innovations. On his way he met an old woman who gave the first jolt to his trust in sutra knowledge, and directed him to the master Lung-t'an. According to the *Wu-mên-kuan*, the woman asked Tê-shan, who wanted to buy some refreshment from her, "Your Excellency, what are those writings you are carrying in your knapsack?" Tê-shan replied, "The *Commentaries on the Diamond Sutra*." Thereupon the woman said, "In the sutra it is written, 'The consciousness of the past is inexpressible, the consciousness of the present is inexpressible, the consciousness of the future is inexpressible.' What consciousness do you wish to refresh?" To this Tê-shan could give no answer, but following the woman's advice he walked the five miles to the home of Lung-t'an. There, as the master blew out the candle and darkness settled about him, the eye of enlightenment opened to Tê-shan instantaneously. The next day he went out and burned the sutras.[41]

Later, numerous disciples gathered around Tê-shan. In the training of his disciples he made much use of his staff. He never ascended the high seat in the Zen hall without this short stick, which he brandished in the air while he called out, "If you can speak, thirty blows! If you cannot speak, thirty blows!" [42] In the Rinzai sect, striking and shouting play a great role. The blows are not intended as punishment, but rather as an incentive and a practical means or artifice (*upāya*) to the comprehension of reality. It is a mistake to see in this striking and shouting mere crudeness. And yet a certain roughness is unmistakable. How little the Zen masters cared about blood and pain can be seen in an account of the severe Chü-chih. Chü-chih had taken over from his master, T'ien-lung, the so-called "One-Finger Zen." In place of all instruction he only lifted his finger and thereby led the disciple to enlightenment. One day a disciple imitated him. In answer to a question about enlightenment, he too, like his master, simply lifted a finger. When Chü-chih learned of this, he cut off the disciple's finger with a sword. Crying out in pain, the monk ran away. But the master called him back. As Chü-chih now lifted his own finger, the disciple attained enlightenment.[43]

The Monastic Life

All life requires form and, if it is genuine, will create forms that are appropriate to it. During the heyday of Zen in the T'ang period, the monastic rule of Pai-chang (749-814), which regulated the life of the Zen monks, was developed. While in India "a robe and a bowl on a stone under a tree" was adequate to the meager needs of a mendicant, in China, with its more rigorous climate and different customs, such simplicity did not suffice. In the earliest years of Chinese Zen, Tao-hsin had already set up certain rules for the life of his five hundred disciples, which stipulated that they should do manual work in order to supply their daily needs. Thus we see Hui-nêng, the newcomer from the South, engaged for eight months in splitting wood and treading the rice mill in the monastery of the Fifth Patriarch, Hung-jên.

Hui-nêng was not the only member of the community who served the common welfare by manual labor. Mention is made in the chronicles of rice-planting, farming, and bamboo-cutting, along with other activities.[44] Begging, however, was not abandoned completely; it subsisted as a reminder of the renunciation of property, one of the spiritual foundations of Buddhist monasticism. In earlier times the monks even renounced the communal possession of land in order to avoid all covetousness. The ethical value of work, within the framework of Zen, was recognized above all by the master Pai-chang, who for his celebrated monastic regulations was given the title "The Patriarch Who Created the Forest" (i.e., the community of disciples).

Since the monastic rules of Mahāyāna lacked clarity, all Buddhist monks in China, including the Zen monks, followed the

Hinayanist rules, which stipulate a strict discipline for the community of disciples (*samgha*). Building on the existing rules of the Mahāyāna and Hīnayāna Vinaya, Pai-chang combined what was good and useful in both and created a new order for the Zen monks. In this way he freed Zen from dependence on other Buddhist schools. The new regulations were practiced in the monastery which he had built. This community of strict Zen observance rapidly reached a high degree of prosperity. Numerous distinguished disciples gathered around the master who had devised the new monastic forms. The communal life of Pai-chang retained something of the simple rigor of ancient Buddhist monasticism, an achievement praised even by Confucianists.

The main precept of the rules is manual labor, a principle pregnantly formulated by Pai-chang: "A day without work—a day without eating." The master put the greatest value on having his monks work, and he himself set the best example. Even at an advanced age, he still insisted on working in the garden. When members of the community, concerned for his welfare, took his tools away, he refused to eat until he was again permitted to work.

Pai-chang's rules regulate the arrangement of the buildings, the hierarchy of offices, the special ascetic practices throughout the year, and the penalties for infringing the rules. They also prescribe in detail the daily routine of the monk's life. Meditation, worship, and manual labor alternate. During the periods of ascetic practice the monks sleep in the meditation hall, where each performs his meditation at his assigned place and takes his meals according to a fixed ritual.

Today's visitor to the Japanese Zen monastery will be deeply impressed by the order, cleanliness, and religious discipline. The Chinese rules were not introduced into Japan in full, and changes have been made during the centuries, yet most of what can be seen today goes back to the legislation of the master

Pai-chang. Significantly, the historical sources give a sympathetic picture of his personality. He is shown as simple and unpretentious in his words, kind and cheerful in his dealings, industrious and energetic in his labors.

Outer work and administrative activities can readily lead to slackening of the spirit and neglect of meditation. New attachments thus created may become real obstacles on the way to enlightenment. Pai-chang was aware of these dangers and sought to combat them. The inner freedom of the enlightened one was the favorite topic of his teaching. "To cling to nothing, to crave for nothing"—this is the basic principle he inculcated in his disciples. "When you forget the good and the nongood, the worldly life and the religious life and all other *dharmas,* and permit no thoughts relating to them to arise, and when you abandon body and mind—then there is complete freedom. When the mind is like wood or stone, there is nothing to discriminate." [45] Thus Pai-chang, through his Zen regulations, passed on the spirit of his master Ma-tsu in whose rigorous school he had been trained. Through these rules, too, he safeguarded the adherents of meditation from the ruin which threatens the spiritual freedom of a life given to idleness and lacking in restraint.

Until the third and fourth generation Hui-nêng and his disciples represent the apogee of Chinese Zen. These enlightened masters burn Buddha images and sutras, laugh in the face of inquirers or suddenly shout at them, and indulge in a thousand absurdities. Though they may behave like fools and possess nothing, yet they feel themselves true kings in their free mastery of enlightenment. They know no fear, since they desire nothing and have nothing to lose.

The adaptation of Indian Buddhist teaching to the Chinese character has been fully achieved, Indian metaphysics has been fused with Taoist thought, and the Chinese feeling for life has been assimilated. Strange actions are performed daily in the

Zen temples, but the movement itself stays within the limits of Buddhism. At no point do the Zen masters deviate from the Buddhist faith and its salient expressions. Certain iconoclastic manifestations may bewilder at first sight, but the burning of the Buddha images and the sutras does not imply an attack on the saint and founder, Shākyamuni. Such gestures are purely symbolic and should not be misinterpreted. Once the intoxication of enthusiasm is over, the Zen monks assemble before the Buddha image for the ritualistic reading of the sutras. This continues to the present day. The Zen school is a branch of the Buddhist tree, and the mysticism of enlightenment is a vital expression of the Buddhist religion.

7 Peculiarities of the "Five Houses"

After the great persecution of the year 845, which was the hardest blow encountered by Buddhism in China, of all the Buddhist schools at the close of the T'ang period only Zen flourished. At that time and during the later period of the Five Dynasties (907-960), South Chinese Zen developed into various traditions or families, usually known as the "Five Houses." When this expression was coined is not definitely known, though it appears to have been soon after the death of Fa-yen (885-958), the founder of the last of the "Five Houses."

Both the need for more closely knit organization and the development of local peculiarities seem to have given rise to the organization of separate sects. Generally the sects followed a uniform line of development, refusing to be led astray by irrelevancies. Two of these sects, the Ts'ao-tung (Jap.: Sōtō) and the Lin-chi (Jap.: Rinzai), developed into the two major streams of Zen, and it is in their tradition that Zen continues today. Both traditions must be regarded alike as legitimate heirs to the patriarchal heritage. We shall here review briefly the stages of development through which the "Five Houses" passed.[1]

The Circular Figures (Wei-yang Sect)

The earliest of the "Five Houses" was the short-lived Wei-yang sect, which took its name from the two mountains, Wei in Hunan Province and Yang in Kiangsi Province, where the temples of the founders were located. Wei-shan (771-853) was appointed by his master, Pai-chang, to head the new monastery, Ta-wei, as soon as he replied to the latter's question to the disciples: "Call him what you wish, only do not say 'water jug'! What will you call him?" Thereupon Wei-shan kicked over the jug and thus indicated his state of enlightenment. For this reason another master, Wu-mên, praised the "rare lad" who "overleaped the bonds of Pai-chang" and could not be held by any monastic regulations.[2]

Among the disciples of Wei-shan, Yang-shan and Hsiang-yen are outstanding personalities. When his parents refused him permission to enter the monastery, Yang-shan struck off two of his fingers to prove his seriousness. Thereupon they acquiesced and he devoted himself to Zen. He followed various masters and finally received the "seal of the Mind" from Wei-shan. When Hsiang-yen was questioned by his master, Wei-shan, about his existence before birth, he could not reply and searched for an answer in the sacred writings, but in vain. At last he burned all his books and withdrew into solitude, still inwardly troubled by this question. Then suddenly, in the midst of his daily chores, he heard the clatter of a falling tile. The sound awakened him to enlightenment. He hurried to the master and reported, "At one stroke I have forgotten all knowledge. There is no further need for ascetic practice." [3] As this episode indicates, Wei-shan and his disciples cultivated immediate experience in the style of the classic masters of the T'ang period. Beyond this, they developed a few special characteristics.

The method of the "perfect signs" or, concretely, of the "circular figures," which was first developed by Huai-jang, the disciple of Hui-nêng, was used by the Wei-yang sect to symbolize the nature of the enlightened consciousness or the "original countenance before birth." It was Yang-shan, himself enlightened instantaneously through the use of the circular figures, who brought this method, already practiced by Wei-shan, into its own among the disciples. "While the master sat there with closed eyes," the chronicle relates, "a monk came and stood quietly by his side. The master opened his eyes and drew a circle on the ground. Within the circle he wrote the character for water, then looked back at the monk. The monk said nothing." [4]

In Zen literature mention is made of ninety-seven circular figures. The use of circles not only became the main practice of the Wei-yang sect but also was widely diffused beyond its immediate limits. Opposition from other Zen sects was not lacking, however. This method, it was argued, had to be rejected, even as a preliminary artificial means (*upāya*)—it naturally would not be more—because it veiled the true nature of reality, namely, "the absolute emptiness and formlessness of all things." Possibly the similarity of this method to the *kasina* practice in Hīnayāna heightened the prejudice of many Zen disciples.

The Pass of a Single Word (Yün-mên Sect)

One of the most famous Zen masters of the later T'ang period and the era of the Five Dynasties was Yün-mên (d. 949). As many references to him in the chronicles and *kōan* indicate, he was much loved by later generations. He attained enlightenment under the master Mu-chou, a disciple of Huang-po, through whose rigorous school Lin-chi had also passed. Three times he asked his master for elucidation of the truth, but without success. The third time, the latter threw him out of the gate and shut it so suddenly and with such force that Yün-mên's leg was caught in it and broken. At the extreme pain Yün-mên attained enlightenment. Afterward he spent four years in the monastery of Hsüeh-fêng (822-908), whose heir he became in the line of transmission. Just as he himself attained enlightenment at a great price, he did not spare his disciples. He was in the habit of striking the novices with his staff and of frightening them by shouting suddenly, "*Kuan!*" A solid and robust character, he gathered many disciples around himself in the Yün-mên monastery, from which he received his name.

One of Yün-mên's original devices was to reply to a question or a request concerning enlightenment with only a single word or a single character. This innovation is known in Zen history as the "pass of a single word." Many examples are recorded. "Of what kind is the eye (essence) of the true Dharma?" "Everywhere." Or, "He who kills his father and kills his mother confesses before the Buddha. But before whom shall he who kills the Buddha and kills the patriarchs confess?" "Obvious!" Or again, "What is the meaning of the Patriarch's coming from the West?" "Master!" [5] (The Patriarch is Bodhidharma, and the question concerning the meaning of his coming from the West, India, in Zen is equivalent to the question, "What is reality?")

The collected sayings of Yün-mên contain two answers of similar character to the question concerning the essence of Zen. In the one instance the master says laconically, "That's it," in the other, "Not a word to be predicated." [6] To give a final example: when a monk asked him, "What is the Buddha?" he received the answer, "A dried-up dirt scraper." The Buddha is everything. It is simply a matter of the right way of seeing.

Yün-mên also gave the classical formulation for the eternal Now in the time-transcending enlightenment. The main section of the sixth *kōan* in the collection of the *Pi-yen-lu* records: "Yün-mên said, 'I do not ask you what was fifteen days past. But can

you say a word about what will be fifteen days hence?' In place
of [the disciples] he himself replied, 'Every day is the good
day.'" "The good day," namely, the here and now of enlightenment, is the central point on which Yün-mên takes his
stand. According to one commentator, the fifteen days past
signify the time of practice from the first awakening of the
desire for truth until the time of ultimate comprehension in experience. The Now of enlightenment is as perfect as the full
moon at the halfway mark of its cycle. Just as the moon wanes
and becomes dark, so during the fifteen days following enlightenment the consciousness of the awakening, which still lingers
in the mind as a residue, fades and disappears. Enlightenment
now equals "every day," and the "every day" equals enlightenment. Thus it becomes useless to distinguish between the before and the after. Reality is one single Now. This Now is every
day. "Every day is the good day." [7]

Yün-mên eschews theory and excels in originality, paradox,
and trenchant repartee in keeping with the tradition of the
great masters of the T'ang period. One finds an anticipation of
dialectics in the so-called "Three Propositions of Yün-mên."
These were set up in the spiritual tradition of the master by his
most eminent disciple, Tê-shan, who presented them, when he
took over the leadership of the sect, as the quintessence of Yün-
mên's teaching. Phrased obscurely, they characterize the state
of enlightenment as freedom from all attachment to the relative world of appearances or to a single Absolute. [8]

The Interpenetration of the Attributes of Being (Fa-yen Sect)

A third sect, of lesser importance than the two preceding ones,
and one which disappeared just as quickly, was that of Fa-yen
(885-958). This learned master, equally versed in the Chinese
classics and in the literature of Buddhism, attracted many dis-

ciples who committed themselves to his firm yet gentle guidance. He excelled in psychological insight and skillful adaptation. His scholarly bent may to some extent have impaired his practice of the true Zen method. He applied neither stick nor shouting with his disciples, but employed sharp repartee and paradox. His favorite practice, the constant repetition of a word or phrase without explanation, reflects in any case the Zen spirit.

Fa-yen studied the *Avatamsaka Sutras* (Chin.: *Hua-yen*) thoroughly, especially the doctrine of the interpenetration of the six basic attributes of being. These are: totality and distinction, identity and difference, becoming and passing away. These attributes are illustrated by a circle, in which are represented the aspects of reality which are neither identical nor different. The following explanation is attributed to Fa-yen:

> The meaning of the six attributes in Hua-yen is that within identity there is difference. For difference to be different from identity is in no wise the intention of all the Buddhas. The intention of all the Buddhas is both totality and distinction. How can there be both identity and difference? When the male body and the female body enter *samādhi*, no reference to male and female body remains. When no reference remains, terms are transcended. The ten thousand appearances are utterly bright, there is neither reality nor phenomena.[9]

This basic doctrine of Mahayanist monism is comprehended in the contemplation of the circular figure which contains the six attributes, a practice that can scarcely be distinguished from certain Hinayanist practices. Fa-yen perpetuated the Zen tradition of the T'ang period, including instantaneous enlightenment, but a certain reversion to the older Buddhist tradition is unmistakable. His emphasis on the teachings of the Mahāyāna sutras constitutes a bridge to other forms of Buddhism with which Zen was later to develop various ties.

The Five Ranks (Ts'ao-tung Sect)

The name of the Ts'ao-tung sect (Jap.: Sōtō) is a contraction of the ideographs of its two founders, Tung-shan (807-869) and Ts'ao-shan (840-901), who in turn had been named after the mountains on which their respective monasteries stood.[10] When the name for this "House" of Zen was first used is uncertain, though it appears to have been soon after the death of Ts'ao-shan early in the tenth century. Tung-shan was not yet ten years old when he left his parental roof and began his unsettled monastic life. He received his first instruction in Zen from a disciple of Ma-tsu and later, at the age of twenty, was ordained a monk. Thereafter he followed the two famous masters Nan-ch'üan and Wei-shan for a short while, finally becoming a disciple of Yün-yen (772-841), whose line he perpetuated. It is related that his master, Yün-yen, taught him to understand the "sermon of inanimate things," which in Zen signifies, not the miraculous power of the Buddhist saint who can hear with his eyes and see with his ears, but the knowledge of the undifferentiated identity of animate and inanimate beings in the unity of Buddhahood. Many brief dialogues between him and his master have been preserved in Zen literature.

After the conclusion of his novitiate, Tung-shan visited the temples of China and became acquainted with the leading contemporary representatives of Zen. These encounters with Zen masters from different traditions afforded him a wide knowledge of the peculiarities in doctrine and method, which at the time displayed a rich variety of forms. His long years of wandering, filled with many vicissitudes, came to an end when at the age of fifty-two he entered the monastery on Mount Tung. There he devoted the brief remainder of his life to the guidance of his disciples, among whom Ts'ao-shan and Yün-chü (d. 902) were the most distinguished.

These two chief disciples of Tung-shan displayed the same

contrast in character that we noted in the rivalry of the two successors of the Fifth Patriarch, Hung-jên, namely, Hui-nêng and Shên-hsiu. Ts'ao-shan,[11] who was familiar with Confucianism from early youth, was a man of strong scholarly bent, and continued his studies after entering the Buddhist monastic life, with parental permission, at the age of eighteen. His novitiate under Tung-shan was brief, perhaps from 865 to 868, and only two dialogues with the master have been handed down, the one at his arrival and the other at his departure. He was especially interested in the Five Ranks (see below) in which Tung-shan formulated the dialectic of enlightenment. He traveled very little. For thirty-five years he dwelt in quiet contemplation in the two monasteries of Ts'ao-shan and Ho-yü-shan, and there exercised his sharp mind in concentration on the Five Ranks, the meaning of which he developed and explained. The chronicles list the names of nineteen of his disciples. Nevertheless, within four generations his line was extinct.

Yün-chü,[12] the other important disciple of Tung-shan, showed little interest in the dialectical teaching of the Five Ranks. He directed his efforts toward the immediate experience of enlightenment, which he embodied in an austerely ethical life. Before devoting himself to Zen he had learned the monastic discipline of Vinaya. He came to Tung-shan two years before the arrival of his colleague Ts'ao-shan, but nonetheless stayed longer and received a careful training from the master, as the many recorded dialogues show. Among Tung-shan's disciples he enjoyed the highest reputation. The many eminent men who later emerged from his school described him as one of the most important and influential men of the time. Furthermore, his disciples and spiritual heirs perpetuated his sect in China, and through Dōgen it was taken to Japan, where it still flourishes today.

The doctrine of the Five Ranks of the Ts'ao-tung sect is characteristic of the dialectic of Zen.[13] In contradistinction to the

Five Ranks of ontological-psychological analysis in Buddhist philosophy, as well as in the Abhidharmakośa or the Vijñaptimātra doctrine, the Five Ranks of Ts'ao-tung all express the same thing, namely, the fundamental identity of the Absolute and the relative, which can be viewed in the various stages of development. This teaching of the Ranks is an outgrowth of the *prajñāpāramitā* doctrine, but was shaped by the Chinese mind, in accord with *The Book of Changes* (*I Ching*). It can thus be regarded as an expression of Chinese philosophy. The basic concepts stem from Tung-shan, who built on the foundation of Shih-t'ou and other Zen masters of the T'ang period. But it was Ts'ao-shan who, grasping the heart of the master's teaching, gave it the final form in which it has come down to us. The following interpretation is based on his commentary.

According to their literal meaning, the two characters which express the Absolute and the relative in their opposition signify the straight (or erect) and the bent (or inclined). These correspond to the concepts of *li* (the Absolute Principle) and *shih* (the phenomenon) in Chinese philosophy, which are also designated the dark and the bright, and are illustrated by a black circle (●) and a white one(○), Tung-shan explains the straight as follows: "There is one thing: above, it supports heaven; below, it upholds earth. It is black like lacquer, perpetually in movement and activity." The straight is also the One, the Absolute, the foundation of heaven and earth and all Being. But this Absolute is dynamic, constantly in motion. The perceiving mind cannot lay hold upon the straight and grasp it as object. It is the true Void, without duality, of which the metaphysics of Supreme Wisdom (*prajñāpāramitā*) speaks.

The Absolute becomes manifest and completely penetrates the phenomenal world. It thus becomes the All and all things. This is the bent or the bright. But the two, Absolute and relative-phenomenal, are not separate, are not two, but one. The Absolute is the Absolute with regard to the relative. The relative, however, is relative with reference to the Absolute. Therefore the relative-phenomenal is also called the "marvelous existence," which is inseparable from the true Void. Thus the expression "the marvelous existence" contains the quintessence of the enlightened view of reality.

The oneness of the Absolute and the relative-phenomenal is the fundamental concept of the Five Ranks of Tung-shan. Their interrelationship is expressed in the character which signifies "middle" or "within." The Five Ranks, then, develop as follows:

1. *The Absolute within the relative*: Because the Absolute merges entirely with the relative, the comprehension of reality is possible by a complete turning toward the relative-phenomenal. In this rank the knower separates himself from the straight, the Absolute or the *li*, and gives himself over entirely to phenomenal existence. The movement is from the Absolute to the relative. In the symbolic representation the upper half of the center of the Absolute (◗).

2. *The relative within the Absolute*: The second rank denotes the movement from the relative to the Absolute. Inasmuch as the relative-phenomenal is such only by virtue of the Absolute, one must of necessity encounter the Absolute in the relative. Any statement concerned with the phenomenal, of necessity goes beyond the purely phenomenal. The explanation of this stage thus states that it means "abandoning phenomena (*shih*) and entering the Principle (*li*)." But since the Absolute and the relative are nonetheless identical, no separation from either is made in these first two stages, in spite of the fact that attention is given, now to the relative, now to the Absolute. Being is the fullness of appearance, and appearance is the fullness of Being. They merge completely. The symbolic representation, the exact reverse of the first, is (◖).

The first two ranks illustrate the interpenetration of the Absolute and the relative, of Being and appearance. One would expect that in the third rank the opposition would merely be resolved back into oneness. But in the scheme of the Five Ranks two more ranks (numbers 3 and 4) are inserted, in which number 3, the Absolute purely as Absolute, and then number 4, the relative purely as relative, are comprehended. The first two ranks, in which the one is fully contained in the other (the two signs of the straight and the bent are united by the sign for "middle" or "within"), are placed in opposition to the other two ranks of "alone," in order that in a fifth rank all contradiction may finally be resolved. Accordingly the third rank is as follows:

3. *The Absolute alone:*   Inasmuch as no other side, nothing relative-phenomenal, appears in this formula, the "middle" symbol has lost its meaning of interpenetration and signifies merely by implication the potentiality of the relative in the Absolute. The Absolute is contemplated in its stark Absoluteness, without reference to or inclination toward the relative-phenomenal. This third rank shows the Absolute before any unfoldment or externalization, but pregnant with all the possibilities of development, like seeds before the first germ sprouts. This Absolute is, at the same time, the terminus of a retrogressive process of evolution, when all development, all words, sink into silence. "The nonword contains the word," says the explanation. The symbolic representation would be a black circle surrounded by a white one signifying potentiality (⊙).

4. *The relative-phenomenal alone:*   The fourth rank signifies, accordingly, the relative-phenomenal alone in its stark relativity. Phenomena, conditional combinations and forces, are viewed in their respective individual forms. In this way Absoluteness becomes evident through the relative. "In the word is the nonword." Tung-shan compares this to two swordsmen fighting with naked swords, neither of whom can force the other to yield, or to the lotus unscorched in the midst of fire.

In the symbolic representation the relative is to be found in the center of the Absolute (**O**).

5. *The Absolute and the relative-phenomenal together:* The fifth rank unquestionably signifies the highest rank, namely, undifferentiated oneness. Perhaps in the structure of the Five Ranks, it may be apprehended as the transcending of the opposites of the first two ranks of "interpenetration" and the following two ranks of "alone." This last transcendence and negation of all opposites becomes the highest absolute affirmation, the final freedom which the Zen masters attribute to enlightenment. The symbolic representation is the black circle (●).

In the commentaries on the Five Ranks comparisons play an important role. The most famous is Ts'ao-shan's parallel of the "Lord and Vassal," in which the dialectic of the ranks in the meaning described above is excellently expressed:

1. The lord sees the vassal.
2. The vassal turns toward the lord.
3. The lord (alone).
4. The vassal (alone).
5. The lord and the vassal in union.

The metaphysics of the Five Ranks is that of the Middle Way of Nāgārjuna, who systematized the doctrine of the *Sutras of Transcendental Wisdom.* But these ranks in Zen are not to be taken as mere speculation, but rather as the "Dharma gate to the opening of the eye of the mind" in enlightenment. The speculations seek to make evident the interpenetration of all things in the mature identity of the one Buddha-reality. When this unity has been experienced, the expression becomes irrelevant. Every word and every gesture, however senseless they may be, can signify reality. In Zen, therefore, the highest dialectical speculation can turn into arbitrary absurdity at any instant.

The Five Ranks exercised a wide influence beyond the Ts'ao-tung sect. Fen-yang (947-1024), one of the most eminent masters of the Lin-chi (Jap.: Rinzai) sect, adopted them with a modification of their sequence and composed a commentary on them. Later, logical trickery brought the Five Ranks into discredit.

Shouting and Beating (Lin-chi Sect)

The most important of the "Five Houses" is the Lin-chi sect. Its founder, Lin-chi, was a man of genius with a brilliant mind and an indomitable will. He enjoyed the esteem of his contemporary Chinese Buddhists and exercised a lasting influence on Zen history. *The Collected Sayings of Lin-chi* reports extensively on his life and work. These sayings belong to the most important writings of the Zen sects.[14]

Lin-chi had already spent three years in the monastery of the famous Huang-po without having once conversed with his master. But he was consumed by an ardent desire for enlightenment. After diligent study of the Vinaya and the sutras, he had turned to Zen in order to have his mind opened to the full truth, and thus to see reality. At the time Mu-chou was first among the disciples of Huang-po. Encouraged by Mu-chou, Lin-chi finally ventured, after three years of waiting, to enter the room of the master and to question him about the essential truth of Buddhism. Instead of an answer he received twenty blows of the stick. In sorrow he returned to Mu-chou to report his experience. On the latter's friendly advice he returned to the master a second and a third time, only to have the experience repeated. He was unable to understand what it all meant. Thinking that his failure was due to an evil *karma* working itself out in his life and that of Huang-po, he decided to leave the monastery and seek another master. Mu-chou concurred in this and accompanied him to Huang-po's room, who in parting directed him to the Zen master Ta-yü.

Thus Lin-chi journeyed to Ta-yü and inquired of him for

what mistakes he had deserved such severe beatings. But Ta-yü explained that actually Huang-po had treated him with consummate kindness, and scolded him for his obtuseness. Then suddenly Lin-chi was awakened. He saw everything in a new light; and in a completely changed tone asserted that the *dharma* of Huang-po was nothing special. Thereupon Ta-yü struck him harshly, saying, "A moment ago this little pipsqueak wanted to know what his mistakes were, and now he makes light of the *dharma* of Huang-po. What impudence!" But undismayed, Lin-chi pummeled him three times in the ribs. Ta-yü now recognized the genuineness of his enlightenment, which he credited to Huang-po.

Ta-yü now sent the young Lin-chi back to his former master, to whom he related his experience. Concealing his joy at the happy outcome he had foreseen, Huang-po pretended to censure Ta-yü's gullibility. If Ta-yü were to come to the monastery, he would taste twenty blows himself, he declared. "No need to wait for that," replied Lin-chi, "here you are!" and dealt the old master a vigorous slap in the face. "This mad fellow!" called out Huang-po. And Lin-chi, in a thunderous voice, roared, *"Katsu!"* He had obtained enlightenment and received the Dharma seal, namely, the succession to the master Huang-po.

Shouting and beating with a stick characterize the way of enlightenment along which Lin-chi leads his numerous disciples to the experience of ultimate reality. He cudgels and cuffs them; he roars at them, for he has experienced in his own body that such harsh encounters with reality can lead more quickly and surely to enlightenment than discourses and disputes. Nevertheless he was aware of the limitations of this method, as the following dialogue with a disciple makes clear. "The master inquired of Lo-p'u and said, 'One man has been using a stick and another resorting to the *katsu*. Which of them do you think is the more intimate to the truth?' Answered the disciple, 'Neither of them.' 'What is the most intimate, then?' Lo-p'u cried out, '*Katsu!*' Whereupon Lin-chi struck him." [15] Many anecdotes in the collected sayings show the master and the disciples in action. Is it sportive play, a burst of manly vigor, or earnest ascetic struggle that here astounds us?

Lin-chi distinguished four types of shouting (*katsu*). "One time the shout is like the precious sword of the Vajrarāja. Another time the shout is like a golden-haired lion crouching on the ground. Another time the shout is like the pole and weeds [with which the fisherman brings the fish together in one place]. Finally there is the roar that is not really a roar." [16] In this explanation of the shout one may venture, perhaps, to recognize characteristics of enlightenment more clearly brought out in other texts. The sword might indicate the keenness of enlightenment; the crouching lion, controlled power; the pole and the weeds, the mystery in the homely things of daily life; and the fourth shout, the paradox of experience.

Lin-chi's sharp mind delighted in dialectics. In his collected sayings there is a text frequently commented upon by teachers of the sect in later periods. The ascent to the grasp of reality by the enlightened one is explained by four attitudes toward subject and object:

> Sometimes take away [i.e., negate] the subject and not the object; another time take away the object and not the subject; yet another time take away both subject and object; and finally take away neither subject nor object [therefore affirm both at the same time].[17]

As to formula, the text depends upon the well-known "Four Propositions" of Indian Buddhist logic (*catushkotika*); as to meaning, it corresponds to the four aspects of reality in the Hua-yen doctrine. In the first and second stages illusion departs first from the subject and then from the object; clinging to subjective intellectual perception and to the objective world is overcome. The third stage negates both subject and object, but their differentiation continues to exist. Finally, in the fourth stage, when the transcending of the opposition of subject and object has been affirmed, the confrontation of subject and object ceases completely. Reality is comprehended in its final oneness.

Analogous formulas are the "Fourfold Relation of Guest and Host" and the "Fourfold Precedence and Subsequence of Light and Activity." With all such formulas the terms must be understood symbolically. We are concerned with a logical or metaphysical dialectic regarding the relationship of subject and object, relative and Absolute, appearance and reality. Another of Lin-chi's expressions regarding the "Three Mysteries and the Three Essentials" was applied by later commentators to the triad of substance, quality, and activity, which are regarded as one and inseparable.

However, one would present a false picture were one to overemphasize the importance of the various doctrinal elements in the Zen of Lin-chi. In the final analysis his chief interest is immediate enlightenment. Boldly he praises the "great freedom" of the enlightened one, who has attained to the supreme self-realization through his own effort. Freed from all fetters, the figure of the enlightened one towers in steep solitude. He asserts his existence at the crossroads of life between being and nonbeing. Nothing can block his way.

The truly enlightened one cares not for the Buddha nor yet for the Bodhisattva or the saints. He rejects mere pious acts. Having freed himself by his own effort from the cycle of things, he adheres to nothing. Even if the universe should collapse, he would not waver for a moment. Should all the Buddhas from the ten heavens come to meet him, no thought of joy would disturb him. Should all the nether worlds and hells be opened, no fear would confuse him. For everything is void: being which changes and nonbeing which does not change. The three worlds are only mind, the ten thousand things are only consciousness, dreams, and illusions.[18]

Lin-chi describes with inimitable vividness the freedom of the state of enlightenment. "Elevated above all external circumstances, the enlightened one does not burn, though he walk in fire, and he does not drown, though he enter the water. In the nether world and hell he plays as in a pleasure garden, and among hungry ghosts and beasts not a hair is disturbed." [19] Freedom in being untouched by birth and death is the true fruit of enlightenment, whereby the enlightened one is like unto Buddha.

During the period here surveyed, of somewhat more than a century, the Zen movement of the T'ang era crystallized into the "Five Houses." This incipient differentiation is important for the development during the Sung period, which gave to Zen its actual form. The earliest of the "Five Houses," the Wei-yang sect, was separated from the latest one, the Fa-yen sect, by approximately a century. Yün-mên was one of the strongest personalities in the "Zen forest," but his House disintegrated rapidly. Only the Ts'ao-tung and the Lin-chi sects were perpetuated. In both these Houses the dialectical impulse, which was present in the beginnings of Zen and was cultivated by the early masters of the T'ang period, above all by Shih-t'ou, was developed further. The inclination to theoretical and intellectual activity, which the use of dialectics encourages, was balanced by an emphasis on the instantaneous character of immediate enlightenment, as well as by the concrete, often paradoxical and painfully harsh, guidance of Lin-chi. But this much is certain: Zen has never existed in pure experience only, without admixture of theoretical teachings or methodical practice, as it has sometimes been idealized. It could not exist in that fashion, for mysticism, like all other human experience, is dependent on the actual conditions of human life.

8 Spread and Methodological Development During the Sung Period

Zen and the Spirit of the Age[1]

Historians point out that during the Sung period of Chinese history, Buddhism in general fell into decline. It was unable to recover from the severe persecution of the Emperor Wu-tsung toward the end of the T'ang period (845), though during the next few centuries no new oppression of any importance followed. The emperors of the Sung period were well disposed toward Buddhism. And yet this time was hardly congenial to the prospering of monastic life, for the empire was beset by political turmoil within and enemies without. The major factor in the decadence of Buddhism, however, was its enervation and loss of discipline.

Only the Zen sects withstood the general decline. After the storm of persecution under the Emperor Wu-tsung, a period of expansion soon set in. During the Sung period Zen was accorded the highest esteem. While the religious rigor and originality of the T'ang masters was not equaled again, the cultural creativity of Zen surpassed all previous attainments. Despite its political instability, the Sung period is one of the most significant cultural eras in the whole of Chinese history. To this Zen contributed greatly. Zen monks were among the eminent painters of the period. The Zen spirit was so fully absorbed by the art of the time that to this day Sung art can be regarded as the typical artistic expression of Zen. In Japan it was the Buddhist monks and their friends who introduced the fine artistic works of the Sung period along with the Neo-Confucian philosophy of Chu Hsi and the Zen way of enlightenment. The three were regarded as of one piece, and together were cultivated and further developed in the Zen monasteries.

The new philosophical creativity of the Sung period was closely related to Zen, in whose quiet temples the leading philosophers of the time practiced meditation. The mode of contemplation which arose at this time in Confucianism, and was practiced by Chu Hsi, is akin to the Zen practice of sitting, and according to authoritative sources was actually stimulated by Zen. Although the Confucian renaissance of the Sung period rejected Zen, Buddhist elements can be detected in its philosophical systems. This is true even of Chu Hsi, who was an avowed foe of the Buddhist religion. The Confucian delight in metaphysical systems was strongly stimulated by Mahayanist speculation, which left as deep an imprint on Chinese thought as did the wisdom of Taoism.

The extensive spread of Zen during this time was not always marked by depth and genuineness of religious experience. Indeed, the rapid outer growth occasioned an inner decline and, in the end, led to a crisis involving the very existence of Zen, in which the *kōan* exercise was organized as a methodical way to enlightenment. Inner impoverishment accompanied outer splendor. Bodhidharma and the great masters of the T'ang era had avoided the capital, and had steadfastly resisted the overtures of the imperial court. But during the Sung period the Zen monasteries maintained friendly relations with the court, were often involved in political affairs, and became focal points in social and cultural life. Particularly eminent were the "Five Mountains" and the "Ten Temples" of the Lin-chi sect. As the number of Zen disciples grew, their quality necessarily declined. The danger of numbers was all the greater since up until this time Zen had known neither doctrine nor systematic exercises, but had transmitted "mind" and experience only.

Another danger of the time was an ascendant intellectualism which, encouraged by the syncretistic tendencies inherent in all Buddhism, aimed at the fusion of Zen with other sects. Admittedly, many of the masters of the T'ang period were well versed in the sutras and shastras, but they had found liberation solely in experience, and inculcated in their disciples the conviction of the superiority of enlightenment over all knowledge of the sutras. But during the Sung era, sutra learning pushed its way more vigorously into Zen and led to divers alliances on both sides.

As long as it was merely a matter of the *Avatamsaka Sutras*, the danger did not seem acute, since these sutras are intimately related to Zen and, indeed, furnish the key to the world-view of Zen. By contrast, the efforts to achieve a *rapprochement* with the highly differentiated and theoretical doctrine of the T'ien-t'ai (Jap.: Tendai) school were unacceptable to Zen. In its encounter with this school, Zen opposition to sutra Buddhism sometimes went to the extreme of rejecting all of the sacred writings. At first glance, the bonds between Zen and Amida Buddhism may seem especially surprising in view of the basic difference in structure between the two movements. But here too the embedding of Zen in Buddhist piety—a piety which Zen may surpass in mystical enlightenment but can never fully deny—becomes evident. Moreover, there is a remarkable psychological similarity between the rhythmic repetition of the Buddha name in the so-called *nien-fo* (Jap.: *nembutsu*) and the intensive practice of the *kōan*. During the Sung period it was above all Yung-ming (904-975) of the Fa-yen sect, one of the greatest syncretists in Chinese Buddhist history, who promoted the unity of Zen and Amida piety, and sought as well to establish contact with T'ien-t'ai.

The Rise of the Kōan in the Lin-chi Sect

During the Sung period three of the "Five Houses" became totally extinct; Yün-mên and Fa-yen declined about the middle of the period, while Wei-yang had already ceased to exist at an earlier date. After having flourished during the T'ang period, the survival of the Ts'ao-tung sect also was for a time in the balance. Gradually it regained considerable strength, but without ever equaling the Lin-chi sect in China. In its beginnings, the Lin-chi sect was of no more importance than the other sects during the T'ang era; from about the middle of the tenth century, however, it rose rapidly and covered the country with its temples and monasteries.

In the seventh generation after Lin-chi a split gave rise to two branches named for two disciples, Huang-lung (1002-1069) and Yang-chi (992-1049). Huang-lung, who gathered a thick "forest" of disciples about himself, was distinguished by his ingenious use of the paradox, as his famous text of the "Three Barriers" shows. The following play of question and answer (Jap.: *mondo*) has been preserved in Zen tradition as an exercise for enlightenment:

> Question: "Everyone has his own native place owing to the causal nexus [*karma*]. Where is your native place?"
> Answer: "Early in the morning I ate white rice gruel; now I feel hungry again."
> Question: "In what way do my hands resemble the Buddha's hands?"
> Answer: "Playing the lute [*biwa*] in the moonlight."
> Question: "In what way do my feet resemble the feet of a donkey?"
> Answer: "When the heron stands in the snow, its color is not the same." [2]

The Lin-chi sect was first transplanted to Japan by the Huang-lung line of transmission. In China, this branch had already died out in the fourth or fifth generation. It was the Yang-chi line of the Lin-chi sect which brought Chinese Zen to its highest development. Many anecdotes, employing paradox, are related about Yang-chi—a man of great charm and goodness. A second-generation disciple of his, Wu-tsu (1025-1104), described the immediacy of experience by comparing it to sensory perception, namely, that of tasting water. He exerted a strong influence upon later generations.

The rise of the *kōan* is connected with the names of Wu-tsu's two successors, Yüan-wu (1063-1135) and Ta-hui (1089-1163).[3] From the end of the T'ang period and the time of the Five Dynasties on, the inner development of Zen had tended in this direction. Men looked up in reverence to the towering figures of the old masters and immersed themselves in the "accounts of the fathers" and "models of the elders" which had been handed down from early days. In a time of spiritual slackening and regression they hoped once more to grasp the true Zen spirit through the aid of the accounts of the fathers. *Kōan* (Chin.: *kung-an*) means, literally, "public notice" or "public announcement." In Zen, anecdotal events or utterances of the masters are given to the disciples as problems for practice. During the Sung period, such problems, suitable as means for methodical guidance to enlightenment, were collected.

The two most important *kōan* collections, the *Pi-yen-lu* and the *Wu-mên-kuan*, date from that period. The main source for the hundred *kōan* of the *Pi-yen-lu* (1125) was the *Models of the Elders*, which Hsüeh-tou (988-1052) gathered from the *Zen Chronicle* of the Ching-tê era. For each model he composed a brief verse or ode (*gāthā*). The third "layer" of this work is formed by the addition of Yüan-wu, who interpolated commentaries on the anecdotes and the *gāthā* and explanations of the *kōan*, and provided an introduction. When a *kōan* is presented to the disciple today, the commentaries of Yüan-wu are usually replaced by the master's own comments, which, however, are based on traditional explanations. Thus an extensive literature accretes around the simple and profound basic texts.

A century after the *Pi-yen-lu*, the *Wu-mên-kuan* appeared (1228); it had been assembled by Hui-k'ai (1184-1260).[4] This collection is less extensive, and the forty-eight *kōan* are more concisely formulated. Beyond this, the explanations of Wu-mên, as Hui-k'ai was named by his disciples after his work, and the verses of enlightenment at the end of each *kōan* are highly concentrated. If the *Pi-yen-lu* is more valuable from a literary viewpoint, the *Wu-mên-kuan* excels in pregnant brevity. This is why Japanese Zen masters like to use it for the wearisome exercises of the hot summer season. Both *kōan* collections exemplify the genuine Zen spirit. Both are true expressions of the Chinese genius and can be regarded as literary works of the highest order. The experience of nature as expressed in the *gāthās* of Hsüeh-tou finds in Japanese Zen literature its strongest echo.

In assessing *kōan* practice one must keep in mind that this is a method which leads to enlightenment but is not the enlightenment itself, and therefore is not the essence of Zen as such. In a significant comment regarding the development of Zen, Ui distinguishes between "doctrine" and "auxiliary means" on the way to enlightenment. By "doctrine" he refers to the theoretical material of the sutras, while by "auxiliary means" he designates the paradoxical words and actions, the beatings and the shoutings, as well as the *kōan* method itself.[5] He finds both elements present in Zen from the beginning; prior to Ma-tsu and the great masters of the T'ang period there was more emphasis on doctrine and less on means, the reverse becoming true as time went on. Yet, Ui says, it would be misleading to judge Zen on the basis of the relationship of doctrine and means, since both possess merely relative value in the Zen scheme. Among Zen followers the auxiliary means are often overestimated, because they are peculiar to Zen, which easily leads to a depreciation of the basic Buddhist teaching. Finally, Ui points out that the two elements are by no means mutually exclusive, but that each actually conditions the other. Auxiliary means are likewise rooted in Buddhist doctrine and presuppose it, while on the other hand many doctrinal statements are used as *kōan* exercises. During the Sung period, the thunderous shout "*ho!*" (Jap.: *katsu!*) served as the adequate expression for the theory of doctrinal stages as taught by the Hua-yen school. The essence of Zen lies not in the method, but in the experience of seeing into one's nature and becoming a Buddha.

In the *kōan* Zen received an effective method for systematic guidance toward enlightenment. While methods and systematization are manifestations of a period of decline, nonetheless they often rescue the cause itself. While the early Zen masters had grasped the *satori* experience spontaneously out of their own original genius, here at last was a suitable means whereby *all* might strive for enlightenment. "Aristocratic Zen was now turned into a democratic, systematized, and, to a certain extent, mechanized Zen. No doubt to that extent it meant a deterioration; but without this innovation Zen might have died out a long time before. To my mind it was the technique of the *kōan* exercise that saved Zen as a unique heritage of Far Eastern culture." [6] Thus Suzuki judges this development.

The Psychological Structure of the Kōan

Many instances of enlightenment and many paradoxical episodes and sayings of the Zen masters which serve as *kōan* have been cited in previous chapters. In all, the number of *kōan* is said to be seventeen hundred. These provide abundant material for historians and psychologists, as well as for specialists in religion and literature.

The *kōan* are clearly introductory, auxiliary means and make no pretense of expressing the inexpressible. What they contain serves merely as an impetus. There is no inner relation between the episode which they report, or the question which they pose, and enlightenment itself. The paradox occurs that "gatelessness becomes the gate to the Dharma. How can one enter by the no-gate?" [7] In almost all the *kōan*, the striking characteristic is the illogical or absurd act or word. A monk once asked, "What is Buddha?" The master replied, "Three pounds of flax." [8] Or a Zen master remarked, "When both hands are clapped a sound is produced; listen to the sound of one hand." Again: "Last night a wooden horse neighed and a stone man cut capers." To take a final example: "Buddha preached forty-nine years, and yet his broad tongue never once moved." [9]

The *kōan* are one great mockery of all the rules of logic. Usually, indeed, the Zen disciple first seeks to solve his problem intellectually. But this proves impossible, a fact which is underscored by the severe rebuff and the sharp blows of the master. During his ceaseless intellectual toil anxiety mounts intolerably. The whole conscious psychic life is filled with one thought. The exertion in the search is as that "if one were fighting against a deadly enemy," or "as if one were surrounded on all sides by raging flames." [10] Such assault against the walls of human reason inevitably gives rise to distrust of all rational perception. This gnawing doubt, combined with the futile search for a way out, creates a state of extreme and intense yearning for deliverance. The tension may persist for days, weeks, and even years, but there must be a reaction.

What occurs in the soul may be likened to the process in shooting an arrow from a stretched bow. In his book *Zen in the Art of Archery*, Herrigel aptly describes the matter psychologically. "When I have drawn the bow," he explains to the master, "the moment comes when I feel: unless the shot comes at once

I shan't be able to endure the tension. And what happens then? Merely that I get out of breath. So I must loose the shot whether I want to or not, because I can't wait for it any longer." To this the master replies, "The right shot at the right moment does not come because you do not let go of yourself. You do not wait for fulfillment, but brace yourself for failure. So long as that is so, you have no choice but to call forth something yourself that ought to happen independently of you, and so long as you call it forth, your hand will not open in the right way— like the hand of a child. Your hand does not burst open like the skin of a ripe fruit." [11] Thus, as in archery, so in the *kōan* exercise everything depends on the proper attitude. Only when the attentive mind is relaxed, free from purpose and the ego, and fully devoted to the task, can it open as of itself.

Suzuki describes this psychological process in terms of the law of accumulation, saturation, and explosion. While the psychological concept underlying this illustration may be partly outdated, it helps to clarify the process, and reveals the danger inherent in it. Even accumulation and saturation to an extreme degree can be harmful. A still greater danger is the premature explosion, more like the bursting of a bomb than the opening of the skin of a ripe fruit. Both in the past and in the present there are plentiful examples where the *kōan* exercise leads to a bad end. It is not without reason that Zen masters warn of self-deception and of "fox-enlightenment" (this is how Zen masters name all kinds of pseudo experiences).

The unnatural suppression of reason is a gamble. It may destroy the psychic structure of a person permanently and irremediably. The inviolable dignity of man sets limits to the *kōan* exercise as well as to the therapeutic process of modern psychiatry. Moreover, a greater similarity between the two exists than appears on the surface. There is in Zen the so-called practice of *sanzen*, in which the learner reports his inner psychic experiences to his master face to face. On this occasion he may utter broken, incoherent words, and the master may suddenly slap him in the face or exhibit other bodily or psychic reactions, a situation similar, to some extent, to what may happen in the therapeutic session when the psychiatrist seeks by free association to coax from his patient the unconscious secret of his soul.

The structure of the *kōan* led C. G. Jung to identify in his highly suggestive Foreword to Suzuki's *Introduction to Zen Buddhism* the "great deliverance" in Zen as the liberation of the unconscious. Evoked by the enormous psychological strain of trying to force a solution of the insoluble *kōan* problem, enlightenment is experienced as the dawn of a new reality, in which the boundaries between the conscious and the unconscious disappear, and conscious and unconscious alike are openly revealed. The Zen disciple realizes the totality of human nature in its primal unity, prior to all discrimination and division. This analysis of Jung's can shed light on the psychological structure of the *kōan* exercise and other related phenomena of natural mysticism. But the mere psychological approach does not give adequate consideration to the historical roots of Zen in Mahāyāna Buddhism, and actually places mere method, namely the *kōan* exercise, at the center of the experience. It is the identification of the *kōan* with Zen *satori* that hinders a true evaluation of the experience as a whole.

The Two Main Streams of Zen

The systematization of the Way of Enlightenment in the *kōan* exercise as developed by the Lin-chi sect determined the character of Chinese Zen during the Sung era. At the same time, however, the Ts'ao-tung sect regained considerable vigor. During the sixth generation after Tung-shan, the famous master Ta-yang (943-1027), of the line of Yün-chü, earned new esteem for the sect.[12] Among his followers it was T'ou-tzŭ (1032-

1083), Tan-hsia (d. 1119), and Fu-jun (d. 1118) especially who achieved distinction. Their wisdom was preserved in collections of sayings, stanzas (*gāthā*), and other writings and thus transmitted to posterity. The leading men of the Ts'ao-tung sect devoted considerable effort to commenting on the Five Ranks of the founder of their sect, Tung-shan. Their doctrine of enlightenment crystallized into "the Zen of silent illumination" (*mo-chao-ch'an*; Jap.: *mokushōzen*), whose great representative was Tien-t'ung (1091-1157), who received the posthumous title "Master Hung-chih." Tien-t'ung exerted an extensive influence, which won for the Zen of his time high esteem, but also evoked indignant opposition.

Ta-hui, the main representative of the Lin-chi sect during this time, called the way of the Ts'ao-tung sect a "false path." The designation "the Zen of silent illumination," which he coined, carried a note of disdain, since he, as a disciple of Lin-chi, rejected the method of quiet sitting to await enlightenment. This attack led Tien-t'ung to set forth, in a brief and spirited treatise of 288 characters, the real meaning of silent illumination, which according to him is the true expression of the tradition of the Buddhas and the patriarchs.[13] For the sitting posture by no means signifies mere silent inactivity, as its opponents falsely suppose. Rather, the two characters for "silence" and "illumination" contain the quintessence of Mahayanist metaphysics, and must be understood in terms of their true meaning. "Silence" is the primal stillness of the ground of the enlightened mind, whose natural activity is to "shine." Tien-t'ung describes this activity in another writing as "knowing without touching the thing [known], and as shining without forming an object." [14] Enlightenment as the mirroring action of the radiant mind is based in the Buddha-nature and is regarded as the imperishable possession of all sentient beings.

Tien-t'ung was not satisfied merely to justify his own position, but passed over to the offensive. Disdainfully he characterized the *kōan* method as "gazing upon the word" (*k'ang-hua;* Jap.: *kanna-zen*), since the learner was required to dwell incessantly upon the *kōan.* Ta-hui, for instance, admonished his disciples: "Just steadily go on with your *kōan* every moment of your life. . . . Whether walking or sitting, let your attention be fixed upon it without interruption. . . . When all of a sudden something flashes out in your mind, its light will illumine the entire universe, and you will see the spiritual land of the Enlightened Ones fully revealed at the point of a single hair, and the great wheel of the *Dharma* revolving in a single grain of dust." [15]

The dispute between the two factions was carried on by means of polemical writings, and harsh words fell on both sides. Still, it did not lead to complete enmity, for, as contemporary sources show, friendly relations continued to exist between Tien-t'ung and the two chief representatives of the *kōan* movement, Yüan-wu and Ta-hui. When Tien-t'ung died at the monastery which he had devotedly and successfully sought to develop into a center of Buddhist monasticism and which bore his name, Ta-hui hastened to attend the final rites of his deserving colleague.

Through the development of their peculiarities, the two major sects of Chinese Zen, Lin-chi and Ts'ao-tung, found in the *kōan* exercises (*k'ang-hua*) and in quiet sitting (*mo-chao*), respectively, their permanent form. Potential opposition extends back to the earlier centuries, when questions about doctrines and attitudes toward the sutras were the main points at issue. The disagreement over the successor to the Sixth Patriarch is typical of the first phase. Late in the T'ang era, the master Yang-shan distinguished between the "Zen of the Perfected One," which aspired to the intuitive grasp of reality (*pratyātma gocara*) in accordance with the *Lankāvatāra Sutra,* and the "Zen of the patriarchs," which alone cultivated the line of spiritual transmission. This distinction was to recur later during the Sung period in the controversy between the two sects, when the radical adherents of the *kōan* tradition for the first time demanded the total rejection of all sutras and even challenged the original relationship of Bodhidharma to the *Lankāvatāra Sutra*.

The two main streams of Chinese Zen were transplanted to Japan, where each retained its peculiarity. In the Rinzai sect we find the dynamic character of the daring *kōan* experiment and of lightninglike enlightenment, while the Sōtō school is characterized by a preference for silent sitting in *zazen* and the quiet deeds of everyday life. In Japan also one can discern no enmity beyond personal rivalries. It appears, rather, that adherence to one sect or the other is determined largely by the spiritual bent of the monks, who are inherently suited to one tradition or the other and pursue enlightenment in a way appropriate to their character. Thus one can find in the temples of the Sōtō sect men of brilliant wit and dynamic character who devote themselves to the *kōan* exercises, while on the other hand certain Rinzai monks of subdued character can scarcely be distinguished from Sōtō disciples.

The respective advantages and disadvantages of the two sects can be gathered from the accusations they bring against each other. The Rinzai adherents reproach the Sōtō sect for its passivity. To sit in meditation only, they say, enervates the mind. Conversely, Sōtō believers are able to point to dangers in the *kōan* exercises. From a general Buddhist viewpoint, they reproach the *kōan* sect for its neglect of the sutras and commandments—indeed, of the whole Buddhist tradition. This accusation is all the more serious since the commandments do not deal merely with regulations of Buddhist religiosity but with general moral norms. The practicer of the *kōan* who awakens in sudden enlightenment may be swept away by a feeling of absolute freedom which readily leads him into the error of ignoring all moral restraint, an error that can have only the most dire results, especially when, as so often happens, he has experienced only partial enlightenment or has been the victim of an illusion. In such cases it is possible that a supposedly enlightened one loses the insight into the truths basic to the Buddhist way of salvation at all stages, namely, the transiency of all earthly things and the nothingness of one's own ego. The danger accompanying the more daring exercises is lessened by the strict treatment of beginners in the Rinzai monasteries. In times of decline, signs of decay usually appear more quickly in the Sōtō sect than in the Rinzai. But all Zen masters of whatever persuasion warn against error and abuse, and the truly enlightened are always few.

9   *The Transplanting of Zen to Japan*

Preliminary Developments

The influx of Buddhism into Japan from the Asiatic mainland begins at the outset of Japanese history. According to
the Japanese chronicles, the first Buddha image was brought
from Kudara in Korea to the imperial court during the reign
of the Emperor Kimmei in A.D. 552. After a brief struggle against
opposition the new religion prevailed, and for many centuries
thereafter Buddhism as a superior religious force superseded
the primitive native Shinto cult in shaping the spiritual life of
the Japanese people.

The Prince Regent Shōtoku Taishi (d. 621), who was the
first great personage in Japanese history and the real founder
of the imperial state, was a devout disciple of Buddhist teaching. With his heart he trusted in the protection of the Hotoke,
which was the Japanese name for the Buddha, while his states-
manship recognized in the Buddhist Law an efficacious means
to elevate the cultural and spiritual level of his people. Among
the three sutras which he particularly cherished, and expounded before a pious circle of hearers, was the *Vimalikīrti
Sutra*, whose influence upon Zen we noted in an earlier chapter. We may rightly assume that the meditative exercises which
characterized Buddhism in all stages of development held a

prominent place from the beginning in the practical piety of Japanese Buddhists.

The first certain information we possess regarding Zen in Japan goes back to the early period of her history. The outstanding Japanese Buddhist monk during that age, Dōshō, was attracted to Zen through the influence of his Chinese teacher, Hsüan-tsang, under whom he studied the Yogācāra philosophy (653). This philosophy was the central teaching of the Hossō school, which Dōshō transplanted to Japan. It was at this time that the followers of Hui-k'o had brought Zen to great fame in China.[1] Dōshō thus came into immediate contact with the tradition of Bodhidharma and brought the Zen of the patriarchs to Japan. He built the first meditation hall, at a temple in Nara. Zen early found a hearth on Japanese soil within the Hossō school.

A century later, for the first time in history, a Chinese Zen master came to Japan. This was Tao-hsüan, who belonged to the northern sect of Chinese Zen in the third generation after Shên-hsiu.[2] Responding to an invitation from Japanese Buddhist monks, he took up residence in Nara and contributed to the growth of Japanese culture during the Tempyō period (729-749). He cultivated contacts especially with the Kegon (Chin.: Hua-yen) and Ritsu (Vinaya) schools, and transmitted Zen meditation to Gyōhyō, who in turn passed it on to Saichō (Dengyō Daishi, 767-822), the founder of the Japanese Tendai school. In China Saichō had already met a master from the Niu-t'ou sect of Zen. Thus the contemplative element in the Tendai tradition, which held an important place from the beginning, was strengthened in both China and Japan by repeated contacts with Zen.

A further step in the spread of Zen occurred in the following century when I-k'ung, a Chinese master of the Lin-chi sect, visited Japan. He came at the invitation of the Empress Tachibana Kachiko, wife of the Emperor Saga, during the early part of the Shōwa era (834-848), to teach Zen, first at the imperial court and later at the Danrinji temple in Kyoto, which the Empress had built for him. However, these first efforts in the systematic propagation of Zen according to the Chinese pattern did not meet with lasting success. I-k'ung was unable to launch a vigorous movement. Disappointed, he returned to China, and for three centuries Zen was inactive in Japan.

During the Heian period (794-1185) the two powerful schools of Tendai and Shingon were predominant, and meditation faded into the background, pushed aside by philosophical speculation and a wild growth of magical rites. Everywhere during that period the marks of decay in Buddhism became evident. Toward the end of the period the secularization at the court had spread to the populace and had permeated even the monasteries.

Eisai

The Buddhist renewal which began at the outset of the Kamakura period (1185-1333) gave rise to new schools and in turn was carried forward by them. The old schools of Hossō, Kegon, Tendai, and Shingon had built up positions of power, had spread esoteric doctrines which were incomprehensible to the common man, and above all had given themselves increasingly to the cultivation and practice of magic. In contrast to this, the new schools of the Kamakura period, born as they were from the distress of the times, answered the urgent religious needs of the people. Aroused by the call for help which, to use the figure of the *Lotus Sutra*, came like "a cry from a burning house," they undertook to save humanity in the apocalyptic atmosphere of the final Dharma (*mappō*).

Hōnen (1133-1212) and Shinran (1173-1268), the founders of the Japanese Amida school, proclaimed the Buddha of Infinite Light and of Great Compassion, a message easily comprehensible to the masses. Nichiren (1222-1282), a prophet both in wrath and in consolation, awakened the national hope of the downcast people. The rising knighthood (*samurai*) found an appropriate religion in the intellectually simple yet practical and aristocratic Zen. During this period all the leaders of the Buddhist movement came from the Tendai school, but they descended from Mount Hiei (near Kyoto, where the first Tendai monastery had been founded by Saichō), broke with the old tradition, and joined themselves to the people.

From the middle of the twelfth century on, a steady exchange of Japanese and Chinese monks developed, which brought to Japan the flourishing Zen of the Sung period in its various branches. To Eisai (Zenkō Kokushi, 1141-1215) goes the honor of being the actual founder of Japanese Zen.[3] As a boy he had entered the ranks of Buddhist monkhood and received his training in the main temple of the powerful Tendai school on Mount Hiei. During his first journey to China (1168) he visited the Chinese centers of his school, but at that time his attention was already drawn to Zen. He was deeply impressed by the spirit of Zen, and gradually the conviction grew on him that Zen, which was now flourishing in China, could also contribute toward a Buddhist awakening in Japan.

At the outset of a second journey to the West (1187) he was determined to pursue the stream of Buddhism to its sources in India. Because of inclement weather, however, and the opposition of Chinese authorities, this plan failed. But this made his efforts to comprehend Chinese Zen the more fruitful. He received the seal of enlightenment in the Huang-lung line of transmission of the Lin-chi sect, which, as the true heir, he transplanted permanently to Japan.

Upon returning to his native land, Eisai built the first temple of the Rinzai sect in Japan, Shōfukuji, at Hakata, a town on the southern island of Kyushu (1191). But when he proclaimed, in word and writing, the superiority of Zen over

Tendai and expounded Zen meditation, he met with opposition. The monks on Mount Hiei were aroused and periodically
succeeded in banning the new school. Eisai, however, found
protection and help in the Shogun Minamoto Yoriie. The
government of the Shogun appointed him head of the new
Kenninji temple in Kyoto, built in 1202.[4] Energetically he now
promoted Zen and composed a treatise on *The Spread of Zen
for the Protection of the Country*. Combining religious fervor
with national aspiration, he looked to Zen for salvation in the
last day of the "final Dharma." He strove for the recognition of
Zen as an independent school, but because of the proximity of
the court and the powerful headquarters of the Tendai and
Shingon schools, he was forced to make concessions.

Initially the Kenninji temple was not a pure Zen center but
included, in addition to the Zen meditation hall, a place each
for the rites of Tendai (*Tendai-in*) and Shingon (*Shingon-in*).
Until his death Eisai recited the sutras of Shingon, and to this
day, while the temple has meanwhile become exclusively Zen, a
Tendai ceremony is still performed. Eisai was able, also, to
bring the Zen tradition to Kamakura, the second residence of
the Shogun, upon whose authorization he became the abbot
of the third temple of the Japanese Rinzai sect, Jūfukuji.

The name of Eisai is associated in Japanese cultural history
with the cultivation of tea. The actual introduction of tea into
Japan is of earlier date, and is attributed to the founder of the
Shingon sect, Kūkai (Kōbō Daishi, 774-835), a figure veiled
in legend. Eisai brought tea seeds from China and planted
them in temple grounds. He wrote a book on tea and is regarded as the father of Japanese tea culture.

The knowledge of the second main stream of Chinese Zen
was mediated to Japan by Dōgen (1200-1253), the founder of
the Japanese Sōtō sect. The centers of this sect in Japan are
the Eiheiji temple in the province of Echizen, which Dōgen
founded, and the temples of Daijiji in Kyushu (founded in

1278) and Sōjiji, which became a Zen institution in 1321. The first abbot of the Sōjiji was Keizan (1268-1325), whose importance in the Sōtō sect is second only to that of Dōgen. Dōgen is undoubtedly the greatest figure in Japanese Zen. Later we shall devote an entire chapter to him.

The Flowering of Rinzai Zen in the Kamakura Period

It was under the patronage of the shogunate that Zen struck root in Japanese soil. The mighty house of Hōjō, which suc-ceeded the warlike family of Minamoto, provided Zen with devoted adherents. The Shogun Hōjō Tokiyori (1227-1263), who himself attained enlightenment under the rigorous school-ing of a Chinese master, attracted additional Rinzai monks to Japan. A Chinese monk named Lan-chi Tao-lung (Jap.: Rankei Dōryū, Daikaku Zenji) became the first head of the newly built temple of Kenchōji (1253), in which Zen was practiced in unadulterated Chinese fashion.

The architecture of the many magnificent temples through-out the wide and wooded territory likewise imitated the Chi-nese style. Unfortunately, nothing remains of the early build-ings. The only ancient structure, the memorial hall of the founder, dating from the Muromachi period, contains an im-pressive handcarving of the master Daikaku which has sur-vived various fires. As the first of a series of "Five Mountains," which were established during the Kamakura period in Chinese style in the two centers of Kyoto and Kamakura, the temple of Kenchōji enjoyed the greatest prominence.[5] Later it lost much of its glory, but it remains one of the most characteristic of Japanese temple sites.

The second shogun of the house of Hōjō, Tokimune (1251-1284), who was immortalized in Japanese history by his coura-geous and successful defense against the Mongolians, had the Engakuji temple (1282) near Kamakura built for the famous

Chinese master Tsu-yüan Wu-hsüe (Jap.: Sogen Mugaku, known as Bukkō Kokushi, "National Master of the Buddha Light"). This temple also was one of the "Five Mountains," and as a cultural center achieved great fame. We are told that, at the approach of the Mongolian fleet, the Shogun Tokimune went to the temple to seek strength in Zen from his master. He said, "The greatest event of my life is at last here." Bukkō asked, "How would you face it?" Tokimune uttered *"Katsu!"* as if he were frightening away all his enemies actually before him. Bukkō was pleased and said, "Truly a lion's child roars like a lion." [6] A "divine wind" (*kamikaze*) scattered the enemy fleet.[7]

During his war-perturbed reign, Tokimune never once had to leave his headquarters in Kamakura. After his early death, his wife retired to the Tōkeiji nunnery, which she had built on a hill opposite Engakuji.[8] But there too, as elsewhere, the wooden structures being so vulnerable to fire, the present buildings are all of more recent date. No nuns remain to honor the memory of the noble foundress. Only a fine bronze bust of Amida, dating from the Muromachi period, testifies still to the worship of the compassionate Buddha of Infinite Light which the devout women combined with the strict practices of Zen.

While at the seat of the shogunate in Kamakura true Zen prospered in the tradition of the Chinese Lin-chi sect, in Kyoto the early stages of its development were marked by difficulties and setbacks. The Kenninji temple, which since the days of Eisai had harbored Tendai and Shingon alongside of Zen, was soon stifled by magic rites and religious formalism. Dōgen stayed repeatedly at this famous temple, but found no scope there for his religious needs and aspirations. Finally he withdrew permanently from Rinzai Zen. While Eisai had stressed the careful observance of temple regulations, discipline deteriorated after his death. Help finally came from outside the

community through the efforts of the first abbot of the Tōfukuji temple—which was begun in 1236, dedicated as a Zen
temple in 1255, and then placed under the direction of Enju
Benen (Shōichi Kokushi, 1202-1280).

The master Shōichi was one of the most remarkable figures
in early Japanese Zen. Like others before him, he had received
his Buddhist instruction in the Tendai school, and was distinguished in both religious fervor and knowledge of the sutras.
He enriched his development further by studies in Confucianism. During a six-year residence in China (1235-1241) he
mastered Zen and received "the seal of the Mind," i.e., the
succession in the Yang-ch'i line of transmission of the Lin-chi
sect. Through him, and a little later through Jōmyō (Daiō
Kokushi, 1236-1308), who attained enlightenment under masters of the same lineage, this line was transplanted to Japan,
where it became the chief exponent of the Rinzai form of
Zen. Among the leading Japanese masters, Eisai alone belonged to the other lineage of Huang-lung.

Under the leadership of Shōichi, the Tōfukuji temple
quickly attained a high state of development. This master
worked pre-eminently in the Zen spirit, yet saw no contradiction in the practice and transmission of esoteric rites. During
the early years Tendai and Shingon found a haven in Tōfukuji. Shōichi had numerous disciples and extended his activity to other temples as well. His name is listed as tenth among
the abbots of the Kenninji sect. Daily at the sounding of the
noontime gong he left his headquarters at Tōfukuji and strolled
to the Kenninji temple—there to carry out his reforms according to the principles of Zen.

The Tōfukuji temple was another of the "Five Mountains"
of the Kamakura period. Built to the south of Kyoto, it is
surrounded by spacious temple grounds. Zen temples are
usually composed of a number of buildings, forming a com-
pound, which are dispersed, whenever possible, over a slope or

a hill; for this reason these establishments are also called "mountains." The layout at Tōfukuji, which is one of the most beautiful and best-preserved temples of the early period, gives a clear picture of the pattern of the "seven halls" (*shichi dō garan*) taken over from China.[9] One enters the temple area through the "Mountain Gate" (*sammon*), which symbolizes the purging of desires and conceptual thinking as one enters the Void, and then mounts directly toward the Buddha hall. But the adoration of the Buddha image must be preceded by cleansing and purgative exercises. In these exercises washing and the purging of bodily filth are necessary. For this purpose there are two wooden buildings between the gate and the Buddha hall, one to the right, the other to the left, namely, the bath (*yūshitsu, furo*) and the latrine (*tōsu*). In Zen monasteries both activities are accompanied by recitative rites.

The meditation hall (*zendō*) and the storehouse (*kuri*) and refectory (*jikidō*) provide for the nourishment of mind and body. These buildings are likewise located to the left and the right, but slightly behind the Buddha hall. The seventh building is the Dharma hall (*hattō*), in which an enlightened monk lectures on the sutras. This hall is situated on the central ascending axis, and constitutes the focal point of the entire complex. This pattern was regarded as analogous to the human body. The realism and consistency with which the idea was carried through is indeed amazing. In Tōfukuji the entrance gate, the Zen hall, and the Treasure House of the Sutras, the bath and the latrine, all derive from early times, and have been entered in the catalogue of national "cultural treasures." [10]

The magnificent Nanzenji temple, which had been transformed from a residence on the eastern hillside near Kyoto at the behest of the Emperor Kameyama (1293), also was an influential cultural and artistic center. The first abbot of the

Diagram of the Tōfukuji temple plan

Explanation:

1. Entrance hall (*sammon*)
2. Buddha hall (*butsuden*)
3. Dharma hall (*hattō*)
4. Latrine (*tōsu*)
5. Bath (*yūshitsu*)
6. Meditation hall (*zendō*)
7. Storehouse (*kuri*)

The measurements of the buildings differ according to the temples. In the Tōfukuji the splendid Buddha hall is the biggest building and the center of the plan. In the Eiheiji temple (Fukui prefecture) founded by Dōgen, which is the center of the Sōtō branch, there is, situated obliquely in front of the main entrance, a special door for the Imperial messenger (*chokushimon*). The steep ascent to the three main buildings consists of a paved stone way and a stone staircase flanked by gorgeous cedars. The Dharma hall is the biggest and most magnificent edifice of this plan. At present, in practically all Zen monasteries the fundamental plan of the seven edifices has been obliterated by numerous additions.

newly established temple, Mukan Fumon (Daimin Kokushi), had spent twelve years under a Zen master in China and there received the seal of the Mind. He was also a disciple of the master Shōichi, whose successor he became as the head of the Tōfukuji temple in the third generation. The Emperor Kameyama appointed him Founder Abbot of Nanzenji, but he passed away during the first year of his tenure there.

In the third generation he was followed by the Chinese Zen master I-ning I-shan (Jap.: Ichinei Issan, d. 1317), a versatile artist of widespread fame. As the first purely Zen temple of the capital, without admixture of Tendai or Shingon, Nanzenji enjoyed the special favor of the Emperor. The abbots were named by the imperial court, and many of them were men of great distinction. In the following century the temple enjoyed the special favor of the Shogun Ashikaga Yoshimitsu and was elevated above all other "Mountains" of Zen (1386).[11]

During the first century of Japanese Zen history occurred the remarkable journey to China of the monk Kakushin (Hottō Emmyō Kokushi, 1207-1298). He had early forsaken the world, was ordained at Tōdaiji in Nara, learned the esoteric doctrines in the Shingon temples on Mount Kōya, and finally was introduced to Zen by a Japanese master.[12] In China he became the disciple of the most eminent Zen master of the time, Wu-mên Hui-kai (1184-1260). From the very beginning the relationship between master and disciple was exceptionally intimate. Master Wu-mên (No-gate) asked the newcomer at their first encounter, "There is no gate here whereby you can enter. Therefore where did you come in?" Kakushin replied, "I came in by the No-gate [Wu-mên]." The master now asked, "What is your name?" "My name is Kakushin [i.e., Enlightened Mind]." On the spot the master Wu-mên composed the following verses:

Mind is Buddha [the Enlightened One].
Buddha is Mind.

Mind and Buddha in their thusness
Are in past and future alike.

On his return to Japan in 1254 Kakushin brought with him
the *Wu-mên-kuan*, which his master had edited and written
commentaries upon. He quickly rose to eminence, built a
temple in the vicinity of Wakayama, and was repeatedly invited to the court in the capital at Kyoto. Under Wu-mên,
Kakushin had become acquainted with the branch of Zen
known as the P'u-k'o sect (Jap.: Fuke), whose origin went
back to Ma-tsu's disciple P'u-k'o, of the T'ang period. This
sect cultivated especially flute-playing. Its adherents were the
itinerant "have-no" monks (*komusō*). There had already been
earlier itinerant monks in Japan, but the sect as such was first
introduced by Kakushin. During the Middle Ages and the
Tokugawa period these monks were able to carry on un-
molested. Early in the Meiji period, however, because of various abuses, their sect was suppressed (1871).[13]

The transplanting of Zen to Japan did not mean a mere
passive acceptance of a foreign tradition, though admittedly
the admiration of the Japanese Buddhist monks for China
knew no bounds. They sought religious guidance and
enlightenment in an unbroken chain of voyages to the mainland. They were likewise gratefully receptive to artistic sug-
gestions. The strongest creative impulses came from the consummate art of Sung paintings, and a considerable number of
works of great Chinese masters such as Liang-k'ai, Mu-ch'i,
and Ma-yüan, escaping the Mongolian invasion, found their
way to Japan. Buddhist disciples, enamored of the art of
China, took scrolls, bells, porcelains, silk embroideries, and
lacquer ware across the sea. Chinese influences sank deep roots
into the Japanese soul.

But it was not a matter of reception and absorption only.
The creative Japanese assimilation of this new cultural substance and its independent development had already begun

during the Kamakura period and reached its peak during the
following Muromachi period. The centers of these cultural and
artistic achievements were the Rinzai temples in Kyoto and
Kamakura. In the religious sphere, however, one can hardly
speak, within the Rinzai sect, of early attempts at further development and adaptation to Japanese peculiarities.[14] It was
Dōgen, the founder of Sōtō Zen, who succeeded with creative
power in giving to Zen a new form commensurate with the
Japanese genius.

10 *The Zen Master Dōgen*

His Life and Work

More than any other religious figure in Japanese history, the Zen master Dōgen (1200-1253) has evoked attention and admiration in modern times. Not only the faithful of the Sōtō sect but Buddhists of all schools venerate him as a Bodhisattva and hold him up as an example. Philosophers derive inspiration from the "incomparable depth of his thinking" which "points the way to contemporary philosophy." Many are proud of this "unique religious personality, arisen from the very heart of Japanese culture," as the embodiment of the best elements in the Japanese genius.[1] Indeed, it may well be that Dōgen is the strongest and most original thinker that Japan has so far produced. Doubtless he was a man of singular magnetism. His writings preserve for posterity his genuine humanity and his creative thought. The crucial element in them is his religious intuition, deeply convincing in its authenticity. We shall present here a sketch of his life and work, stressing, as befits the framework of this study, some of the outstanding characteristics of his thought and his original religious genius.

Like all other Zen masters, Dōgen is known in history by his monastic name rather than that of his family. His family belonged to the court nobility. His father, Kuga Michichika, held high government offices; his mother was descended from the distinguished house of Fujiwara, from which the emperors liked to choose their spouses. The highly gifted youth received the careful literary training befitting the son of a noble family. At the age of four he read his first Chinese poems. However, though in his further education Chinese influences were predominant, they exercised little influence on his later intellectual development. His writings show only faint traces of his early contacts with Chinese literature, which seem to have provided him with the knowledge of certain forms rather than with their substance.

Dōgen lost his father at the early age of two and his mother when he was only seven. The tender disposition of the child experienced its first deep religious shock. In grief and solitude he realized the frailty of all earthly things. His biographer relates: "At the loss of his beloved mother at the age of seven his grief was profound. As he saw the incense ascending in the Takao temple he recognized the arising and the decay—the transitoriness—of all things. Thereby the desire for enlightenment was awakened in his heart." [2] On her deathbed his mother had called him to her pillow and urged him to take up the monastic life, to follow the Dharma, to pray earnestly for his deceased parents, and to labor for the salvation of all sentient beings. These experiences left indelible impressions in his mind and confirmed his decision to renounce the world.

After his mother's death, Dōgen was adopted by an older brother of his mother, a powerful aristocrat, who wanted him to become his heir and successor. Informed of the fate in store for him, the twelve-year-old youth fled from his uncle's house just before the date set for the rites of puberty and his entrance upon a secular career, and joined a younger uncle who lived as a hermit at the foot of Mount Hiei, engaged in Buddhist studies and esoteric practices. After some hesitation this uncle

was won over by Dōgen's persistence and agreed to help him
enter the monastic life. As early as the following year (1213)
Dōgen was ordained a Buddhist monk by Kōen, the chief
abbot of the Tendai school.

In a monastery on Mount Hiei he devoted himself fully to
the religious life and to the study of the sacred writings. Soon
he encountered a tormenting and seemingly insoluble problem. "Both the exoteric and the esoteric doctrines teach the
primal Buddha-nature of all sentient beings. If this is so, why
then do all Buddhas and Bodhisattvas arouse the longing for
enlightenment and engage in ascetic practices?" This question
of the relationship between the Buddha-nature and enlightenment, or, in technical Mahayanist language (e.g., in the *Mahāyāna Śrāddhotpāda Shastra*), between innate and acquired
enlightenment, disturbed the inquisitive mind of the young
Dōgen and drove him from his solitary cell on Mount Hiei
where no one could give him a satisfying answer.

Dōgen took his problem to the famous monk Kōin (1145-
1216) of the Tendai temple Miidera on Lake Biwa. Kōin
was a deeply sincere, religious man who at an advanced age
still pursued the quest for truth; late in life he burned the
writings of his early years and turned from the speculations
of Tendai to the simple faith of Amida. Kōin recognized the
earnestness of his young inquirer and directed him to Eisai,
who, since his return from China, now taught the new way
of enlightenment through immediate intuition. It is not certain that Dōgen actually met Eisai,[3] for at that time (autumn,
1214) Eisai may already have been living in Kamakura. In any
case no record shows indications of an encounter with Eisai.

About this time Dōgen entered the Kenninji temple and
enrolled in the school of Myōzen, who had succeeded Eisai
there as abbot. At this temple Zen was amalgamated with
Tendai and Shingon. According to the chronicles, Myōzen
transmitted "the three religions of the exoteric doctrines, the

esoteric teachings, and Mind," i.e., knowledge of the sutras, Tantric rites, and Zen.⁴ But on Mount Hiei Dōgen had already become acquainted with the sacred writings and the widespread esoteric practices. Zen alone was new to him; in Kenninji it was taught in the strict manner of Rinzai, that is, with the *kōan*, and with shouting and beating. A warm relationship sprang up between Myōzen and his new pupil, but Dōgen's religious aspirations remained unfulfilled. Feeling increasingly drawn to China, he readily received permission from Myōzen to go there. Indeed, the teacher decided to accompany his pupil, and together they set out on their journey in the spring of 1223.

After a difficult sea voyage they landed in April at a port in central China. Dōgen, in order to adjust gradually to the new environment, remained temporarily on board ship. He received his first profound impression of Zen from the kitchen steward of a temple who had come to the city to buy provisions. This worthy Buddhist monk declined Dōgen's urgent invitation to visit the ship because he felt it necessary to return to his work in the monastery. In Zen, daily work in the kitchen is a religious practice which can lead to enlightenment. The steward thus embodied the living tradition in Chinese Zen which, since the days of the Fourth and Fifth Patriarchs and of the master Pai-chang, regarded not only sitting in meditation and reading of the sutras, but also daily service to the community, as exercises and manifestations of enlightened conduct.

Soon Dōgen had the opportunity to experience personally the monastic life of Chinese Zen. In the flourishing temple of Tien-t'ung-szŭ, which, according to contemporary witnesses, accommodated about five hundred monks and whose abbot at the time was the master Wu-chi, Dōgen devoted himself fervently to the religious practices and gained lasting impressions of the community life. And yet, despite extreme effort, he did not achieve the seal of enlightenment. So he left once more, wandering now from temple to temple. In this way he made acquaintance with many schools and sects of Chinese Buddhism and came in contact with the noted masters of the time. As he was preparing to return to Tien-t'ung-szŭ, he learned of the death of the master Wu-chi. In his disappointment he decided to embark on the homeward journey to Japan.

At this point Dōgen met an old monk who told him that a famous and experienced master named Ju-ching (1163-1268) had become the abbot of Tien-t'ung-szŭ, called there by the royal court to head the temple and the monastic community. Returning to the temple on May 1, 1225, Dōgen saw his new master for the first time. Immediately, his spirit soared: Dōgen finally had found a worthy leader. Ju-ching received the Japanese novice warmly, and gladly gave him permission to visit the master at any time, regardless of the normal regulations.

An impressive figure of great height, Ju-ching continued, after a life of distinguished service to Zen, to labor with great energy up to an advanced age. He was a strict ascetic. Simple and unpretentious in his habits, he loved the crude temple diet and his coarse monastic robe. An enemy of honors and decorations, he kept aloof from the royal court and devoted himself unstintingly to the training of young monks. But he combined his rigor with geniality. Through the testimony of Dōgen we learn how he carried out the exercises:

> My deceased master, Ju-ching of Tien-t'ung-szŭ, as abbot of the temple, censured those who had fallen asleep during the meditative exercise in the Zen hall. He kicked them with his shoe and scolded them with insulting words. And yet all the monks lauded him for having struck them. Once he spoke to them in the hall as follows: "I am now growing old and should retire from the community into a hermitage to nurse my old bones. But since I know the community, I remain in office in order to help each one to break through his passions. For this reason I chastise with in-

sulting words or strike with the bamboo rod. This saddens me. But it is to carry out discipline in the place of the Buddha. Brothers, forgive me!" Thereupon all the monks wept.[5]

At Tien-t'ung-szŭ the disciples meditated literally day and night. The aged master set the pace, struck the drowsy ones, and admonished them by citing the hardships endured by people in worldly callings, the dangers suffered by soldiers, and the sweat of the peasants. How disgraceful, therefore, if the monks fell asleep in the midst of such exalted pursuits as theirs! He would not give ear to a proposal to shorten the periods of meditation, and complained rather that because of his age his arm was growing weak, which prevented him from disciplining as vigorously as had been his wont.

The matchless zeal at this temple was an exception in China at that time. In this atmosphere Dōgen gave his utmost, and soon he was prepared for the great enlightenment. Once more the monks were seated in nighttime meditation. One of them had gone to sleep. Ju-ching noticed him and remarked, "In Zen, body and mind are cast off. Why do you sleep?" On hearing this, enlightenment suddenly broke upon Dōgen. He rushed to the Dharma hall, kindled some incense, and gave thanks to the Buddha. Convinced of the genuineness of Dōgen's enlightenment, Ju-ching rejoiced. Dōgen, liberated from all illusion, passion, and ego-clinging, exulted in the freedom of an enlightened one. From Ju-ching he received at once the seal and the mantle of succession to the patriarchate of the Sōtō sect. This episode occurred during the summer, soon after Dōgen's return to Tien-t'ung-szŭ. He stayed on, however, for two more years of training. The return journey to Japan he had to undertake alone, since Myōzen had meanwhile died.

Contrary to the practice of other Buddhist pilgrims to China, Dōgen returned to Japan in 1227 literally empty-handed, without new sutras, rites, or sacred images. On his return he went first to Kenninji, where he interred the bones of his fellow pilgrim, Myōzen. He had no intention of founding a new sect but wanted to devote his life to the realization of the true Dharma in meditation. To this end he wrote his first treatise, *Fukanzazengi* (*General Teachings for the Promotion of Zazen*), a brief introduction to the practice of meditation (*zazen*), in less than a thousand Chinese characters.

Owing to the moral disintegration of a period of upheaval, conditions in the Kenninji temple had deteriorated greatly after Myōzen's departure. Dōgen, not feeling called to the role of a reformer, preferred to retire to the small rural temple of Anyōin near Fukakusa (1230). Soon this temple became an important center for the practice of Zen, as many earnest seekers left the capital city of Kyoto to journey there. Dōgen taught his disciples to sit in meditation and to realize their innate Buddha-nature. He inspired them with confidence. Even during the degenerate days of the decline of the Law (*mappō*), peace might be enjoyed by the country if the true Dharma was observed. It was at this time (1231) that Dōgen produced the first chapter of his great work *Shōbōgenzō* (*Treasury of Knowledge Regarding the True Dharma*) on the practice of *zazen* (*bendōwa*).[6] Soon after, he moved to a larger building called the Kannondōriin on the site of the adjacent decrepit Gokurakuji temple (1233). There he won his most faithful follower, Ejō (1198-1280), who transmitted to posterity his master's literary work.

But the Kannondōriin building eventually proved inadequate. A new temple, Kōshōhōrinji, with a meditation hall was built, actually the first fully independent Zen temple in Japan (1236). Dōgen's joy was indescribable. The regulations which he formulated for the Zen hall testify to his ardent zeal for the meditation exercise as well as to his high moral attainments.[7] The disciple who seeks the Way must free himself from all thought of personal honor and gain. Fearless of the future, he is to concern himself only with the present. All are to live together in harmony, carrying out the exercises of the way of liberation. In the meditation hall neither the study nor the reading of the sutras is permissible. There are to be no recitations or invocations of the name of Buddha (*nembutsu*). Each is to follow the instructions of the abbot and to speak softly. It is futile to dwell on the shortcomings of another. The Buddha chastises the shortcomings, but he does not hate them.

During the years at Kōshōhōrinji, Dōgen was at the height of his powers. Many gifted disciples were attracted to him, and numerous lay people, both men and women, entrusted themselves to his guidance. In spite of all this he was finally moved to relinquish his fruitful activities and leave the monastery because the hatred and envy of the monks on Mount Hiei threatened him and his community. As in 1243 he followed the suggestion of his faithful lay disciple and friend, Hatano Yoshishige, to journey to the province of Echizen, he may have found consolation in his love of mountain solitude. He remained for a while in small rural temples (Yoshiminedera and Yamashibu) until the completion of a new temple in 1245, whose name, Eiheiji, means Eternal Peace.

But now only a brief span of time was allotted to him. His fame had spread throughout the whole country. The Shogun Hōjō Tokiyori invited him to his residence in Kamakura. In the winter of 1247-1248, Dōgen accepted this invitation, but he soon returned happily to his mountain solitude. By now his health, which had always been precarious, gave occasion for serious concern. He was often confined to his room. Inspired by the last teachings of the Buddha,[8] he now wrote the final chapter of the *Shōbōgenzō*, on the "Eight Thoughts Which a Buddha or Bodhisattva Should Awaken" (*Hachi-daininkaku*). At the insistence of his friends he went with his trusted colleague Ejō to Kyoto to seek medical care, but his illness, apparently a pulmonary disease, was already in an advanced stage. He died on August 28, 1253.

Dōgen's life was overshadowed by the sorrowful awareness of the transitoriness of all things. He sought consolation in nature and poetry, and knew how to express a purified, all-embracing feeling of compassion in both Chinese and Japanese verse. Two Japanese poems written shortly before his death are alive with his spirit. Nature, though subject to change and death, is beautiful even in its decay since it is transfigured by the spirit. Like the dew, world and man pass away, and yet in the evaporating dewdrop the mind is reflected like the moon. These parting lines are:

Asahi matsu	On leaf and grass
kusa-ha no tsuyu no	Awaiting the morning sun
hodo naki ni	the dew melts quickly away.
isogi na tatte so	Haste thee not, O autumn wind
nobe no akikaze	who dost now stir in the fields.
Yo no naka wa	To what indeed shall I liken
nan ni tatoen	The world and the life of man?
mizutori no	Ah, the shadow of the moon,
hashi furu tsuyu ni	When it touches in the drop of dew
yadoru tsuki kage	The beak of the waterfowl.[9]

Zazen

Dōgen is the master of *zazen*. Not only did he give himself utterly to this exercise, practicing it above all others and teaching the right way of sitting in meditation to his disciples, but he saw in *zazen* the realization and fulfillment of the whole Law of Buddha. Among Buddhists his approach is called the religion of *"zazen* only" (*shikan taza*) and is regarded as the return to the "pure tradition of Buddha and the patriarchs" and the "true Dharma of Shākyamuni." [10] Nothing was more odious to Dōgen than the sectarian divisions in Buddhism and in Zen, the disastrous consequences of which, such as spiritual decline, formalization, and envy, he had witnessed in the China of the Sung era. Admittedly, he himself, through the patriarchal line of the master Ju-ching, stood in the tradition of the Sōtō sect, but Ju-ching was a free and independent man who despised sectarianism and castigated the abuses of the Buddhism of his time.

It was from Ju-ching that Dōgen inherited his critical attitude toward the historical development of Zen during the T'ang and Sung periods in China. The extreme rejection of the word of Buddha as found in the sutras he regarded as erroneous. There is no special Buddha-mind to be transmitted mysteriously apart from the texts. The false designation of the "Zen sect" he considered harmful. "One must realize that the term 'Zen sect' is a designation of Māra. Those who use the devil's terminology are the accomplices of the devil and not followers of the Buddha and the patriarchs." [11]

Whereas Eisai sought to introduce Zen as a special school in Japan, Dōgen regarded *zazen* as bound to no particular school and as nothing other than "the great way of the Buddhas and the patriarchs." It is thus an irony of history that the Sōtō sect, which was transplanted to Japan by Dōgen, became the strongest of all Japanese Zen sects.

Zazen is the meditation in which the disciple sits upright with legs crossed. Dōgen found this mode of meditation already hallowed by Buddhist tradition. Sitting meditation provides the basis for the various forms of concentration to be found in both Hīnayāna and Mahāyāna. The example of Bodhidharma, the founder of Zen, who sat in meditation before a wall for nine years, inspired his disciples to strive for perfection in *zazen*. In his early treatise entitled *General Teachings for the Promotion of Zazen*, Dōgen describes the sitting meditation and gives lucid instructions on how to achieve it:

If you wish to attain enlightenment, begin at once to practice *zazen*. For this meditation a quiet chamber is necessary, while food and drink must be taken in moderation. Free yourself from all attachments, and bring to rest the ten thousand things. Think of neither good nor evil and judge not right or wrong. Maintain the flow of mind, of will, and of consciousness; bring to an end all desires, all concepts and judgments. Do not think about how to become a Buddha.

In terms of procedure, first put down a thick pillow and on top of this a second (round) one. One may choose either a full or half cross-legged position. In the full position one places the right foot on the left thigh and the left foot on the right thigh. In the half position only the left foot is placed upon the right thigh. Robe and belt should be worn loosely, but in order. The right hand rests on the left foot, while the back of the left hand rests in the palm of the right. The two thumbs are placed in juxtaposition.

The body must be maintained upright, without inclining to the left or to the right, forward or backward. Ears and shoulders, nose and navel must be kept in alignment respectively. The tongue is to be kept against the palate, lips and teeth are kept firmly closed, while the eyes are to be kept always open.

Now that the bodily position is in order, regulate your breathing. If a wish arises, take note of it and then dismiss it. In practicing thus persistently you will forget all attachments and concentration will come of itself. That is the art of *zazen*. *Zazen* is the Dharma gate of great rest and joy.[12]

The final word in this instruction, which in the combination of Chinese characters expresses repose and delight, is especially important in Dōgen's view. *Zazen* is an easy way to enlightenment, not like the pious invocation of the name of Amida Buddha but because it is the natural position for man to assume. In an Indian Mahāyāna text it is already stated that "among all the manners of sitting the full cross-legged position is the most restful, and does not tire. While hands and feet are thereby brought under discipline, consciousness is not dissipated. Of the four positions which the body can assume, this is the most restful." [13] The body thus finds itself in that state of relaxed attention in which sense and mind remain awake and yet are released in complete rest. The room is kept in subdued daylight, since bright sunlight is just as detrimental to concentration as soporific darkness. A Zen master or another monk passes through the hall continuously, dealing blows to awaken those who become drowsy.

The disciple sits upright as a candle, with eyes open and body at attention, with the senses under full control and yet without unnatural strain. So that the body may rest at relaxed attention, breathing must be correct. The breath, which is the basic vital activity of the organism, provides the foundation for all repose and motion of body and mind, and thus also in *zazen* for the fully tranquil yet unconscious motion. When the breath flows uniformly through the body, tension is released. Therefore the practitioner, after taking his place on the pillow and adjusting his body into the proper upright position, must breathe deeply and regularly until the body has found the corresponding rhythm and the organism rests in equilibrium.

It must be emphasized that this exercise is something other than the Indian Yoga practice which seeks to drive from consciousness the act of breathing as the elementary movement of life. The goal of the regulation of breathing in *zazen* is not to eradicate it from consciousness but to achieve the full and tranquil equilibrium of the organism. In this the ancient Indian concepts of anthropology and anatomy do play a role, according to which "the mind lies a handbreadth below the navel," where "the home of our true being is to be found."

Dōgen tirelessly taught the right sitting position by the spoken and the written word and gave detailed instructions as to the proper bodily posture during meditation. In keeping with the Indian tradition, he conceived the bodily attitude itself in religious terms and attributed magical powers to it. He once considered the question of why the recitation of the sutras and calling on the name of the Buddha are not the most appropriate means to enlightenment. "How is it that one attains to enlightenment by mere idle sitting?" His answer is: "To call the great Dharma of the supreme *samādhi* of all Buddhas mere idle sitting is to slander the Great Vehicle. Is it not highly meritorious to sit in the peace of concentration which all Buddhas have experienced?" [14] Sitting is the authentic attitude of all Buddhas and Bodhisattvas as well as of the patriarchs, and is the most mighty of all the wonderful body positions (*prabhāva*) of which the sutras boast. The full cross-legged position is called the "seat of conquest of Māra" since "at the glimpse of this position the heart of the wicked one is saddened and frightened."

In Dōgen's view the traditional magical concepts are combined with deep insights into the unity of the physical and the psychic nature of man. He declared expressly, "The Way is attained through the body," because of "the unity of mind and body." [15] "According to the Law of Buddha, body and mind are originally one; essence and form are not two." [16] As essence and form are inseparable, so also are body and mind. When the body assumes the Buddha-form in taking the upright and motionless seated position, the mind is likewise in the dwelling of the Buddha. The cross-legged sitting position, which permits the blood to circulate freely throughout the body, and stills the passions of anger, vexation, and selfishness while composing and emptying the mind, is not merely the prerequisite to the experience of enlightenment but in itself already constitutes enlightenment. For the enlightenment is embodied in the person who in *zazen* takes the form of devotion to the Buddha. *Zazen* as revelation and as exhibition of the Buddha-nature is an eminent religious act of well-nigh infinite worth.

We have already noted the mental attitude in *zazen* as stipulated by the basic text. "Free yourself from all attachments.

. . . Bring to an end all desires, all concepts and judgments. Do not think about how to become a Buddha." The purposelessness upon which Dōgen insists above all else is not difficult to comprehend if one grasps that enlightenment is already present in *zazen* itself. Why should one harbor desires and dream about the future when in every instant of the sitting exercise one already possesses everything? Dōgen, of course, does recognize enlightenment as experience, but this is not different from the enlightenment in the exercise itself. Every moment of *zazen* exists in the realm of Buddha and is infinite. Dōgen censures the disciples who, devoid of understanding, await a great experience and thereby neglect the present moment. Nothing is more harmful than the conscious purpose of seeking Buddhahood by means of meditation.

We noted, too, Dōgen's practical instructions on how conscious mental activities are to be brought to rest. First those thoughts which arise spontaneously are brought into the light of consciousness and noted in order that they may then be put aside. Thereupon the disciple reaches that state of concentration in which he knows of both his thinking and his nonthinking, and yet adheres to neither. In this connection Dōgen elucidates a dialogue which is contained in the Chinese Zen *Chronicle:*

> Once a monk asked the master Yao-shan, "Of what does one think while sitting?" Yao-shan replied, "One should think of nonthinking." To this the monk answered, "How does one think of nonthinking?" "Through superthinking," [came the reply].[17]

Enlightenment is to be found in thinking as well as in nonthinking, since originally thinking is without object or a nature of its own, while nonthinking connotes no mere void. Thinking and nonthinking are rendered translucent in a transcendent state in which both thinking and nonthinking are contained. During the sitting exercise the mind is fully at rest as the mirrorlike surface of a lake stirred by no breeze, transparent to the bottom and composed in itself. This difficult degree of composure, through which the negation of thoughts and concepts is expressed, is a prerequisite to the perfect, immediate knowledge in Zen, without admixture of subjectivity, since the ego now finds itself in motionless repose. In this state one can "know without touching things," that is, without making things into objects in one's consciousness. It is in this way that things can be known in their proper essence, just as they are, not as objects in relation to subject but in their primal thusness.

In Dōgen the *zazen* exercise is endowed with high ethical spirit. By constantly emphasizing the transiency of earthly things he sought to instill in his disciples the taste for the ascetic life which had inspired him from early youth. "In the morning rosy cheeks, in the evening a pale skeleton." With his monks he led the simple and strict life of the Zen hall, which is well suited to promote deliverance from earthly attachments.

This rule of life continues to be observed almost without change in Zen monasteries today. The morning and evening meals consist of a light serving of rice, and the noon meal of a wheat porridge with vegetables. Animal foodstuffs such as meat, fish, eggs, and milk are not taken. The clothing is light and simple. During the seasons for special religious exercises, in summer and winter, the monks do not leave the temple grounds. For four periods daily—early morning, forenoon, late afternoon, and after sunset—they sit in meditation. The relatively short night, from nine P.M. to three A.M., is interrupted at midnight and again at one and two o'clock in the morning for brief periods of sitting.

This brief sketch is sufficient to show that he who would enter the "Dharma gate of great rest and joy" cannot avoid painful exertion. And yet Dōgen was convinced that he was leading his disciples the easy way. The following lines, the moral earnestness of which is not to be missed, contain the essence of his wisdom about life and the guidance of man:

> This is the easy way to become a Buddha:
> Not to create the various evils,
> Not to cling to life and death,
> To have deep compassion for all sentient beings,
> To venerate superiors and to sympathize with inferiors,
> To hate nothing,
> To desire nothing,
> Not to reflect on anything,
> Not to sorrow about anything—
> This is what I call the Buddha.
> Do not seek anything else! [18]

Religious Metaphysics

Like all great religious geniuses, Dōgen accorded religious practice precedence over all else. Practice, i.e., *zazen*, alone is sufficient. And yet he was a thinker who probed the depths and whose daily life was inspired by ultimate insights. The key to his exclusive emphasis on *zazen*, which we have just described, is to be found in his view of the identity of *zazen* and enlightenment, a viewpoint which in turn springs from his metaphysical speculations on the Buddha-nature. The primal enlightenment—the innate Buddha-nature—is the *a priori* basis of the practice which is a single progressive enlightenment. Dōgen elaborates as follows:

> In Buddhism, practice and enlightenment are one and the same. Since practice has its basis in enlightenment, the practice even of the beginner contains the whole of original enlightenment. Thus while giving directions as to the exercise, [the Zen master] warns him not to await enlightenment apart from the exercise, because this [the exercise] points directly to the original enlightenment. Since enlightenment is already contained in the exercise, there is no end to enlightenment, and since it is the exercise of enlightenment, it has no beginning.[19]

The relationship between exercise and enlightenment is clarified in Mahāyāna philosophy by the important distinction made between "original enlightenment" and "acquired enlightenment." It is the primal enlightenment which makes the exercise possible. The exercise or practice is necessary since without it, and without the enlightenment gained thereby, the Buddha-nature does not become manifest. As the exercise of the enlightened one, *zazen* is regarded as the self-manifestation of original enlightenment. The Zen disciple who comprehends this does not seek the Absolute outside himself; he does not gaze upward toward some Supreme Being, nor does he seek to bring down the Eternal to himself, but rather he finds in himself the Buddha-nature as the foundation of his own being. "Let the light be reflected so it falls back and irradiates the self," admonishes Dōgen. Then "mind and body will of themselves disappear and the original countenance will become manifest." [20]

The four Chinese ideographs of the *Mahāparinirvāna Sutra*, in which the basic Mahāyāna idea of the cosmic Buddha-nature is expressed most clearly, can be read, depending on the combination, either as "The being possesses the Buddha-nature perfectly" or "All being is the Buddha-nature." According to the first and more common rendering, the Buddha-nature is regarded as the essence of being. In the second reading Dōgen sees a somewhat different meaning. [21] It is not that the Buddha-nature is believed to be hidden in men and things, but rather that the total reality as it lies before our eyes is Buddha. The world is like an infinite ocean of the Buddha. Since the Buddha-nature cannot be limited by any thing, all things must be transcended continuously. By means of dialectical negation the mind attains the formless Buddha-nature which reveals itself in every form. In a famous hymn, Hakuin sings, "It is like ice and water." Just as there is no ice without water, so nothing exists apart from the Buddha-nature. The whole of reality and all *dharmas*, in Buddhist terminology, are Buddha. The unity of practice and enlightenment is rooted in the one Buddha-nature. Just as the Neo-Platonists boasted of their monistic metaphysical system as the crowning achievement of all Greek wisdom, so Dōgen and his disciples saw in the monistic doctrine of *zazen*, which embraced both metaphysics and ordinary phenomena, the essence of all Buddhism. Since the Buddha Law and *zazen* are not two but one, it is enough to say *zazen*, or, as Dōgen says with subtle nuance, "to know *zazen* as *zazen*." "Even though one should know *zazen* as the Buddha Law, yet if he does not comprehend *zazen* as *zazen*, how then can he know the Buddha Law as Buddha Law?" [22] Everything is comprehended in *zazen*.

Dōgen's disciples delightedly praised this simplification of Buddhism, as it eliminates the endless stages on the way of salvation. Foundation, roof, and center of the building all become one. In the simultaneous interpenetration of practice and enlightenment, the nature of being unfolds itself. As in the enlightened vision the opposition of subject and object dissolves, so in the life of the Zen disciple no distinction remains between means and end, between desire and object. The practice is enacted, not in the hope of something to be achieved, but to manifest continuously the enlightenment which is present in the practice.

In the viewpoint of Dōgen, Zen is a way of perfect unity. The first and basic Zen experience concerns the unity of body and mind, which is expressed in the sitting position. This position carries into the realm of enlightenment, since of necessity corporeality is bound up with the mind; for all Buddhas exhibit the enlightened state of their nature in their sitting.

The enlightened one experiences himself further in his unity with nature and mankind. Dōgen's love for nature was nourished by his enlightened vision. In the *kōan* exercise, which

Dōgen does not reject but merely relegates to secondary importance, he wishes the student not to strive desperately to penetrate the paradox. Rather, the student is asked to grasp in the concrete problem of the *kōan* the great problem of the universe.[23] As he sits undisturbed in the solitude of nature, he experiences the unity of all things which is the solution of all *kōan* problems.

The experience of unity extends itself into life. All things are transparent to the enlightened one who sees the One in all things. For him there is no longer a distinction between the "wonderful" and the "ordinary." The wonderful world of which all the sutras speak is this ordinary world which spreads before our eyes, a world of trees, grass, and flowers, of mountains, streams, and oceans. Likewise, the meditating figure undergoes no special change in mind or body and yet, to the initiate, is "marvelous" and has the "full-moon shape" of enlightenment. Nor does it matter whether, during the sitting exercise, distractions or desires arise which are merely noted and emptied, or whether the mind sinks into unconsciousness or even the "Great Enlightenment" occurs.

A second hallmark of the monistic doctrine of Mahāyāna philosophy is the equation of the cycle of becoming in *samsāra* with the absolute rest of *nirvāna*. The endless becoming in the sequences of birth and death is at one with the reality of the Buddha-nature. No distinction is to be made between name-and-form and voidness, between phenomenon and absolute reality. Dōgen explains: "All being is the Buddha-nature. A part of all being we call 'sentient beings.' Within and without these sentient beings there is the sole being of the Buddha-nature." [24] From this view Dōgen derives the equation of being and time. All being is fused with time. Apart from time there is no being. To exist is to become. "When we say being and time, time already is being. All being is time." [25] Time is the motion of absolute being. The juxtaposition of objects in the universe corresponds to the juxtaposition of points in time. Dōgen sketches this relationship concretely: "Colors are not limited to flowers, for all times likewise have their colors, such as blue, yellow, white, etc. Spring draws the flowers after it, while the flowers also draw the springtime." [26]

In this conception time is accorded neither substance nor continuity. Like objects, moments of time stand side by side in the universe. Every moment is self-contained. In every moment only the present exists without relationship to past or future. For this reason Dōgen admonishes, "You must fix your heart on the exercise only today in this moment, without losing the light of time." [27] The *now* is absolute. Just as Buddha is contained in the tiniest particle, and the whole is present in every grain of rice or drop of water, so the whole of enlightenment is contained in every moment. Therefore every moment of exercise is of infinite worth. To the enlightened one the whole of life is but a single unadulterated exercise. To the one who practices, the Buddha innate in original enlightenment comes into being at every moment of time. To experience one's fleeting life without illusion and in accordance with the truth of the Buddha is to actualize the present in the present. This and nothing else is Zen.

Dōgen put his doctrine forward as a monistic-pantheistic or cosmotheistic metaphysics within the general framework of Mahāyāna philosophy. In modern times Japanese philosophers have frequently placed this philosophy alongside the modern European pantheistic or existentialist systems. In so doing, however, the thoroughly religious character of Dōgen's thought has not been sufficiently recognized. For the concept of faith belongs to the basic tenets of his doctrine.[28] The exercise must be performed in faith. He who does not awaken faith in his heart cannot live in enlightenment. The word "faith," which Dōgen uses frequently and with varying significance, may at first sight seem surprising. What place is there for belief in a system of radical monism? Above all, how can believing sub- sist side by side with practice and enlightenment?

Just as, in the view of Dōgen, practice and enlightenment are related finally to the Buddha-nature, so also is believing. The pantheistic vision of reality is not surrendered. Yet this vision is attained through a religious process which is triggered and impelled by the act of believing. By experiencing the tran- sitoriness of all things, the disciple's religious capacities are aroused and set on the way to enlightenment. The "believing heart" is awakened, to comprehend that the teaching of Buddha opens a door out of the sorrow of transience, and that there is a true reality in which becoming and passing away are overcome. This reality is attested in the sacred Bud- dhist writings, which are to be received with due respect. In conscious contradiction of many Chinese masters, Dōgen urges the diligent reading of the sutras.[29] Familiarity with the sutras and faithful adherence to them are the hallmarks of a true son of the Buddha.

The sacred objects of the Buddhist religion are to be handled with respectful veneration. Says Dōgen:

> One should cultivate the hidden virtues. He who does so is as- sured of grace and beneficence. Even a Buddha image made crudely and without artistic distinction from clay or wood is to be venerated. Even though a sutra scroll be yellow or red or made from valueless material, one must hold in esteem the sutra doctrine. Should a Buddhist monk brazenly break the command- ments, his profession must nonetheless be held in respect, in faith. He who venerates him with a believing heart will assuredly be blessed. He who in the face of a fallen and shameless monk, a crude Buddha image, or a worthless sutra scroll lacks respect will assuredly be punished. For according to the Dharma left us by the Perfected One, Buddha image, sutra, and monk contribute to the blessedness of both men and gods. He who respects them will assuredly be blessed, and he who lacks faith commits a transgres- sion.[30]

The reverence which Dōgen brings to image, scripture, and monk is the expression of his believing heart. In veneration he embraces the whole Buddhist tradition, even other forms such as the *nembutsu* and the Tantric rites, which he replaces by *zazen* only in his own practice. The following text shows his pious devotion to the master:

> The traditional way of comprehending the teachings of Zen consists in gradually improving the things one has grasped and thought in one's own heart by ever greater conformity to the instructions of the master. Thus, for example, we know the figures of Shākya and Amida as Buddha, endowed as they are with distinguishing bodily traits, with a halo and the gift of preaching for the salvation of sentient beings. But should the master say that frogs and earthworms are likewise Buddha, the disciple would be required to surrender his usual ideas and hold that frogs and earthworms are Buddha. . . . For he who follows instructions and corrects his sentiments in accordance with the word of the master will come to agree with him. Since the scholars of recent times, however, adhere to their own views and on the basis of their concepts hold the Buddha to be such and such, and none other, and reinterpret other ideas according to their own feelings, they make no progress on the path of the Buddha.[31]

Dōgen interprets the absolute subjection of one's own judgment to the guidance of the master, who is regarded as the representative of tradition, as an act of religious faith. Through this faithful yielding, the disciple attains to truth, which, as is shown in the text quoted above, is nothing other than the existence of the Buddha-nature in all sentient beings. Believing leads into the pantheistic world-view of the vision of enlightenment which is achieved, not in philosophical thought, but by religious experience.

At various points the religious metaphysics of Dōgen approximates Plotinus' Neo-Platonism. The essence of man and of all things is the Buddha-nature, though it be encrusted and soiled by the dust of passion. Purification is imperative, above all purification of the ego and of selfish desires. There must be self-surrender. With profound insight Dōgen states, "To learn the Buddha-way is to learn to know oneself. To learn to know oneself is to forget oneself. To forget oneself means to be enlightened by all the *dharmas*."³² This passage has been interpreted as a call to self-realization. If this were true, Dōgen's way of enlightenment would at heart be a doctrine of self-discovery and self-actualization. But such an interpretation is misleading. Dōgen knows nothing of the self-assertive demands which are associated with the modern concepts of self-realization. His attitude toward reality is humble and reverent. There is here no Promethean struggle for the liberation and elevation of human nature, but rather reflection and purification with a view to exhibiting the metaphysical basis of human existence in the holy and immaculate Buddha-nature. Dōgen expressly rejects concepts in Chinese Zen which approximate the modern views of self-realization. To become a Buddha is not to be equated with comprehending one's own nature. Thus he writes:

> Where did the seven Buddhas and the twenty-eight patriarchs ever teach that the Buddha Law consists only of contemplating one's own nature? The phrase "seeing into one's own nature" is admittedly to be found in the sutra of the Sixth Patriarch, but this is an apocryphal writing.³³

Further:

> Since certain uninformed people do not know what Arhathood and Buddhahood signify, they do not know that they are neither Arhat nor Buddha, but foolishly suppose they are Buddha. This is a great error and a serious transgression.³⁴

To Dōgen's sense of the divine, the Buddha-nature is like a higher reality which he reveres. This must be kept in mind in any evaluation of his metaphysics. He himself was probably unaware of the irreconcilable contradiction between his religious devotion to the Buddha and his philosophical system, which in its equating of the phenomenal world with the Absolute leaves no room for transcendence.

The Zen master Dōgen is a towering figure in Japanese Buddhism and a sympathetic and attractive personality to boot. Of incorruptible integrity, he combined a sharp and penetrating mind with sincere devoutness. His noble qualities won him many friends and disciples even after his death. He belongs among the great creative figures of mankind.

11 *The Cultural Influence of Zen in the Muromachi Period*

The Spread of Zen Under the Rule of the Ashikaga

The Kamakura period was the greatest religious epoch in Japanese history, and also the time in which Buddhism exerted its strongest influence on all strata of the population. Under the protection of the Shoguns of the house of Hōjō, Zen was able to strike deep roots into Japanese soil. The influx of Chinese culture during this early period was chiefly of a religious and intellectual nature.

In the following Ashikaga period, which embraced both the Yoshino (1333-1393) and the Muromachi (1393-1573) eras, Chinese cultural influence reached its highest level. Important trade relations with the Asiatic mainland, carried on chiefly by Buddhist monks, began to develop. In contrast to the serious marks of decay in other Buddhist schools at that time, Zen displayed extraordinary vitality and spread out along broad fronts. The great Zen temples which were built during the Kamakura period in Kyoto and Kamakura became focal points of religious and cultural life, while new temples entered into competition with those already in existence.

The temple of Daitokuji owed its founding (1324) to the Emperor Go-Daigo, an ardent advocate of Buddhism. The first abbot to be called to this temple was Myōchō (Daitō Kokushi,

1283-1337), who had been trained by his master, Jōmyō (Daiō Kokushi), in the strict Chinese Zen of the Yang-chi sect. The extensive collected sayings of the masters Daiō and Daitō, which were compiled in Chinese style, transmit Chinese Zen as it was taught by the masters of the T'ang dynasty and the schools of the Sung period. From the very beginning the temple of Daitokuji was held in high esteem, and occasionally was counted among the "Five Mountains" of Zen in Kyoto. Later, however, it was not included in the official lists, but assumed a special position.[1] Names such as Ikkyū, Shukō, and Kobori Enshū testify to the powerful influences on Japanese culture emanating from Daitokuji.

It was from the Daitokuji temple that during the lifetime of its first abbot, Myōchō, and at the instance of the abdicated Emperor Hanazono, the temple of Myōshinji was established (1335). An imperial villa in Kyoto served as temple. The master Daitō proposed his best disciple, Kanzan, as first abbot. After his initial enlightenment, Kanzan had retired to a quiet rural temple in the district of Gifu to devote himself to further practice. In spite of his protests, he was forced to comply with the call to the capital. Once there, he inspired the temple of Myōshinji with the spirit of strict discipline which characterizes that institution to this day. The wide temple area is distinguished by quiet simplicity. Both land and buildings are devoid of ornamentation, and neither gardens nor works of art attract the visitor.[2] The founder of the most important modern Japanese school of philosophy, Nishida Kitarō, is buried in the temple grounds.

After the lonely death of the dethroned Emperor Go-Daigo in Yoshino, the victorious Shogun Ashikaga Takauji erected the temple of Tenryūji on the western edge of Kyoto (1339) for the consolation of the former's spirit and for the atonement of his own sins. He entrusted the guidance of the new temple to the most famous Buddhist monk of the time, Soseki

(Musō Kokushi, 1275-1351), who had been on terms of intimate friendship with the deceased emperor.[3] His brilliant talent and wide experience fitted him for the important and honorable position. A native of Ise, Soseki had entered the monastic life at the age of nine, and through the study of the sutras and of Tantric rites he had mastered the field of religious knowledge of his time. He attained the seal of Zen enlightenment under the master Kennichi (Bukkoku Kokushi, d. 1314), a son of the Emperor Go-Saga, who early in life had renounced the world and chosen the Way to Enlightenment. During long years of vicissitudes and peregrinations Soseki stayed in various great temples and hermitages, driven by religious longing and love of nature and mountain solitude. For a certain period (1334-1336) he was also in charge of the Nanzenji temple.

After being called as abbot to Tenryūji, Soseki became the central figure in the Buddhist movement in the capital. Together with Gen'e (1269-1352), Shūshin (1321-1388), and his highly gifted disciple Zekkai (d. 1405), he represented the "Literature of the Five Mountains," which devoted itself to the study of the Chinese classics of the Sung period and the Neo-Confucian philosophy of Chu Hsi. In an earlier chapter we noted the reciprocal influence of Neo-Confucianism and Zen in China during the Sung period. Though no inner affinity between the two ways of thought is discernible, Japanese Zen disciples were most receptive to Neo-Confucian metaphysics, which they characteristically interpreted in a naturalistic sense. Through their efforts Chinese philosophy became highly and widely appreciated in Japan.

The admiration of the master Musō (Soseki) for China was not limited to art and learning. On his advice the Shogun sent a party by ship, under the guidance of the monk Sakugen of the Tenryūji temple, to purchase jewelry and consumer goods in China (1342). This was the beginning of trade relations which, thanks to the efforts of assiduous monks, at times reached a high state of development. The episode is referred to in Japanese history as *Tenryūji-bune*, "the ship of Tenryūji."

Musō's name is associated with many of the newly established temples and artistic creations of the time. He induced the Shogun to issue a general decree in 1338 which led to the building of Zen temples in sixty-six localities—"temples to pacify the country" (*ankokuji*). This was actually a continuation of the old system of provincial temples (*kokubunji*) which during the Nara period assured the spread of Buddhism throughout all Japan. It was by means of these provincial temples that Zen achieved its great influence over the general populace. While the master Musō and after him other monks maintained positions, often of political power, at the court of the Shogun, the provincial temples attracted disciples from all walks of life.

The high point in the development of Japanese Zen was achieved during the long rule of the third Shogun of the Ashikaga, Yoshimitsu (1367-1395). At his request, the Shōkokuji temple monastery was founded in 1383 as a branch of Tenryūji. Its first abbot was Myōha, the nephew and most beloved disciple of Musō, otherwise known as Master Fumyō (d. 1388). This new temple, in the classification of Zen centers, was included in the "Five Mountains" of Kyoto. In 1386 the Shogun established the hierarchy of the Zen temples definitively.[4] Above the two groups of "Five Mountains" in Kyoto and Kamakura stood Nanzenji as the foremost Zen temple in the country. As the fourteenth century came to a close the establishment of new temples and the spread of the movement likewise came to an end. The provincial temples received their inspiration and spiritual direction from Kyoto and Kamakura.

Two Zen temples, arising in the magnificent residences of the Shoguns Yoshimitsu and Yoshimasa, must be noted here especially, though less for their religious significance than for

1. *Bodhidharma, by a painter of the school of Mu-ch'i. Original in the Daitokuji, Kyoto.*

2. *Hui-k'o, by Minchō. Original in the*
   Tōfukuji, Kyoto.

3. *Eisai, wooden sculpture, worshipped in the Kenninji, Kyoto.*

4. *Lin-chi, by Jasoku. Original in the Daitokuji, Kyoto.*

5. OPPOSITE: *Hakuin, self-portrait.*

6. Dōgen, *self-portrait.*

7. *Tōfukuji (Kyoto), Butsuden.*

8. *Tōfukuji (Kyoto), Zendō, of the Kamakura period.*

9. *Ryōanji (Kyoto), stone garden by Sōami.*

11. *Landscape, spring, by Sesshū.* 10. OPPOSITE: *Shinjūan (Kyoto), entrance to the tearoom.*

12. *Landscape, winter, by Sesshū.*

13. *Monks at the* dokusan, *"going alone" to visit the Zen master for spiritual guidance.*

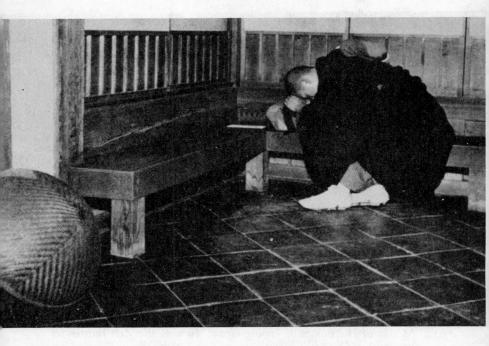

14. *Novice asking for admission in the Zen monastery.*

15. Monks going to beg alms (takuhatsu).

16. FOLLOWING PAGE: *Zen monks at manual work.*

the splendor of their art. Both were born of the spirit of Musō and are associated with his name, despite the fact that at the time of building he was no longer alive. The palace Kinkakuji (Golden Pavilion [1397]), into which Yoshimitsu retired late in life, became after his death the Zen temple Rokuonji, but it is Musō who is honored as the founder.[5]

Following the example of his great ancestor, Yoshimasa built a costly palace, Higashiyama-dono, on the East Mountain, though this was a time of catastrophe when thousands of his subjects perished through famine, fire, and sword. After his death in 1490 this palace was transformed into the Jishōji temple. Though the monk Suimei was the original abbot, Musō again is celebrated as the founder. The residence, Tōgudō, to which the Shogun retired, devoting the last years of his life to aesthetic pursuits, houses the oldest existing tearoom of the four-and-one-half mat size (*koma*: about ten feet square), which later became standard. Only a few steps from this house, Yoshimasa had constructed the two-story "Silver Pavilion," Ginkakuji. The adjacent garden was planned by Sōami, who lived from about 1450 to 1530, and unites the chief motifs of earlier patterns. It contains in profusion formations of sand and water, trees and rocks. While other gardens may reveal a higher degree of spiritualization, at Ginkakuji buildings and gardens are fused with nature in unique harmony, forming a work of art of enchanting beauty.

Approaches to the People

It was during the Kamakura period that Zen first found entrée among the Japanese nobility. The virile discipline and the courage and indifference to death which Zen inculcates by its stern training appealed to the warrior class. But from its earliest origins, Zen had also tended toward the people.[6] Eisai was familiar with the ideal: "To possess in one's heart the great compassion of the Bodhisattva and to become the kindly father of all sentient beings." [7] He recruited his disciples primarily from among the Daimyo (feudal lords) and the noblemen, but we also know that the poor turned to him for help. His compassion for the people had two sources: the religious ideal of the Bodhisattva, and his concern for the welfare of his country. Dōgen's religious genius was by its nature universal and therefore appealed to the hearts of rich and poor alike. The major portion of his work is written in Japanese style. Among his followers were many laymen and even women. The Chinese Rinzai master, Lan-chi Tao-lung of Kenchōji, also admitted women to the exercises and, since he did not speak Japanese, instructed them through interpreters.

With the beginning of the Muromachi period the ties with the populace were on the increase. The provincial temples disseminated the influence of Zen throughout the country. Eminent masters used a fluent Japanese style (*kana-hōgo*) that could be readily understood, and adapted their message to the comprehension and needs of the unlettered. Through this new mode of proclamation Zen reached the broad masses, while no perceptible change in the content of the doctrine is discernible. The metaphysical subsoil remained, as before, the Mahayanist philosophy centered upon the doctrine of the Buddha-nature and the Buddha-mind.

With little originality, the masters of this time repeat the same thoughts, give the same psychological advice, and use the same figures of speech. As in the Japanese poems (*waka*) of the period, only rarely does a new motif emerge to enrich the old modes of expression. All the more astounding, therefore, are the contagious enthusiasm and the persuasive conviction of the masters which kindle the vital spark in their disciples.[8] With increasing development, however, certain dangers cannot be avoided. The road from popular appeal to superficiality and worldliness is often a short one. In the final phase of the period we find some Zen masters dangerously sympathizing with the weaknesses of the people, and drawing from the basic harmony between the Buddha Law and the ways of the world disastrous conclusions for daily life.

In the Zen masters' teaching methods at this time, Chinese elements fade into the background. Dropping the use of the paradox, they declare forthrightly what Zen is about. They demonstrate why it is of great intellectual benefit, and by what means it is practiced. Freely interpreting the doctrine of the direct transmission of mind, they leave room for the sutras. Musō, the outstanding figure of the early Muromachi period, skillfully presented his religious teachings in simple Japanese terms that were readily understood. His major work, the *Muchū-mondō*, explains the core of Zen in the form of questions and answers. As with Dōgen, his faith developed from the experience of the transitoriness of all things earthly, which gives the impulse toward a change of heart. The believing heart is first awakened when one

. . . comes to recognize the inconstancy of the things of the world, and gives up pursuit of honor and gain. The thoughts of yesterday pass away, and the life of today possesses no substance. The breath of life is disrupted, and whether old or young, everything which lives must die. The number of the dead grows, the flowering blossoms are scattered, and the leaves of the trees fall. All things, like foam on the water, are but the image of a dream. Like fish which flounder about in shallow water, so life still lingers briefly as the day ebbs away. Parents and children, husband and wife who lived together, cannot accompany each other. Of what value are high rank and possessions? In the morning cheeks are rosy, but at night there remains only a pale skeleton. Not to trust the transient things of the world, but to seek rather the Way of the Buddha, that is to awaken the mind which seeks the Way and believes in the noble Law.[9]

How much originality in thought and expression is contained in this text is difficult to determine, but apparently not

much. Nonetheless, one can assume that Musō had experienced
and understood what he here set forth. Inspired by a deep
Buddhist faith, and in keeping with the syncretistic tendencies
of his time to regard the Japanese *kami* (gods) as manifestations (*avatar*) of the primal Hotoke or Buddha,[10] he co-
ordinated his native Shinto cult with Buddhism. Thus the un-
alterable cosmic law of *karma* was seen as overarching both
kami and Hotoke. He says further:

> One can be certain that even the *kami* and Hotoke [Buddha]
> will not violate the compensations in the world to come. . . . If
> one's heart is noble and upright, it corresponds of itself to the
> exalted heart of the *kami*, and thus even without prayer there
> will be a token of recognition. *Kami* and Hotoke are inseparable
> as water and wave. One *kami* is like ten thousand and the
> ground of all *kami* is one. . . . The *kami* are to be worshipped
> since they are everywhere present in the universe. The hearts of
> sentient beings, the hearts of the *kami* and of Hotoke, do not
> change. Invisible, they yet appear in heaven and on earth; they
> are mutely present in grass and trees, clouds and wind. Outside
> the hearts of sentient beings there are no *kami*. To revere the
> *kami* is to revere the heart. The controlled heart is like infinite
> space.[11]

While Musō became the central figure in the flourishing Zen
life of the capital, Kyoto, the more popular masters, Bassui
(1327-1387) and Gettan (1326-1389), labored in the provinces. Both wrote in the simple Japanese *kana* letters and addressed themselves without distinction to both monks and laity.
Along with strict obedience to the laws of Buddha, ordinary
life in the world also has its place. But enlightenment transcends all else, and it teaches that "all things which arise in
the mind should at once be cut asunder as with the diamond
sword." "When the things of this world approach, they must
be severed. When the things of the Buddha-world approach
these likewise must be severed." [12] Enlightenment is like awakening from a dream. "In this instant [of enlightenment]

flowers bloom on the dry tree and flames spring up from the ice. In this instant the things of the Buddha-world and the things of this world, all good and all evil, are like a dream of yesterday. Only the Buddha of primal nature appears." [13]

Bassui succeeded in making the difficult doctrine of the universal Buddha comprehensible in simple language and illustrative comparisons. He once comforted a dying person by pointing to the emptiness of all things, the unreality of his sickness, and the transcendence of the Buddha-nature over all pain and passion, saying:

> The Buddha-nature of your mind was neither born nor does it die, it is neither being nor nonbeing, neither emptiness nor form. It experiences neither pleasure nor pain. If you desire to know but do not know what it is that thus in this sickness experiences pain, and if you meditate on what the mind is that experiences the pain of this sickness, and beyond this one thought you do not think, desire, know, or ask anything; if your mind evaporates like a cloud in the ether and comes to nought, the way to rebirth is cut off and the instant of immediate release has come.[14]

Gettan did not shirk the effort of explaining the basic idea of Zen to a laywoman. This devout Buddhist still clung to the externalisms of her religion and to the popular concepts of Buddha-lands, of heavens and hells. In a letter Gettan stresses sharply the emptiness of such concepts and refers to the greatly venerated *Lotus Sutra*.[15] To a lay disciple he explained the self-forgetting way to enlightenment as follows:

> In the *zazen* exercise one must concentrate on but one thing from the very beginning, on the illumination of the Buddha Law, while keeping the mind clear of any single thought. If the mind applies all energy to make the Buddha Law clear, it will of itself forget itself, and when nothing remains but the position and motion of the body in *zazen*, the instant will arrive as suddenly as one awakens from a dream. And in this instant all attachment to concepts will disappear, whether concepts of being or nonbeing, of becoming or decaying, and the way of escape into living freedom will be opened.[16]

The enlightenment remains in day-to-day life, transcending the Law of Buddha and the law of the world. Gettan seeks to lead even the lay disciples to this highest stage of enlightenment.

The most popular figure during the latter half of the Muromachi period was the Zen master Ikkyū (1394-1481),[17] who, much like Musō a century earlier, gathered around himself the religiously stirred and the artistically creative of the capital city. A comparison between these two leading personalities of the fourteenth and fifteenth centuries shows clearly the growing secularization of Zen. For where Musō's art is for the most part religiously inspired, Ikkyū surrenders largely to the spirit of his age. This is the autumn of the Japanese Middle Ages. The feudal order is tottering, the court nobility is decadent, and the shogunate is declining. Social distress and political unrest announce the rapid approach of the end of the epoch.

Ikkyū's origin cannot be determined with certainty. The tradition, however, that he was of imperial blood can apparently be accepted. His mother, who came from the noble family of the Fujiwara, was a favorite of the Emperor Go-Komatsu. Becoming pregnant, she was exiled from the court and gave birth in a poor citizen's house. The boy was turned over at a tender age to be educated in the temple, where he learned the basic concepts of Buddhism and acquired also some literary and scientific knowledge. He loved poetry, and the volumes of his collected poems testify to his native talent in this field.

Ikkyū's devotion to Zen grew out of an aesthetic-religious experience. At the age of twenty-four he heard a blind minstrel sing the story of a king's daughter who fell into disgrace and renounced the world. Three years later the call of a crow in the deep of night stirred in him the desire for the great awakening. After a long life full of vicissitudes, he died at a great age in the temple of Daitokuji in Kyoto, of which he had been abbot during the last eight years of his life.

Ikkyū went far, perhaps too far, in his identification with the people.[18] He mixed with persons of all classes. He ate fish and meat, loved sake and women, and begot children. An enemy of all narrowness and hypocrisy, he spread a naturalistic religiosity which appealed strongly to the common man. If he complained about degeneracy among the monks, it was only to exert himself the more for the lay adherents to Zen:

> In bygone days, those whose hearts were awakened to faith entered the monasteries, but now they all forsake the temples. A careful observer readily discovers that the bonzes are ignorant. They find that to sit in meditation is burdensome, and they neglect the practice of the *kōan*. They enjoy outward frills and spend much time in the decoration of their cushions. With much satisfaction they glory in their monastic robes, and though they wear the habits of a monk they are only laymen in disguise. Let them put on cloaks and robes, and the robe becomes a rope which binds the body, while the cloak becomes an iron rod to torment it.[19]

In these last words there echoes the contemporary image of hell which, however, Ikkyū regarded with skepticism.

Ikkyū also is moved by the transitoriness of all things and teaches indifference toward life and death. On New Year's Day he paraded through the streets of the city carrying a bamboo rod to which he had affixed his treatise on the "Skeleton." To the questions of the astounded onlookers he replied, with an untranslatable play on words, that only the skull is a happy omen. "If you have not come to terms with death like this skull, there can be no happiness for you."[20] He sharply challenged the ideas of the afterlife cherished by the Amida believers. The paradise expected by the pious is more fleeting than a stream of water which hurries by. "If a person purifies the ground of his own mind and beholds his own nature, there remains no Pure Land for which to hope, no hell to fear, no passions to overcome, no duality of good and evil. He is free from the cycle of rebirths. He will be born in every life as his mind wishes."[21]

From this view of enlightenment, Ikkyū drew practical conclusions for day-to-day life. He discarded old customs and mocked at the superstitious practice of kindling lights at the death festival, or of making food offerings to the deceased and reciting the sutras. Rain and dew—the sacrificial gifts of the universe; the moon dispensing light; the breeze rustling in the pine trees; the gurgling of waters in the fountains: these are the true reading of the sutras. In a Japanese song he sings, "Bring melons and eggplants as a sacrifice, or the water of the Kamo River."

Ikkyū called himself the "son of the errant cloud." There was much in him that was eccentric, but also a high-minded liberality and the laughter close to tears characteristic of popular humor. Both the pride of the aristocracy and the destitution of the poor aroused his anger, which he expressed in biting irony. Many anecdotes about him have come down to us. Once when he was begging, dressed in his old clothes, a half-penny was given to him at the door of a wealthy landlord. Thereupon he visited the same house dressed in the ornate garb of his office. He was received in an inner room and offered a sumptuous meal. Instead of eating, however, he arose, took off his robe, and placed it before the food, declaring that the festive meal belonged not to him but only to the robe. His originality, his independent thinking, and his compassion endeared him to the people. He must be counted among the most outstanding bonzes of the Japanese Middle Ages. His puns and *gāthā* live to this day. The following verses typify his manner:

Hetsuraite	Though subtle flattery
tanoshiki yori mo	May bring pleasure, rather
hetsurawade	without falsehood and deception
mazushiki mi koso	Would I dwell in poverty, with
kokoro yasukere	my heart cradled in peace.

The Unfolding in Japanese Culture

The Zen movement has made significant and abiding contributions to Japanese culture.[22] This cultural effect springs from the very substance of Zen. In turn it sheds further light on the nature of Zen and displays various aspects of its spiritual content. In the following pages we are concerned, not with an aesthetic evaluation of the refined culture of the Muromachi period, but with the spirit of Zen from which its art was born.

Even before the introduction of Zen into the land of a thousand islands, the Japanese people, artistically gifted and sensitive to beauty, had been stimulated by Indian and Chinese influences during the early Nara (645-794) and Heian (794-1185) periods, and had produced some great works of art. The deepest inspiration was derived from Buddhism. Even in later times, not all the great works of art in Japan are to be credited to Zen, as some overenthusiastic panegyrists claim. But it is correct to say that from Zen an influence of unparalleled scope entered Japanese daily life, permeating the whole of life, in house and garden as well as in social usage. The Chinese Zen influence entered deeply into the Japanese soul, greatly enriching the appreciation of nature, while Zen as a technique of living immeasurably raised the level of the cultural life of the people. Against a religious background there developed in the Zen temples a mundane culture of a genuine folk character. The spiritual and the secular were close neighbors. Things remain things, and as things are earthly, and yet they are illumined by the rays of the Absolute.

All arts or "ways" (Jap.: *dō*) inspired by Zen were fostered in the Zen temples, whether fencing, wrestling, or archery, which appealed to the warriors; gardening, flower-arranging, and the tea ceremony, which breathe the tranquillity of the temple; or poetry, calligraphy, and painting, which in the European sense belong to the arts. Noble lords and knights retired

periodically to the monasteries to prepare themselves by meditation for their military vocation. Learned scholars sought the
tranquillity of the temples to study Chinese literature. The
major preoccupation was concern for the artistic transfiguration
of life. Abiding works of art were produced, and even more so,
countless beautiful objects for daily use. In ornate temples
there developed the Japanese cult of the beautiful even in utili-
tarian things, whose simplicity and harmonious appropriateness
reflect nature and man's handiwork transfigured by the spirit.

At the beginning of the Muromachi era, the master Musō
was a distinguished artist and the initiator of creative work in
his circle. He was famous for his brush writing, but it was in
his garden that his artistic talent found its foremost expression.[23]
Gardening has been considered an art in Japan since the earliest times. Here, too, the first impulse came from China, but it
found a ready soil in Japan. According to the ancient chronicles, well-cultivated, pleasant gardens date back to the Nara
period and even before. In the Heian period we find vast, luxurious parks, their narrow paths animated by merry strollers,
their ponds dotted with small boats carrying glittering, festive
parties along under arched stone bridges—the picture of a refined, sophisticated society. Under the influence of Zen a new
style in garden-planning developed, aiming at the spiritualization of the nature lover. The gardens of Musō are the oldest
that have been preserved, and belong to the most beautiful in
all Japan. In style they represent the transition from the landscape gardening of the Heian period to the symbolic stone patterns of the late Muromachi era.

Musō was not content merely to imitate nature; within the
vast, all-encompassing framework of nature he placed an image
and reflection endowed with new meaning and spirit. The
garden planned by Musō for the temple of Tenryūji is set
within a glorious landscape of wooded hills and near and distant mountains. The spontaneity of nature is combined with

symbolism. At the outer reaches there is the suggestion of a waterfall, though there is no real water there. This is the focal point of the garden. At the center is a lake, fed by a natural spring and shaped like the Chinese ideograph for "heart." The pure, transparent water in the lake signifies the mind of man as it ought to be and, in enlightenment, indeed is. In the middle of the lake there is an "isle of paradise." Groups of stones depict turtles and storks, animals that are believed to be omens of good fortune. A bridge rests on stones rising above the water; they are spaced at intervals corresponding to the numbers 3, 5, and 7. In the Chinese view these numbers signify the perfect form of human life.

An indescribable stillness reigns over the garden. The many insoluble difficulties which beset human life are here symbolized by the spring, a figure taken from the Chinese artistic tradition. And as the water wells up from the ground to rise in the lake, so the human spirit draws strength from the tranquillity of nature. The white sand at the border of the pond has the same purifying power for the mind as has the pure water. From this purity springs the triumphant courage displayed by the young carp when in the spring he leaps upward against the waterfall, a figure familiar to the Japanese, since it is featured in the Boys' Festival on May fifth, when this event (*koi-nobori*) is celebrated. The feelings that animated Musō as he created this garden can be sensed in a poem of his written in Chinese style:

> Constantly and inexhaustibly flows the stream;
> The one stream flows deep and wide.
> Gaze not upon the curved bank!
> When night falls, the moonlight is mirrored in the heart of the
> waves.

Equally famous is Musō's moss garden at the Saihōji temple, an old historical site at the foot of Arashiyama (Storm Mountain) in Kyoto. This garden, too, is planned around a pond shaped like the character for "heart." It is distinguished further by splendid trees, by rare flowers, and above all by impressive groupings of stones. The garden is actually a symbolic representation of the ideal Land of Zen as described in *Hekiganroku.* Because of the more than twenty varieties of moss to be found on the grounds, this temple came to be known popularly as the "moss temple" (*kokedera*).

Musō's gardens have exerted a lasting influence on Japanese landscaping. At many places throughout the country can be found gardens laid out with the heart-shaped pond (*shinji-ike*) and the characteristic stone arrangements. Frequently these gardens, too, are credited to Musō, though his connection with most of them is doubtful. The Japanese bent toward imitation guaranteed every new artistic motif numerous reproductions.

With the increase of secular culture the artistic activity of the Zen temples spread ever further. For a considerable time the Daitokuji temple took a leading role. Ikkyū, the popular and art-loving abbot, exerted a lasting influence during the fifteenth century. His lay disciple, Shukō (1422-1502), who had been placed in the monastery as a child, and who returned to the world at the age of twenty-four, was the actual founder of the Japanese tea ceremony. As we have already noted, the tea plant had been introduced from China in early times and during the Kamakura period the custom of tea-drinking grew in popularity. This drink, soothing and stimulating as it is to the mind, was especially suited to Zen, since its disciples sought to perfect themselves in quiet but alert meditation.

In his hermitage, called Shinjuan, situated on the grounds of the temple of Daitokuji, Shukō developed further the Chinese elements of the tea ceremony in accordance with Japanese taste. Among his disciples it was Jōō, especially, who further enriched the Japanese forms and accessories of the art. His disciple, Sen no Rikyū (1521-1591), who was descended from a wealthy merchant family of the harbor city of Sakai near Osaka, learned the tea ceremony from a monk of Daitokuji; and later, as tea master under the Shogun Hideyoshi, brought the art to its consummate form. The ceremony as he perfected it came to be accepted generally as a model. Rikyū's teahouse was situated on the grounds of Hideyoshi's luxurious palace, Jūrakutei. After the tea master's death this house was dismantled and erected near the temple called Jukōin within the precincts of Daitokuji, with which Rikyū had been in closest relation. Along with the small three-mat house, a stone lantern and steppingstones were also taken to the new location.

The tea ceremony (*cha-no-yu*) is intimately interwoven with Zen. In China the ritual was "instituted by the Zen monks of successively drinking tea out of a bowl before the image of Bodhidharma, which laid the foundations of the tea ceremony," which is "a cult founded on the adoration of the beautiful among the sordid facts of everyday existence." [24] The few friends meeting in the dim tearoom are imbued with an exalted and gravely happy mood. What they engage in here is actually a continuation of their meditation. The small and meticulously clean teahouse is still marked by the tranquillity of the Zen hall, but the stark loneliness of the experience of enlightenment is here softened by the sense of communion with like-minded friends.

Since the days of Rikyū the furnishings of the tearoom have been fixed. A single scroll graces the *tokonoma*, under which stands a vase holding a single rare flower or blossoming sprig. A small hole is sunk in the floor for the teakettle. The asymmetrical forms and varied colors of all utensils are selected with fine artistic taste. A path (*roji*) leads from the tearoom to an outer waiting room for the guests and to the well which provides fresh water for the tea. The space around the path and the well is developed into the tea garden, which constitutes in its peculiarities one of the important types of Japanese horticultural art.

An example of this type of layout is the "garden of a hundred stones" at Jukōin, designed by Rikyū. Moss-covered turf, rocks, and three slight hills surrounded by green hedges give this tiny spot the appearance of a peaceful garden. A group of stones suggests the eternal symbolism of a bridge which leads to the "opposite shore." The enlightened contemplator has already attained the other side. The garden, the well, and the low, tile-roofed teahouse are fused into a perfect unity.

Rikyū achieved distinction also in other fields of art such as ceramics and flower arrangement. Chronologically he belongs to the subsequent Momoyama era (1573-1614), but in the tea ceremony he brings the Zen-inspired culture of the Muromachi period to its highest state of development.

The precedent for the tea garden was the so-called style of the "flat landscape" (*hira-sansui*) or "dry landscape" (*kare-sansui*), which represented the highest degree of spiritualization attained at the time. In this style, mountains are depicted by rocks, while instead of water, a plain of moss or sand signifies the endless ocean or the universe. Such a garden, like the *kōan*, poses a question to the viewer. What does it stand for? It means, of course, the Buddha, whose body is the universe of nature. In the garden of the Shinjuan hermitage, which goes back to early times and is ascribed to the tea master Shukō, the ground surface is formed by an exquisite, luminous coat of moss. Natural rocks of rare shape, arranged in the 7, 5, 3 series, give one the impression of power and security. To view this garden purifies the heart, pacifies the mind, and directs the eye inward.

The most famous Zen garden of all is the level stone garden adjoining the Ryōanji temple in Kyoto. This garden was planned in about 1499, for General Hosokawa Katsumoto, who spent his declining years at the temple which he founded. It was designed by Sōami, the author of many important works of art during that period. The garden is rectangular in form, about 102 by 50 feet in size, and is enclosed by a low clay wall. One's gaze naturally rises beyond the wall, where an adjoining pine forest and distant hills and mountains provide a harmonious view. The garden consists of nothing but sand and fifteen natural stones arranged in five groups surrounded by a meager growth of moss. The sand symbolizes water, the stones signify mountains or islands, while the moss suggests a forest. The surface consists of coarse snow-white sand. There is neither path nor steppingstone, since no foot falls upon it. Void of all animal life and nearly all vegetation, this stone garden is a symbol of the pure mind purged of all forms. It represents Nothingness, or what Meister Eckhart called the "divine desert."

Nevertheless this desert garden is mysteriously animated from within. The stones live. With their curious forms, they bring a rare movement into the sand waste which, when viewed from the seat of the contemplator, appears to extend to infinity. In full sunlight the rising flood of light blinds the eye, but when the silver moon glides over the white sand, the mind of the contemplative pilgrim is carried to the world beyond, where there are no opposites and the unadulterated Nothingness of pure Spirit dwells in eternal light. In vulgar usage the garden at Ryōanji is called "the garden of the wading tiger," since these living stones resemble the heads and backs of tiger cubs whom the mother tiger is leading through the ford of a stream. This interpretation, of course, does not meet the intent of the artist, who in his work visualized above all the effect of the flat surface, succeeding thereby in combining the greatest abstraction with concrete reality. With the simplest of means he evoked an inexhaustible depth of spiritual meaning.

Another famous garden, projected in the same symbolical-spiritual style, is located at Daisenin in the temple district of

Daitokuji. It is uncertain, however, whether this one is likewise the product of Sōami's hand. The buildings were erected in 1509, which must also be taken as the approximate date of the founding of the garden. Nature in all its grandeur and multiplicity of forms is here compressed into a tiny space. Carefully trimmed trees combined with upright stones depict crags and a waterfall. Broad flat stones represent bridges and riverbanks, with only a trace of sand to indicate the stream. In this simple way the manifoldness of the world with its ten thousand things is set forth symbolically. Perspective is achieved through variation in the size of tree and plant. Like a rich painting the garden contains many motifs, and yet the total impression is less grandiose than that of the stark rock garden at Ryōanji.

It is in the realm of painting, however, that we find Zen art at its highest.[25] The landscapes of the Chinese and Japanese painters, inspired by the religious world view of Zen, are the most abiding contribution of Zen to the fine arts. Early in the thirteenth century Ma-yüan, Hsia-kuei, Liang-k'ai, and other painters under Zen influence were active in China. About the mid-century, Mu-ch'i, a Zen monk in a temple near Han-chou, produced some outstanding paintings which, on being brought to Japan, exerted there a lasting influence on Japanese ink drawing (*sumi-e*).[26] In Japan this art found its true home in the Zen temples where talented monks expressed their enlightenment by their brushwork.

One of the pioneers of the new style was Kao (d. 1345), who according to a doubtful tradition was a monk at the Kenninji temple in Kyoto, and of whose paintings several excellent examples have been preserved. Almost a century later, Minchō (or Chō Densu) of Tōfukuji (1352-1431) created, in addition to huge religious works such as "The Five Hundred *Arhat*," a *nirvāna* sketch and a portrait of Shōichi Kokushi, and also black-and-white landscapes in the Chinese style. His disciple Josetsu followed Ma-yüan and Mu-ch'i in their style without, however, achieving the level of his Chinese models. A good comparison is his "Hyōnen," a humorous and spirited sketch of a husky old man who tries in vain to catch a catfish with a gourd,[27] and Ma-yüan's "A Fishing Boat," one of the greatest artistic symbols of all time of the grandeur and loneliness of human existence.

During the first half of the fifteenth century, the efforts of Shūbun, who was attached to the Shōkokuji temple in Kyoto, made the *sumi-e* popular and widely appreciated. The Shogun appointed Shūbun as head of the government office for painting (*e-dokoro*). He was both sculptor and painter. His ink drawings are for the most part imitations of pictures of the Sung and Yüan periods in China which were imported to Japan. His influence can be seen in many distinguished masters such as Sōtan, Nōami, Shōkei (or Kei Shoki), Dasoku, and others. The fame of Sesshū (1421-1506), who apparently also began his career under Shūbun, excels them all.[28]

Among Japanese and European authorities alike Sesshū is regarded as "the greatest painter, or at least the greatest landscape painter, that Japan has produced."[29] Indeed, he has been called "the most powerful of all Japanese artists."[30] His life and art were formed by Zen. Born in the province of Bitchū, in the district of Okayama, he entered the local Buddhist temple at the age of twelve. He received his Zen training in the temple of Shōkokuji in Kyoto, while a later sojourn in China under the Ming dynasty was of decisive importance to his artistic development. The Chinese properly recognized his great talent. Nonetheless he did not submit himself to the influence of contemporary Chinese painting, but sought inspiration rather in the great masters of the Sung period, above all in Ma-yüan and Hsia-kuei.

Returning to his homeland after a period of wanderings, Sesshū settled in the quiet hermitage of Unkokuan, in Yamaguchi. It is here that his talent soared to its full height and maturity. He produced his masterworks late in life, giving abiding form to his realization of Zen. The technique of the *sumi-e*, which permits no subsequent correction, demands the mental control which the Zen disciple acquires by rigorous practice. Every stroke of the brush remains as it was originally. Beginning delicately, it moves boldly across the white paper, and then fades out or ends abruptly. The certainty and vigor of the brush of Sesshū are unexcelled. His piety, nourished by Zen, speaks out of the spiritual animation of his nature scenes. If nature is the body of Buddha, the Buddha-body is constantly becoming. He who would depict nature from within must comprehend this endless becoming. Precisely this is the intent of the paintings of Sesshū, who like no other painter grasped the change of the seasons and comprehended the exquisite life of the plant world.

Among the descendants of Sesshū, it was Shūgetsu and Sesson of the school named after the last home of the master, the Unkoku school, who most nearly approached his genius. Zen painting was still popular, but artistic tastes generally now turned more to secular and decorative themes. During the latter part of the Muromachi period, the great family of painters, the Kano, achieved fame. The founder of this school, Masanobu (1454-1550), was taught by Shūbun and Sōtan, and was influenced by Zen. Nonetheless his pictures show a pronounced turn toward the secular style. His son Motonobu (1476-1559) painted with ink as well as with light colors. In a painting that has as its theme the three exemplars of enlightenment, Shākyamuni, Bodhidharma, and Lin-chi, he showed his veneration for Zen. But in his works generally, he displayed a tendency to lighter themes and to the soft tints of early Japanese painting (*yamato-e*).

The further development of painting during the Muromachi period illustrates the growing secularization of Japanese culture, which drew Zen in its wake. The temples, which as potent spiritual centers of inner renewal had radiated throughout the nation a refined and religiously inspired culture, degenerated into spiritual stagnation and moral decadence. We thus arrive at the dawn of the modern era in Japan.

12 The First Encounter Between Zen and Christianity

It is a matter of more than mere historical interest to learn how Zen presented itself in its first encounter with Europeans, and how it was judged by them. The brief period of Christian evangelization in Japan, from the middle of the sixteenth to the early seventeenth century, provides us with a wealth of informative material which supplements our knowledge of Zen at various important points. European missionaries during this time recognized in Zen the most significant and highly esteemed, and perhaps also the most widespread, school in Japanese Buddhism—unrivaled in vigor and influence. As religious persons who had made the proclamation of the Christian message the purpose of their life, they manifested great interest in the religions they encountered in Japan. At the same time they were the children of their century, a century which, despite the Renaissance and humanism, was still far removed from ideas of tolerance. "The sixteenth century in Europe was the belligerent age of advancing conquistadores, the age of religious wars and religious intolerance." [1] Especially the hot-blooded sons of the Iberian Peninsula, which furnished the majority of the missionaries to Japan, were little inclined in their uncompromising zeal to recognize pagan religions. In spite of this, however, we are indebted to them for various impartial descriptions of the wisdom and virtue of Buddhist monks, and especially of several distinguished Zen masters.

Two circumstances, however, seriously impaired the encounter between Zen and Christianity at the dawn of the modern period. In the first place, at the end of the Muromachi period, Zen was in a state of decline. Not only was religious impulse stifled by cultural and artistic interests, but as a result of the unremitting political and social confusion, temple life was corrupted by both spiritual decay and moral degeneracy. The picture was thus a dark one, which precluded a fair evaluation of the movement as such. Zen followers appeared to the missionaries as atheists and nihilists. Missionaries were scandalized at the widespread practice of pederasty in the temples.[2]

On the other hand, the brief period of undisturbed evangelization provided little opportunity for Christianity to come to full development. Our knowledge of the deeper penetration of Christianity into Japanese culture at that time is limited. The chief historical sources for the period are the detailed letters and reports of the missionaries. On the other hand, the Japanese answer is scarcely heard. The cruel persecution of the Christians buried the Japanese sources regarding the Christian mission, which in the biased historical writings of the Tokugawa period appeared as a foreign political threat. It does not seem that in its first encounter with Western intellectual and cultural influences, Zen was stimulated to inner renewal or any noticeable enrichment.

Friendly and Hostile Contacts

On November 5, 1549, Francis Xavier wrote in his first long letter from Japan to his brethren in Goa:

I have spoken often with several learned bonzes, especially with one who is held in high esteem here by everyone, as much for his knowledge, conduct and dignity, as for his great age of eighty years. His name is Ninshitsu, which in Japanese signifies "Heart of Truth." He is among them as a bishop, and if his name is appropriate, he is indeed a blessed man. In the many conversations I had with him, I found him doubtful and uncertain as to whether our soul is immortal or dies with the body. Frequently he would say "Yes," but again, he would say "No." I fear that other learned monks are like him. But it is a marvel how good a friend this man is to me.[3]

Ninshitsu, who was abbot of the Zen temple Fukushōji, founded near Kagoshima in 1394, was one of the most highly esteemed men of his sect. His intimate friendship with the first Christian missionary to Japan testifies as much to his sincerity as to the candor and humaneness of his friend. The disciples of Ninshitsu related many details of this friendship after his death. In a stroll through the temple grounds the two friends came across the monks seated in meditation. Deeply impressed by the modesty, the concentration, and the repose they displayed, Xavier asked the abbot, "What are these monks doing?" The abbot laughingly replied, "Some are calculating the contributions received from their followers during the past months. Others think on how they might obtain better clothing and personal care. Still others think of vacation and pastimes. In short, no one thinks of anything of importance." [4] On another occasion Xavier asked his Buddhist friend, "Which period in life do you regard as better: youth or the old age in which you now find yourself?" After a moment's reflection, Ninshitsu replied, "Youth." When questioned as to the reason for this preference, he answered that then the body is still free from sickness and infirmity, and one has still the liberty to do what one desires. To this the Father replied, "If you see a ship which has sailed out of harbor and must of necessity, therefore, enter another, at what point would the passengers experience the greater happiness: when they are still in mid-ocean and exposed to wind, waves and storm, or when they approach the harbor and already cross the bar, there to rest from past shipwreck and storm?" Thereupon Ninshitsu said, "Father, I understand full well. Of course I know that the view of the harbor is more pleasing to those who have begun to enter it. But since it is not yet clear to me, and I have not yet decided which is the better harbor, I do not know where or how I should put to shore." [5] The metaphorical language of Xavier is a good proximation of the Buddhist style. Quite effortlessly the great apostle found his way into the heart of his Oriental friend, though he did not succeed in bringing him to baptism.[6]

Ninshitsu was not the only Zen bonze with whom Xavier made intimate acquaintance during his brief stay in Japan from 1549 to 1551. The missionaries whom he left behind in Japan as heirs of his spirit and work followed his example and sought friendly contact with the Buddhist bonzes. The abbot of the Zen temple Nanrinji, a disciple of Ninshitsu, befriended Brother Almeida, and desired to receive baptism from him secretly. Because of his high position he could not bring himself to an open profession of the Christian faith.[7] It was otherwise with a monk at Daitokuji:

[He] was an old man, almost eighty years of age who, because of his age and uncouthness, lived alone in a house in Miyako. He was of a generous nature and inclined to works of charity and compassion. Arriving at the simple house [of Father Vilela] he began asking the usual questions which most people ask out of sheer curiosity. . . . After the Father had replied to his inquiries, he in turn asked the old man whether he would like to hear something of the law which he preached. The old man answered laughingly that he already knew the things of salvation, and only wished to hear of the strange things in India and Europe. . . . And since he took pity on the Father, he returned the next day and brought a small gift of food, attractively and well prepared. While he was in the house they closed the door, since the boys in the street persisted in mischievous pranks and threw stones at him. The Father expressed his gratitude and then immediately spoke to his guest of God, of the soul, and of eternal life. In this way [the old monk's] interest was awakened and he began to listen. Our message aroused in him the greatest admiration and amazement, and since he listened further to our preaching, the good old man received holy baptism and was given thereby the name of Fabião Meison . . .

This upright and amiable octogenarian pitied the Father whom he saw drinking cold wine out of a silver cup at the early morning mass. He therefore offered to send him a clean teakettle with a small copper stove. This, he said, "will serve him on the altar, both to keep his hands warm and to warm the wine which he has to drink. For to drink cold wine in the morning would certainly be harmful to him." [8]

It caused a great sensation in the capital when the Zen master Kesshu, whose enlightenment had been confirmed by two outstanding authorities, was converted. Frois cites, in Portuguese, the verses which he had composed on his enlightenment:

Ah, dry tree, who hath planted thee?
Whose beginning is nothing and shall return to nothing.
My heart possesses neither being nor nonbeing,
It neither comes nor goes nor subsists.

This monk, too, came first to the missionary's house out of mere curiosity. Yet soon he listened "with great interest and great satisfaction to the preaching. Finally he became a Christian and a very good one at that." [9]

Yamada Shōzaimon, of the district of Mino, a nobleman and a lay disciple of Zen, who had sought salvation in the Buddhist schools of Tendai, Jōdo, and Shingon, as well as in the native Shinto cult, had turned finally to Zen and yielded to complete skepticism. To Brother Lourenço, who sought to make clear to him the difference between the Creator God of Christianity and the *kami* and the Buddhas of the pagan religions, he explained that for a long time already he had regarded both *kami* and Buddhas as "figments of the imagination, and ridiculous." Since he was an earnest seeker he finally summarized his doubts in eleven questions. "Solve these doubts for me and I shall become a Christian," he declared. The answer which was given him, first orally, and then, at his request, in writing, satisfied him and he accepted baptism.[10]

Yengennan, an eminent bonze from the Zen temple Kenninji, showed himself to be an unselfish benefactor, who as Frois remarks, "God our Lord chose, though a heathen, to aid the Father." [11] He freely offered to obtain an audience with the Shogun for Father Vilela, and then protected him on the way from the impudent tricks of the street boys and made way for him into the palace. During this procession "the bonze who . . . was well known throughout the city suffered more than the priest, since he could not calm the disturbance made by the rabble as they saw them pass." Later he was again helpful in arranging a second visit with the Shogun to obtain permission to preach in the city.

Frois's history of the mission mentions numerous other encounters with bonzes whose sectarian affiliation he does not report. Undoubtedly many of these likewise were Zen adherents. Often mere politeness or curiosity incited such visits, while in other instances there was also the desire for the exchange of opinions and intellectual broadening. In all cases these friendly contacts bore good fruits, and despite lowering clouds that already foretold the coming storm, the mission visitor Valignano recommended polite and amiable association with the Buddhist monks; indeed, if possible, the missionaries should "cultivate friendship with some of them." [12]

From the early days of the mission, however, friction and enmity began to arise. In his first letter from Kagoshima, Francis Xavier speaks already of the possibility of persecution by the bonzes. It was ill received when with apostolic candor he rebuked the monks at the Shōfukuji temple in Hakata, founded in 1191 by Eisai, for their "abominable vice." [13] In Kyoto the monks of Daitokuji came, often in the guise of courtiers, to probe into the life and teachings of the missionaries. On one such occasion they asked questions which in the opinion of Frois "revealed clearly the malice of the devil who incited them." [14] The enmity heightened in time, and when overly zealous adherents on both sides began reciprocally to set fire to churches and temples, the period of friendly accord came to an end. Yet even then in individual cases good relations were maintained between missionaries or Christian believers and Zen disciples.

Doctrinal Disputes

Francis Xavier regarded the Japanese as "the best nation yet discovered," [15] and praised especially their intellectual abilities. He writes that they have "a very sharp mind and respond to reason." [16] He had a high opinion of their universities. Even a man like Father Cosme de Torres, who was "distinguished in talent and knowledge," [17] was not regarded by him as equal to the disputations to be held at the great universities. For this purpose, therefore, he appealed to Ignatius Loyola to send "well-experienced men" who had been presented to him personally for approval.[18]

Xavier left Father de Torres in charge of the work which he had begun in Yamaguchi. Torres likewise praised the reasoning powers of the Japanese. "If one can explain to them on rational grounds," he writes, "that only He who created their souls is able to save them, and that while their souls had a beginning they have no end—if one can make all this clear to them in well-chosen and reasonable words, they will in that instant . . . forget their gods . . . and become Christians." [19] His own unshakable confidence in the power of reason was surpassed only by his patience and zeal for the cause of evangelization. Day and night he received visitors who were eager to learn, and disputed with them regarding religious matters. "Ever since Father Master Francis arrived in this city, which is now more than five months ago, there has never been a day in which from early morning until deep in the night there have not been priests and laymen here to ask all sorts of questions . . ." [20] Detailed reports of these disputations in Yamaguchi give a picture of vigorous intellectual exchange.[21]

In these encounters with Buddhism the major issues were the existence of God and the immortal soul. Zen believers denied the existence of the soul with particular vigor. Thus they were known among the missionaries as those who deny the soul. Torres found among them various approaches to this question.

> Some say that there is no soul and that when a man dies, everything dies. For they hold that that which is created out of nothing returns to nothingness. . . . There are others, however, who say that the soul has always existed, and that when the body dies, just as the four elements then return to their original state, so too the soul returns to the condition which it had before it animated a body. There are still others who say that after the death of a body the soul in turn inhabits another body. In this fashion souls are perpetually born and then die.[22]

The first viewpoint represents the nihilistically colored Buddhist negation of the substantial existence of the soul. In the second we find, not quite correctly expressed, the basic monist thesis of Mahāyāna, while in the third case we have the Indian doctrine of the transmigration of souls assimilated into Buddhism. The good Father, schooled as he was in European logic, could not bring these contradictory concepts into accord, and concluded that the Zen school held various "species" of doctrines.

In the records of the disputations made by the Spanish brother Fernandez, who, because of his good knowledge of the Japanese language, served as interpreter, questions and answers are treated from many angles. All basic religious problems come under discussion: the existence and attributes of God, the immortality of the soul, the difference between man and animal, the presence of evil in the world, the existence of the devil, the mercy of God, and redemption. Above all the missionaries seek "to maintain clearly that there is a principle (*principio*) which gives to all things their beginning (*principio*)." [23] The adherents of Zen admit this. But according to their view, Nothingness is this principle.

> After the great Nothingness has entered existence, it can do nothing other than to return to that same nothingness. . . . This is a principle from which all things proceed, whether men, animals, or plants. Every created thing contains this principle in itself, and when men or animals die, the four elements revert into that which they had been at first, and this principle returns to that which it is. . . . This principle is neither good nor evil. It possesses neither bliss nor pain. It neither dies nor lives, so that it is truly nothing. [24]

The Father replies by appealing to man's natural knowledge of God. He insists on the moral law which reveals itself in the conscience, and which receives its sanction in heaven and hell, in reward and punishment in the life beyond. The nihilistic version of Buddhism recurs in all the disputations of Jesuits with Zen disciples after Torres. The Jesuit theologians could not grasp the monistic-idealistic Mahāyāna philosophy, for which they found no counterpart in European thought as they knew it, and which in any case was difficult for them to comprehend in the Japanese language. But with their strong emphasis on morality they were able to bring decisive arguments against the naturalistic-pantheistic world-view of Zen, and were able thereby to convince many of their hearers.

Out of these continuous doctrinal discussions with representatives of the Buddhist schools arose the necessity for the creation of adequate polemical weapons. This was the period in

Europe in which the catechisms of a Canisius and a Bellarmine achieved great success. Nothing was therefore more natural than the development of a catechism especially adapted to Japan, which as a polemical treatise would oppose the Christian doctrines, in clear, concise formulation, to the errors of the unbelievers. The mission visitor Valignano undertook this work with the help of some capable Japanese who were familiar with the Buddhist teachings.[25] But the undertaking proved to be extremely difficult. Valignano complains about the multiplicity of various schools and sects which "deal with these matters so confusedly that one can scarcely grasp or understand what they say." [26]

The catechism mentions none of the schools by name, not even Zen, but the basic attitude of Zen is clearly outlined. The philosophical elaborations are restrained and to the point, but when it comes to the Buddhist distinction between appearance and reality and between exoteric and esoteric, Valignano becomes indignant. The postulate of a double truth, one for the unlettered people and the other for those who are wise and enlightened, he regards as "false, mendacious, and deceptive to the people." He will not accept the argument that the common people cannot grasp the truth and must "be pacified like crying children with small and worthless but glittering gifts." "For it is the duty of the upright and wise man to instruct the ignorant and inexperienced, to lead those who go astray, and not to introduce new inventions or schemes to deceive people and to make them still more ignorant." [27]

The moral discipline of the common people likewise does not require such devices. It is absurd to believe that a false pretense has more power to incite men to the good than does the truth.[28] The Buddhist concept of the "artificial means" (Skt.: *upāya*; Jap.: *hōben*), which is at stake here, was considered by Valignano to be not only contradictory to the truth but morally ambiguous.

Valignano's catechism served as the basis for many slightly varied versions which the missionaries used in giving religious instruction. Beyond this there were a great number of treatises which undertook to refute Buddhist teachings. One such treatise by Father Luis Frois, which dealt with Japanese religions, and of which only the table of contents has been preserved, was evidently also intended as an introduction for missionaries into this difficult area. Two chapters dealt specifically with the Zen school.[29] In the annual report of the year 1604 mention is made of a special curriculum in the Jesuit college of Nagasaki designed to prepare Japanese members of the order for Buddhist polemics.[30] The Japanese brother entrusted with the supervision of this course had visited many temples, listening there to the lectures of eminent bonzes and making extracts of Buddhist writings.

The central figure in the disputations with Buddhism during this time was the Jesuit lay brother Fabian, who had spent his childhood at a Zen temple. Becoming a Christian at the age of seventeen, he rendered the order valuable service for more than twenty years. Finally, however, perhaps because his wish to be ordained as a priest was not granted, he apostatized.[31] His treatise, *Myōtei Mondō*, composed in 1605 as a dialogue between two Japanese women, was designed to instruct Japanese women of the upper classes in the Christian religion, since the customs of the country forbade them to receive regular instruction. The first two parts consist of a refutation of Buddhism and Confucianism, while the third part is a positive presentation of the Christian faith.

The few fragments of the chapter against Buddhism which have been preserved are adequate to show the line of argument. Buddhism is a doctrine of negation, and Zen especially has been nihilistic from the moment of its birth, when Buddha turned the flower and Kāshyapa smiled. "Then spoke Shākya: 'The *nirvāna* of the true law is inexpressible. I hand it over to

Kāshyapa.'" Fabian continues: "This is the beginning of the Zen sect which distinguishes between an esoteric and an exoteric teaching." Thereupon he cites the verses:

The true law of the law—no law,
This law—no law—is nonetheless law . . .[32]

Fabian interprets this paradox as negation, but then has the opponent say, "The nothingness which reveals itself in the Buddha-nature is empty but real." [33] How he answers this objection we do not know because of a gap in the text. In any case he is familiar with the terms of Zen philosophy, and according to him they all point to nothingness. Buddhism teaches the return to the Void and is itself empty. "Understand that in the last analysis, the final goal of Buddhism is nothingness." [34]

The missionaries regarded the Zen school not only as the most important form of Japanese Buddhism, but also as that school "which of all the [Buddhist] schools in Japan is most contrary to the law of God." [35] This resulted in their relentless opposition to this "bulwark of Satan," for according to the religious views of the West at the time, all pagan religions were regarded as "inventions of the devil." [36] It may seem surprising that the missionaries could overlook so completely the mystical element in Zen when at the same time they demonstrated sympathy for its ascetic achievements. Repeatedly they speak with undisguised admiration of the "great meditations" of the Zen disciples, and they praise their concentration of mind and perfect control of the body. But if the mystical side of Zen remained hidden from the view of the missionaries, the rational side became the more evident. To answer the objections raised by Zen disciples was no mean task. "The people who make the great meditations state questions which neither Saint Thomas nor Scotus could satisfactorily answer to the unbelievers." [37] The missionaries fought with sharp logic but paid little attention to the mystical side of Zen. It is regrettable that the circumstances of the time did not permit the development of a better mutual understanding.

Cultural Adaptations and Influences

However inflexible and uncompromising the Jesuit missionaries may have been in matters of faith, they were very receptive in their attitude toward Japanese culture. It was not merely that it was to their own advantage to accommodate themselves to indigenous customs, but also that they admired the Japanese genius which despite all its strangeness exerted a strong fascination over them. Here, too, it is Francis Xavier who determines the course. After his return from Japan he related with great enthusiasm to his friends in Goa the brilliant traits of this newly discovered people. "In their culture, their social usage, and their mores they surpass the Spaniards so greatly that one must be ashamed to say so." [38] To his successor in Japan, Father Cosme de Torres, he left instructions that in the way of life, "in clothing, eating, and similar matters . . . nothing is to be changed, unless a change would contribute to the greater glory of God." [39]

This laid the basis for a missionary method of cultural adaptation. After some wrestling within the missionary community and various experiments and consultations with Japanese Christians, Valignano worked out applications of the principle of accommodation with astounding boldness.[40] Of greatest importance, however, was the admission of Japanese into the order and their appropriate training for the missionary task. If these young Asiatic Christians were to feel at home in their new way of life, and if some day they were to render significant service as apostles for the conversion of their country, it would not do to tear them out of the Japanese social fabric. Therefore the way of life in the colleges and houses of the order had to be assimilated to the Japanese pattern of living. Furthermore, it was deemed desirable that the mission should proceed to establish contact with the upper social classes. Violation of the customs was to be scrupulously avoided. In the execution of this missionary method, according to the intention of Valignano, imitation of the Zen temples was to play an important role.

The *Instructions Regarding the Customs and Modes of Living in Japan,* which Valignano passed on to the missionaries after his first stay in the country (1579-1582), are a unique example of ingenious cultural adaptation in Christian missionary history. The European *bateren,* as the Fathers were called, must have seemed as remarkable and strange to the Japanese as did the wonderland of Japan to them. They had not come as travelers or explorers, however, but rather with the purpose of planting the Christian faith in the Japanese heart and of founding the Church in Japan. Everything depended on their establishing the dignity of the Christian Church in a country in which many other religions had been hospitably accepted and were fructifying the culture.

The titles of the first two chapters of Valignano's memorandum make his concern clear: "How To Achieve and Maintain Esteem Among the Japanese"; and "How To Gain the Confidence of the Christians." Authority and confidence presuppose adaptation to the Japanese mind, and especially the corresponding integration into Japanese society, in which all forms of social usage are regulated according to social rank. A sharp distinction was made between the secular classes and the religious. For the missionaries, adaptation to these customs seemed advisable. Valignano chose the Zen school as his model in ceremonial matters, since this one "was at that time regarded as the most important of all religious communities in Japan and enjoyed the widest contact with all classes of Japanese society." [41]

The difficulty in practicing this ceremonial pattern lay in the problem of determining a hierarchy within the missionary staff, with its corresponding titles and forms of courtesy. Valignano solved this problem by assigning the missionaries to ranks similar to those in the Zen community. The head of the mission for all Japan became equivalent to the abbot (*jicho*) of Nanzenji, while the heads of the missionary districts of Shimo, Bungo, and Miyaki were accorded the dignity of the abbot in one of the "Five Mountains" of Kyoto. The Catholic Fathers became the counterparts of the head of a temple (*chōrō* or *tōdo*). The Japanese brothers (*irmaos*), who carried a great deal of the actual missionary responsibility, were placed on the level of the overseer or guide of *zazen* (*shuso*), while neophytes and catechists were ranked as were the treasurers (*zosu*) and shaven novices (*jisha*) in the Zen school.[42]

Through this ingenious and bold arrangement the Christian missionaries attained high standing in Japanese society. Naturally opposition and criticism against this new order of things were not lacking. The chief opponent among the missionaries to the policy of accommodation was Father Cabral, who was removed by Valignano from his position as head of the mission in Japan. Cabral rightly observed that the abbacy of the Nanzenji and other leading temples in Kyoto was usually held by the sons and brothers of Japanese princes, or by other members of the high nobility, and that these titles were bestowed by the Emperor. How successful the ranks set up by Valignano were in practice we do not know, but it seems safe to assume that many modifications and exceptions had to be made.

Other instructions also reveal Valignano's sincere effort to adapt to Japanese customs. In every mission house a tearoom was to be set up near the entrance, where tea was to be served in Japanese style. Guests of whatever class were to be received in a manner appropriate to their station, so that all of them might acquire sympathy and esteem for the Christian mission.

Indeed, the Jesuits have been accused of addressing themselves too exclusively to the upper classes of old Japan, at the expense of the common people. However this may have been, their impact on the upper classes was extraordinary. Numerous lords (Daimyo) and members of the high nobility as well as knights and bonzes were converted. At times Christianity was in the forefront. Portuguese dress became stylish in the capital, and all things European were admired. This flourishing cultural interchange was to vanish quickly once the storm of persecution arose, but nonetheless the contact of the best Japanese tradition with Christianity through members of leading families remains a significant feature in the history of culture.

The Christian Daimyo and the Way of Tea

In Japanese history the period from the end of the shogunate of the Ashikaga family in 1573 until the definitive seizure of power by Tokugawa Ieyasu in 1600 is known as the "Time of War" (*sengoku-jidai*). The "Way of Tea" (*sadō*), which during this time reached the epitome of its development, survived as an island of peace amid the horrors of continuous wars, which destroyed many of the art treasures of the Muromachi period. Two branches of the art of tea-drinking developed in Japan, the knightly and the bourgeois, since the merchants of Sakai and Osaka demonstrated no less interest in the art of tea than did the nobility. The ruler, Hideyoshi, himself loved the ceremony and instigated brilliant tea gatherings. The quiet hermitage of his tea master, Sen no Rikyū (see Chapter 11), was a major center of Japanese cultural life. According to the conception of Rikyū, the tea ceremony is substantially bound up with Zen. It was he who asked his disciples "first to perfect themselves in the practice of the Buddha Law." Without earnest ascetic discipline the religiously inspired ideal of the tea cult cannot be realized.

The flowering of the Way of Tea during the periods of Eiroku (1558-1570), Genki (1570-1573) and Tenshō (1573-1592) coincided with the flourishing of the Christian mission. As a result the Christian faith and the Way of Tea became memorably associated in the lives of many eminent representatives of Japanese society.[43] One finds the names of outstanding Christians on the guest lists of tea gatherings, and not infrequently tea companions found their way together to the teachings of the Christian gospel. As the regulations of Valignano and the many reports which the missionaries sent home testify, the European missionaries sensed the importance of *cha-no-yu*, the tea ceremony, for the Christian Church of Japan. Father Rodriguez Tçuzzu (1561-1634), one of the leading missionaries at the turn of the seventeenth century, in his chapters on "The Art of Tea" shows a remarkable understanding of the religious significance and the spiritual value of the tea ceremony. He regards the ceremony as an act in which the religious ideal of Zen is carried over into the natural artistic realm.

> This art of tea is a kind of religion of solitude. It was established by the originators in order to promote good habits and moderation in all things among those who dedicate themselves to it. In this way they imitate the Zen philosophers who live in desert hermitages and according to their peculiar tradition use no books or treatises of famous masters and philosophers in their meditation as do the philosophers of the other schools of Indian wisdom. Much rather they hold the things of this world in low esteem, they break away from them and deaden their passions through specific exercises and enigmatic, metaphorical devices which at the outset serve as guides. They give themselves to contemplation of natural things. Of themselves they arrive at the knowledge of the original cause in that they come to see things themselves. In the consideration of their mind they eliminate that which is evil and imperfect until they come to grasp the natural perfection and the being of the First Cause.
>
> Therefore these philosophers customarily do not dispute or argue with others, rather allowing each person to consider things

for himself, in order that he may draw understanding from the ground of his own being. For this reason they do not instruct even their own disciples. The teachers of this school are also imbued with a determined and decisive spirit without indolence or negligence, without lukewarmness or effeminacy. They decline the abundance of things for their personal use as superfluous and unnecessary. They regard sparsity and moderation in all things as the most important matter and as being beneficial to the hermit. This they combine with the greatest equanimity and tranquillity of mind and outer modesty—better to say, consummate hypocrisy—after the manner of the Stoics who thought that the consummate person neither possesses nor feels any passion.

The adherents of *cha-no-yu* claim to be followers of these solitary philosophers. Therefore all teachers of this art, even though they be unbelievers otherwise, are members of the Zen school or become such, even if their ancestors belonged to some other persuasion. Though they imitate this Zen ceremony, they observe neither superstition nor cult, nor any other special religious ritual, since they adopt none of these things from it. Rather they copy only their cenobitic solitude and separation from the activities of life in the world, as also their resolution and readiness of mind, eschewing laxity or indolence, pomp or effeminacy. Also in their contemplation of natural things, these practitioners imitate Zen, not indeed with regard to the goal of the knowledge of being and the perfection of original being, but rather only in that they see in those things the outer tangible and natural forms which move the mind and incite to solitude and tranquillity and detachment from the noise and proud stirring of the world.[44]

In this text, which displays a genuine and lively interest on the part of the European missionary for the Way of Tea, we note significant thoughts for the interpretation of the essence of Zen. The Christian participant in the ceremony can replace the Buddhist background of this art by his own faith, without falsification. Might this also be possible with the actual Zen exercise? For the moment this question must remain unanswered. As Rodriguez Tçuzzu further points out, instruction in the tea ceremony was conducted in a manner similar to that used in the transmission of Zen, namely, without explanatory words and only by concrete experience. Understanding is achieved by doing in the manner "in which the Zen masters proceed, whom the followers of this art emulate." [45]

The first missionary goal of Francis Xavier and his immediate successors had been to win the universities of Mount Hiei and of the "Eastern Country" (Kanazawa), the importance of which they somewhat overestimated. Partly because of the burning of the monasteries on Mount Hiei by Nobunaga in 1571, a change in missionary policy was now brought about, in which tea gained in importance. The intimate interaction of persons engaged in the tea ceremony, and the society which grew out of it, provided unparalleled opportunities to exert religious influence. Important conversions were achieved among the tea-loving merchants of the cities, who from their capital or even from the sale of tea utensils contributed notable sums of money to the building of churches and hospitals.[46] Even more significant and no less successful were the efforts to reach with the Christian message the higher nobles and knights, who for the most part were adherents of the tea ceremony and Zen disciples.

The contacts of the Daimyo of Bungo, Franciscus Ōtomo Yoshishige (or Sōrin, 1530-1587), with Christianity reach back to the days when the Church was founded in Japan. The decisive event of his life was his early encounter with Saint Francis Xavier. Though it took decades for him to arrive at the point of baptism, Yoshishige nonetheless constantly showed himself a friend and benefactor of the Fathers. He understood and mastered the tea ceremony and possessed a collection of artistic tea utensils.[47] He was a man of religious leanings and a sincere seeker after truth, susceptible, it is true, to worldly honors and sensual joys, but never exclusively so, for these things could not satisfy him for long. The cares of his office and his adherence to Zen hindered his conversion to Christianity. Yoshishige was kept from making up his mind until he had ascertained the relative value of Zen and Christianity by his own experience. He called a noted Zen master from Kyoto to his new residence at Usuki, where he built a magnificent temple for him. Placing himself under the guidance of the master, he engaged zealously in the Zen exercises. He worshipped the images of the Zen patriarchs Kāshyapa and Bodhidharma, which adorned his house altar, and endeavored to send his second son, Chikai, into a Buddhist monastery. But on no account would the young prince consent to become a monk. "If the king absolutely insists on making me a bonze," he said, "I will slit open my body and kill myself, or I will jump into the ocean and drown." [48] This son, who because of his violent character aroused some anxiety, inclined rather to the Fathers, receiving from them Christian instruction and finally also baptism, this latter with the approval and in the presence of his father. A short time afterward Yoshishige also reached a decision and became a Christian (1578).

The letters of the missionaries describe the dramatic episode at the court of Bungo, which has been recorded in the Japanese chronicle of the house of Ōtomo. The book *The Flowering and Decline of the House of Ōtomo*, which appeared during the second half of the seventeenth century, hints darkly at the happenings.

Toward the end of the Genki and at the beginning of the Tenshō era the Zen master Etsu from the Daitokuji temple of Kyoto lived at the court of Bungo. While Prince Sōrin occupied his mind with the study of the *kōan*, a stranger named "Nowhere" came and caused obstacles to the *dharma* of the master. Thereafter from somewhere came the two masters, Inga and Jorō. After a short while Inga disappeared. Master Jorō taught Zen during many months and years. Everyone said that Master Ikkyū had been reborn and praised him beyond measure. . . .

All things possess the Buddha-nature. All 1,700 *kōan* are but different names for the same mind. In this way he taught in a manner easy to be understood. . . . But during the effort to grasp clearly the moon of the Absolute [Being] clouds arise and obscure the light. Furthermore, there are insolent persons who on hearing the doctrine that on the basis of the exercises the disciple can be likened to the true temple, i.e., the Absolute—that apart from the true temple nothing exists—destroy Shinto shrines and Buddhist temples, and then decorate their own houses with the spoil which they gather. What Jorō sets forth they regard as nothing.

The course of the world is thus corrupted. The *kami* [Shinto gods] are no longer worshipped. People rather follow their own humor. Whether one regards being or nothingness as the principle of Zen, in our country of the *kami*, one dare not oppose the will of the *kami*. Did Sōrin in his study at the temple of Suwa succumb to the view of nothingness? He did not honor the way of the *kami*. His fame flourished and spread through the nine countries and even to China. Nevertheless "between lips and rim of the cup sways the hand of sinister powers!" The form of the sky fills up and decreases.[49]

While his country was sinking ever more deeply into the miseries of war, Yoshishige maintained his Christian faith to the end of his life. After his death his house declined rapidly, typical in its rise and fall of many great families of the time. But in spite of persistent war disturbances, cultural activity in and around Kyoto survived. Valiant nobles found in the tea ceremony the necessary mental relaxation from the bloody business of war. An elite gathered around Sen no Rikyū. Among his seven best disciples, who have gone down in history as "the seven wise men of tea," were five Christians.[50] Their recognized leader was Justus Takayama Ukon (d. 1615), who, by combining the military (*bu*) and the cultural (*bun*) skills, was the incarnation of the Japanese ideal of knighthood. Deeply cultured and a delightful personality, he belongs to the greatest men of his century. While he enjoyed the favor of Hideyoshi and held the important fief of Takatsuki, in the heartland of Japan between Kyoto and Osaka, his influence led many of the nobility to adopt Christianity. The extravagant praise with which the missionaries speak of him in their letters is adequately justified in the long list of his converts that has come down to us. Father Cespedes concludes his report of the work of Ukon as follows:

> Justus Ukondono is a rare phenomenon. He increases daily in virtue and the perfection of life. Through his brilliance the Lord has illuminated also the above-named nobility, who were here baptized . . . His life makes such an impression on the unbelievers that they generally love and esteem him. Hideyoshi likewise speaks often of him and says that no one else can equal his attainments. He loves and esteems him greatly, and counts him among his closest confidants and protégés.[51]

Takayama Ukon was a person of many gifts. He mastered the various forms of Japanese poetry—the poem (*waka*), the chain verse (*renga*), and the epigram (*haikai*). He also excelled in calligraphy. Above all, he was distinguished in the art of tea. Rikyū valued him more than any of his pupils,[52] for his strength of character as much as for his other gifts. Sent by Hideyoshi, Rikyū besought him in vain to recant his Christian faith,[53] but Ukon set his faith higher than the art of tea or political power. His friendship with Rikyū survived his fall from Hideyoshi's grace. Later, in times of difficulty, he sought out his beloved tea master in secrecy, and was kindly received by him.[54]

Ukon reached the height of his artistry in the years of his exile. In Kanazawa he became the center of a circle of tea friends, to which belonged also the powerful prince Maeda Toshiie and his son, Toshinaga. The spirit of the art of tea described in the biography of Shukō, the first great Japanese tea master, as intimacy, respect, purity, and tranquillity, found in Ukon a Christian transfiguration. "He loved to pray in the teahouse," Father Rodriguez Tçuzzu narrates, "and held this ceremony to be useful in acquiring the virtues of purity, simplicity, and judgment." [55] As the dark clouds of persecution began to lower, his faith strengthened him for suffering, but the art of tea provided him natural comfort.

The other Christian nobles in Rikyū's tea circle were led to the faith by Ukon. The most eminent of these was the Daimyo Gamō Ujisato (1557-1596), a famous commander and a favorite of Hideyoshi. "Being descended from an ancient noble family from the province of Ōmi, he was a prince of great and unusual talent. He was cordial in his social contacts, amenable to good advice, and zealous for souls." [56] In addition to the tea ceremony, he was well versed in the composition of poetry and in designing gardens. He had studied Buddhism and Confucianism under the master Nange, at the Zuiryūji temple, a center of the Rinzai sect in Gifu.[57] After initial resistance he was won by Ukon to the Christian faith. Because of his intellectual gifts and his high position, his conversion drew particular attention. Nonetheless he fulfilled few of the hopes which the missionaries had placed in him. He was able, however, to retain his Christian faith until death (1595), right through the time of persecution.

The three remaining Christians in the circle of "the seven wise men of tea" are more famous in the history of the tea ceremony than in the history of the Church. Seta Kamon was an eccentric who introduced innovations in the art of tea and liked to astound his friends.[58] Oda Yūraku wrote his Christian name, Juan, in Chinese characters, which are pronounced "jo-an," and which can mean the hermitage of a teahouse.[59] About the last one, Shibayama Kenmotsu, little more than his name is known.

To the "seven wise men" belonged also Hosokawa Tadaoki (1564-1645), one of the most powerful men of the period. He was a descendant of the Minamoto family, which gave a series of brilliant names to Japanese history. His father, Fujitaka,

who was also known under the pen-name of Yūsai, was renowned alike as poet and as warrior. His school of poetics,
which was the transitional bridge to the modern age, had as
its most illustrious pupil a Christian named Peter Kinoshita
Katsutoshi, or Chōshōshi (1570-1650).[60] Tadaoki was deeply
attached to Ukon, and often engaged him in long conversations about the new religion, in which he demonstrated much
interest. Through Ukon's influence his high-minded wife,
Gracia, became a Christian. A woman of outstanding gifts and
intelligence, she first demanded answers to a number of objections, traceable to her Zen beginnings, before she could bring
herself to accept baptism.[61] In loyalty to his house, Tadaoki
cultivated the virtues of the knight and the artist. He showed
kindness to the missionaries without himself accepting the
faith. After the early and tragic death of his heroic wife he bequeathed rich gifts to the church of Osaka and had a Mass celebrated for the dead which he himself attended.[62]

The Christian Daimyo Augustine Konishi Yukinaga, who
like his liege lord, Hideyoshi, had risen to the rank of noble
through his own efforts, is a wholly different kind of figure.
Yukinaga's personality is characteristic of the sixteenth century:
he combined the contradictory elements of modern humanism
fostered by the Christian faith with the temper and manner
of feudalism. The Konishi family belonged to the merchant
class, and apparently had originated in Sakai, but by the time
of the visit of Francis Xavier in the sixteenth century it was
settled in Kyoto. The father, Ryūsa, took the decisive step
and became a Christian. In the service of Hideyoshi he filled
the office of treasurer or of finance minister, and in this capacity supervised the precious tea utensils of his lord.[63] The oldest
son continued in the merchant tradition of the family and
was a devotee of the tea ceremony.

The second son, Yukinaga, on the other hand, in his youth
scorned artistic refinement and domestic comfort. After being

adopted by a lesser noble he entered upon a naval career and rose rapidly to the rank of admiral. As one of the leading figures in the campaign against Korea, he participated closely in the political events of his time. His name appears only occasionally on the list of Rikyū's tea guests. After the decisive victory of Ieyasu at Sekigahara he had to pay with his life for his loyalty to the minor son of the deceased Hideyoshi. Since as a Christian he could not commit suicide (harakiri), he accepted the shame of execution at the hands of the hangman. Yukinaga in his own way was also a person of stature, both as a man and as a Christian.

Simon Kuroda Yoshitaka, or Josui (1546-1604), became a Christian first, and was only subsequently introduced to the art of tea. He, too, was descended from a family of the old nobility and was distinguished in the arts of war. First introduced to the faith by Konishi Yukinaga, he was prepared for baptism by the two friends Takayama Ukon and Gamō Ujisato.[64] Ever closer ties of affection linked him with his tea companions. His tolerant and engaging disposition helped him to exert a strong influence on people around him, and greatly contributed to the spread of Christianity. His faith proved strong enough to survive a religious crisis, and came out fortified from the ordeal. As he grew old, he managed, in the teeth of enmity and oppression, to live according to his conviction, despite the troubled times. The following words, addressed to his son Nagamasa, reflect an inner state of resignation and maturity, the fruit of his practice of the Christian faith and the Way of Tea:

> In this life I desire nothing further than tranquillity. I need neither gold nor silver, and regard them rather as filth and stone. Nor do I long to attain to fame in the service of men. I need neither beautiful furniture nor clothing, nor yet a delicious meal morning and night. If only I may pass my life without hunger or cold and may refresh my mind![65]

As he had wished, Yoshitaka was buried in the magnificent church of Hakata. His son, Nagamasa, apostatized from the faith, destroyed the church, and persecuted the Christians. His tomb is in the Zen temple of Shōfukuji, located in the same city of Hakata.

The last-noted name from the circle of tea-loving Daimyo who were Christians or who were sympathetic to the faith is Furuta Oribe (1545–1615), who held the office of tea master under the second Shogun, Tokugawa Hidetada.[66] The new school of the tea ceremony named after him, Oribe-ryū, is distinguished by transparent clarity, respect for the individual, and its deliberate effort to free the Way of Tea from its former Buddhist embrace. Sen no Rikyū had remained to the end a devotee of Zen. Even though the many Christians among his followers created the impression that he had secretly embraced the faith and thereby incurred the disfavor of Hideyoshi, there is no clear evidence for this.[67] Rikyū's Way of Tea, with its inclination toward the obscurity of mysticism, was the child of Zen.

Oribe, by contrast, kept the tea ceremony free from the influence of traditional Japanese religions. He paid no attention to the Buddhas or the *kami*, since to him they were no more than mere men and possessed no power of retribution, either for good or for evil. It was the moral worth of personality that he valued. Therefore he stressed the purification and strengthening of the will. Because of his personal emphasis and his dissociation of the tea ceremony from Buddhism, he was counted among the Christians. It is doubtful, however, that he ever received baptism.[68] But he certainly stood under strong Christian influence. He was an intimate friend of Ukon and may even have been connected with his family by marriage. From the available sources one may safely conclude that Oribe carried the dissociation of the Way of Tea from Buddhism further than any of his contemporaries. One also finds in his ideas intimations of the modern view of man. Unfortunately, however, his school could not come to full development. In the Tokugawa period that followed his death, the Way of Tea, together with all intellectual activity, was forced into rigid molds.

Many notable beginnings of spiritual comprehension mark the first encounters between Zen and Christianity at the dawn of the modern era. Two points are of particular importance. First to be noted is the strong influence toward refinement and "inwardness," or, more accurately, toward Orientalization, which the Christian mission experienced at the instance of Zen and the art of tea. This was true despite the fact that the turbulent century of civil wars and religious conflict provided no congenial climate for the development of these impulses, and that the storm of persecution soon destroyed these germs of new life. In the second place, Christianity promoted the development of personal self-awareness. At the end of the feudalist Middle Ages new energies were stirring in Japan which foretold the coming of the modern era.[69] The harsh rule of the Tokugawa shogunate, however, not only suppressed and destroyed Christianity, but also delayed for a considerable length of time the dawn of the modern era with which Christianity was allied.

13 *Zen in the Modern Japanese Age*

During the Japanese Middle Ages Buddhism was able to wield genuine religious power among the common people, thanks to the simple faith of Amida and the energy of Zen. Brilliant works of art and cultural advances combined with notable contributions in education and refinement among wide circles of the populace. But at the dawn of the modern era the intellectual life of Japan came to a standstill, and social conditions generally became sterile and rigid. Under the stern rule of the Tokugawa regime, the living sources of culture dried up. In a narrow and authoritarian political framework, religion and religious bodies were degraded into instruments of politics.

In the course of a comprehensive new legal order, a list of all temples and shrines was drawn up. Buddhist schools and sects were classified according to major temples (*honji*) and branch temples (*matsuji*), and all families were forced to join a Buddhist group. This was done in order to facilitate the execution of the edict against the Christians. In return for state protection, Buddhism had to submit to strict controls which extended even to doctrinal questions.[1] Innovations in teaching were no longer tolerated. The central government nearly always resolved tensions and contradictions within Buddhist schools in favor of the major temples, at the expense of the smaller rural institutions. The political unification and pacification of the country and the resultant economic prosperity, on the other hand, brought outward gain to the Buddhists. Many new buildings were now erected in temple districts. Yet despite this material prosperity, Buddhism lost more and more of its vitality.

The Tokugawa political order was based on Confucian ethics, which the Neo-Confucianists of the upper classes interpreted rationalistically. The political ideal of the absolute state overshadowed intellectual life, thus choking off all independence of thought. The promising beginnings of a new concept of personality and a new scientific attitude, which had been encouraged by the Christian missions during the transitional period, could make but little progress during the whole Tokugawa period from 1600 to 1868. In any case, Zen, like all other Buddhist schools, sided with the reactionary forces throughout the entire period.

The regulations set up by the shogunate to control the organization of Buddhism applied equally to Zen. It will be recalled that Dōgen had condemned the sectarian system of Buddhism and had refused specifically to recognize the existence of the Sōtō sect as such, although he himself stood in its line of succession. Rinzai Zen had developed without definite organization around the "Mountains" of Kyoto and Kamakura, and at the chief provincial temples. At the beginning of the Tokugawa period, however, the Zen school with its branches was for the first time clearly designated and fitted into the total Buddhist scheme. The registration of the temples and monks of all Buddhist schools was introduced by the Zen monk Sōden of Konjiin (d. 1633) at the Nanzenji temple in Kyoto, who under the rule of Ieyasu achieved a position of power and participated in the persecution of the Christians.[2] Along with the Tendai monk Tenkai (d. 1643), he was the most influential

Buddhist leader of his time. A man of iron will and inexhaustible energy, he not only co-ordinated the religious bodies with
the authoritarian Tokugawa regime, but just as successfully
entered into foreign politics and trade. The Shogun rewarded
him richly for his services.

Another Zen master deeply enmeshed in political events was
Takuan, who lived from 1573 to 1645. He, too, stood in the
service of the shogunate, performing important political trans-
actions and enjoying close relations with the Shogun Iemitsu.[3]
He had received his training at the Daitokuji temple in Kyoto,
but later, at the instance of the Shogun, transferred his residence to Edo, the rising center of Tokugawa rule. Takuan
lived, worked, and died at the Tōkaiji in Shinagawa, where he
was also buried. He was the most important Zen figure at the
beginning of the Tokugawa period. A man of wide learning
and brilliant gifts, Takuan expressed himself as readily in the
fluent Japanese *kana* style as in the highly condensed Chinese
ideographs, and as a result found ready access to all classes of
people. His affection belonged to simple rural folk, among whom
it was easiest to find the pure heart and the childlike reverence
pleasing to Buddha. In the vicissitudes of life, Takuan held
fast to the religiously motivated detachment from all things
earthly and never wavered in charity to his fellow men.

Suzuki, in his study *Zen and Japanese Culture*, quotes a long
passage from the treatise on swordsmanship addressed by
Takuan to Iemitsu's master, Yagyū Tajima no kami, in which
he clearly sets forth the affinity between Zen and this military
art.[4] In swordsmanship, as in Zen, everything depends on the
proper attitude, namely, that the unperturbed mind should find
itself in perpetual motion. No distracting or inhibiting concept must cloud the pure mirror of the mind, which must
respond immediately to every stimulus, "not a hair between."
The secret of swordsmanship is the mental spontaneity of the
uninhibited, enlightened consciousness. Just as the enlightened

one allows events to present themselves as they arise, and responds to each according to its character, so in the genuine sword-battle stroke follows upon stroke in seamless succession. All inhibiting thoughts are cast out of consciousness, above all the concept of life and death. Only he who has passed beyond the border line of this dualism attains the total fearlessness which distinguishes the perfect fighter.

In a seventeenth-century handbook on Bushido (the Way of the Warrior) entitled *Hagakure* and influenced by Zen, the way is shown to an overcoming of the fear and the concept of death. Zen contributed considerably to the full development of the Way of the Warrior which, based on Confucian principles, had been practiced since the Middle Ages and finally, in the Tokugawa period, was codified by the Confucian Yamaga Sokō (1622-1685). The Japanese knights practiced the basic principle of Zen, namely the transcendence of life and death. Obviously, fearlessness in the face of death is not the highest human virtue, as a glance at history makes clear. The play with life and death can degenerate into intolerable cruelty. So Iemitsu, the Shogun and devotee of Bushido, wandered at night through the streets of Edo and tried the edge of his sword on human bodies both living and dead.[5]

The Ōbaku Sect

The introduction of the Obaku sect from China brought a fresh impulse into the stagnant life of Japanese Zen.[6] Actually the exchanges with the Chinese Buddhist temples had never been entirely broken off. With the merchant ships there had continued to come also Buddhist monks with new writings and teachings. Numerous Chinese Zen monks were to be found in the three "temples of bliss" (*fukuji*) at Nagasaki—Kōfukuji, Fukusaiji, and Sōfukuji—and at the Shōfukuji temple as well. All these temples were incorporated into the Ōbaku sect during the stay of the Chinese Zen master Yin-yüan (Jap.: Ingen, d. 1673).

Though more than sixty years old, Yin-yüan finally responded to repeated invitations to cross the water to Japan. His disciple Yeh-lan had suffered shipwreck in his passage a short while before and died at sea. After his arrival in Japan in 1654, Yin-yüan stayed first in Nagasaki at the Kōfukuji temple, but the following year moved on to Kyoto. There he undertook the establishment of a chief temple for his sect on Japanese soil. The foundation was easily achieved and even the government of the shogunate, which as a rule showed little sympathy for Buddhism, took a favorable attitude. The new temple, near Uji in the southeastern part of Kyoto, was named Ōbakusan Mampukuji (Temple of Ten-thousandfold Bliss on Mount Huang-po), following the Chinese pattern.

Despite the stringent regulations of the Tokugawa regime, the new sect spread rapidly. Yin-yüan had brought with him about twenty disciples, half of whom, however, returned to China. But the remaining monks were soon reinforced by new arrivals, among them Mu-an (Jap.: Mokuan, d. 1684), who received from Yin-yüan both the seal of enlightenment and the rule of the order. At the outset the majority of the monks were Chinese, but the religious fervor engendered by the new movement soon attracted a rising generation of Japanese followers.

One of the outstanding Japanese monks was Tetsugen (1630-1682), a native of Kyushu, who on hearing the fame of Yin-yüan hurried to his temple and eventually attained enlightenment under the guidance of Mu-an.[7] Tetsugen dedicated himself with great energy to the propagation of the Ōbaku sect. He initiated an edition of the sutras which embraced the sacred writings of all the Buddhist sects and comprised 6,956 volumes of Chinese woodcut prints. No trace of contempt for the sutras can be found in this master, who considered the propagation of the Buddhist Canon as his main task in life.

The sutras likewise play a role in the doctrinal form of Ōbaku Zen. Obaku rejects the crude forms of syncretism, but does promote the unity of scriptural teaching with Zen (*Kyōzen itchi*). In its ascetic practice, very little distinguishes this sect from Rinzai. But alongside the sudden enlightenment of highly gifted disciples a gradual way for those of medium or lesser talent is also admitted. *Zazen* and the practice of the *kōan* are the most useful means for the sudden attainment of *satori*. The gradual way to enlightenment also makes use of calling upon the name of Buddha (*nembutsu*). However, the followers of Ōbaku understand the veneration of Amida in monistic-idealistic terms. Amida is not regarded as a transcendent being, who is supplicated with confidence in the miraculous power of his vows, but rather as the Buddha-spirit in every sentient being. There exists no Amida outside one's own mind, nor is there a Pure Land outside one's own heart. Like the *kōan*, the *nembutsu* aims at the realization of the Buddha-nature.

The Ōbaku sect has preserved the Chinese spirit in teachings, religious ceremonies, and way of life down to the present. The sutras are recited in the Chinese intonation of the Ming period, to the accompaniment of Chinese musical instruments. The buildings of the Mampukuji temple, which are imitations of the Chinese style of that period, are strikingly different from other Japanese Zen buildings. In time the Chinese forms were slightly accommodated to Japanese styles, however. Thus, for example, Japanese straw sandals came to replace Chinese shoes. The manner of eating has remained Chinese. The monks eat from a common bowl into which each dips with his chopsticks.

The effect of the Chinese influence which Ōbaku Zen brought to bear on Japanese life is not to be compared either culturally or religiously with the profound impact of the Chinese Zen masters and their disciples during the Middle Ages. Apparently the Chinese monks who came to Japan during the declining Ming era were not the equals of the towering personalities who had come in the earlier centuries. The main reason, however, for their failure to achieve a genuine breakthrough was the change in circumstances. Under the Tokugawa rule, Japan was an isolated country under police control, which tolerated no significant stirrings of the spirit or creative cross-fertilization of culture. The introduction of the Ōbaku sect, therefore, was a mere episode, and the Mampukuji temple and those dependent upon it remained a Chinese island in the Japanese empire.

Renewal of Zen

A distinct characteristic of the intellectual life of the Tokugawa era was the movement of renewal which sought new life in the heritage of the past. The study of ancient Confucian literature in the Kogaku movement and the Kokugaku sect of Shinto arose from the desire for rebirth by living contact with the sources. Though the capacity for a truly new creativity, in the sense of the European Renaissance, was lacking, the efforts were genuine enough. In Buddhism the striving toward regeneration is mainly discernible in Zen, which at the time occupied a leading role among the Buddhist schools. After the middle of the seventeenth century, notable Zen masters came to the fore as reformers and as heralds of new religious life. The healthy piety of the people, never quite extinguished, responded to a genuine call even in the shallow and hardened society of Tokugawa times. Only a few names from this period can be mentioned here, and all of these are overshadowed by the fame of Hakuin.

Manzan Dōhaku (1636-1714), a member of the Sōtō sect, vigorously intervened against the abuses in the transmission of offices which, since the end of the Middle Ages, had crept in and become rampant owing to the greed of many bonzes.[8] He wrested from the shogunate new directives regulating the succession in the temples. His influence extended widely and achieved notable improvements. A generation later another Sōtō monk, named Tenkei (1648-1735), labored successfully for a religious renaissance.[9] The attraction and comprehensibility of his preaching won him a large audience.

Bunan (1603-1676), a disciple of the Abbot Gudō (d. 1661) of Myōshinji, from whose line of descent Hakuin was to come two generations later, spent his declining years at the hermitage of Shidōan.[10] He loved the people and warned them against a practice which, concerned only with personal enlightenment, seeks out the solitude of mountain fastnesses and looks down on people in the world. Such bonzes are "the greatest evil in heaven and on earth. They pass through the world without doing any useful work and are thus great thieves." He summarized his understanding of Zen in the following terms:

> Man builds a house and lives in it, while the Buddha dwells in his body. The householder resides constantly in the house, and the Buddha resides in the heart of man. If through compassion things and deeds become easy, the heart becomes clear, and when the heart is clear the Buddha appears. If you wish to clarify your heart, sit in meditation and approach to the Perfected One. In meditation turn over the evil saps of your body to the Perfected One. If you do this, you will surely become a Buddha. . . . The enlightened one follows nature whether in walking or standing, in sitting or reclining.

Bunan wrote in the fluent Japanese *kana* style and composed well-known *kōan* in the thirty-one syllables of Japanese poetics. A collection of "*dharma*-words" from his pen has been preserved.

The Rinzai master Bankei (1622-1693)[11] was a man of the people. Powerfully eloquent, he was unequaled in attracting multitudes of hearers. His audience reputedly reached fifty thousand. Bankei dispensed with complicated citations from

the Buddhas and the patriarchs; in explaining the Way to simple people he spurned artificial devices such as beating and
shouting. He laid all emphasis on the "unborn Buddha-heart."
"If you live in accordance with the Buddha-heart and do not
become confused, you need seek no further enlightenment.
Only sit with the Buddha-heart, be only with the Buddha-heart,
sleep and arise only with the Buddha-heart, and dwell only with
the Buddha-heart! If your normal walking and standing, your
sitting and reclining, are the work of a living Buddha, nothing further remains to be done. To sit contentedly in the consciousness of the Buddha-heart is *zazen*. It is *zazen* perpetually,
and not merely during the time of the practice called *zazen*."

Guided by his mystical concept of single-mindedness, Bankei succeeded in finding an answer for the difficulties of daily
life, and was able to show the simple and uninstructed an attitude of mind that would overcome them. A peasant once asked
him, "By nature I am impulsive and easily angered. As a farmer
I am absorbed in my chores and find it difficult to follow
the Buddha-heart. How can I follow the unborn heart?" The
master replied:

Since all men possess the unborn Buddha-heart from their
birth, you are not now seeking for the first time to follow it. If
you perform your chores with all your might, you are practicing
the unborn heart. Also if while hoeing in the field you speak with
the people and hoe at the same time, then you hoe while speaking and you speak while hoeing. But if you hoe in anger, your
anger is an evil work which deserves the punishment of hell, and
your work is toilsome and painful. But if you hoe without the
clouds of anger or other passions, your work will be easy and
pleasant. This comes from the Buddha-heart and is unborn and
eternal labor.

High and low alike received from Bankei directives for their
lives. To all he showed the enlightened wisdom of appropriate action to overcome passions in harmony with the unborn,
imperishable Absolute.

The renewal of Japanese Zen during the Tokugawa regime reached its apogee in Hakuin (1685-1768); he had attained a high degree of enlightenment and restored Rinzai to its original strictness. Suzuki considers him the "founder of the modern Japanese Rinzai school of Zen." [12] All Zen after him shows clear traces of his influence. But however great his significance for Zen may have been—this is the theme of the following chapter—the intellectual life of the Tokugawa period was nonetheless basically shaped by Confucianism. In addition, only the Restoration ushered in by the scholars of the Kokugaku school of Shintoism and the historical school of Mitō attained any importance.

Buddhism and the Zen sects were restricted in their activity to the narrow scope permitted them by state control. After the reopening of Japan, the situation deteriorated further. Only gradually Buddhism managed to free itself from the oppression it had suffered at the outset of the Meiji period (1868-1912). The peak of its power was irredeemably past, its cultural radiation inhibited. During the periods of Meiji and Taishō (1912-1926) the influence of Zen was limited to isolated circles formed around eminent masters. Each new generation produced venerable masters, hardy and original, yet amiable and unpretentious, whose lives were spent in the quiet of temples, comparable to the fading glow of an evening sky. One still finds such monks today, especially in the country, where with unabated conviction they perpetuate the paradoxes which during the T'ang period came from the lips of the Chinese masters.

The next important chapter in intellectual history would be the modernization of Zen which is now taking place under Western influence and in interchange with Western culture. But the time is not yet ripe for a historical assessment of this period of development.

Bashō and Zen's Love of Nature

Japan's greatest poet was engendered by the spirit of Zen. Matsuo Bashō (1644-1694), while not a monk, was a lay disciple of Zen.[13] He received his literary training in the school of Danrin, which developed his poetical genius. He was able to instill the essence of his enlightened view of nature, for which he was indebted above all to Zen, into the spare, strict form of the seventeen-syllable epigram (*haikai* or *haiku*). After long years of experiment and study, he had reached mastery of an art which he felt to be in the tradition of the uniquely Japanese style of *fūga*. His famous lines on the artistic power of *fūga* as a means to transform life creatively contain his self-estimation as poet and man. He speaks of himself as a monk in a robe fluttering in the breeze (*fūrabo*), and says:

> For a long time he loved poetry till finally it became his fate. At times he wearily thought of giving it up; at other times he felt again that he must excel in it. While this struggle went on, his mind was restless. If he tried for a time to make progress in the world, his poetry stood in the way. If for a time he applied himself to the task of instructing the ignorant, he was likewise inhibited. Finally he was powerless and void of all achievement. So he attached himself to the one line [of tradition]. What Saigyō seeks to express in the Japanese song, Sōgi in the chain poem, and what Sesshū aims at in the painting and Rikyū in the tea ceremony—all these ways are permeated by one single thing.
>
> He who comprehends *fūga* follows nature and becomes a friend to the four seasons. In whatever he sees, he beholds the flower. In whatever he thinks, he thinks the moon. He to whom a form is not a flower is a barbarian. He whose thoughts are not the moon is like an animal. Depart from barbarism and leave the beast behind. Follow nature and return to nature.[14]

Of the names mentioned by Bashō as his forerunners, only the last two are Zen disciples in the full sense. Saigyō (1118-1190) had lived in Japan as an itinerant monk and poet, in closest contact with nature, before the arrival of Zen. Several centuries later the poet-monk Sōgi of the Tendai school followed in his footsteps (1421-1502). More than any other artist, Sesshū is spiritually akin to Bashō. Both comprehend nature from within, both instinctively respond to the rhythm of life in the changes of the moon, and repeatedly find the appropriate term for this pulsation in their art. In many of his *haiku* Bashō hints at the seasons whose peculiarity he feels and loves. He sings of the splendor of the morning and of flowers in the spring. But in the Land of the Rising Sun, where the cherry blossoms fade after only a few days, no season speaks so forcefully to the heart as autumn, whose dying beauty is transfigured by the glow of eternity. But even autumn has no heartbreaking melancholy for the enlightened Zen disciple. To him death and birth are equally parts of life which come from Nature and are reabsorbed by her. In many songs Bashō develops variations on the motif of the autumn wind. When he mourns the death of his young poet friend Isshō, the autumn wind breathes the pure sorrow of death:

Tsuka mo ugoke	Grave, bestir thyself!
wage nakigoe wa	My mournful voice weeps
aki no kaze	Like the autumn wind.

In the mute image of the dry, leafless boughs, in the complaining melody of the wind, in the first wave of cold which makes the body shiver, autumn breathes loneliness into the soul, which the poet relishes contemplating.

Karaeda ni	On a dry branch
karasu mo tomarikeri	A raven is perched—
aki no kure	Autumn eve.[15]

Mono ieba	If I but speak
kuchibiru samushi	My cold lips tremble
aki no kaze	In autumn wind.

White is the color of emptiness and solitude. The poet sees the white of the cliffs, and in an unusual transmutation attributes this whiteness to the autumn wind:

Ishiyama no	White gleams the stone
ishi yori shiroshi	Of the mountain rock; whiter yet
aki no kaze	The wind of autumn.

Loneliness is the feeling in which the soul touches the Absolute. Zen practices the loneliness and silence of the Void in long, somber hours of meditation. Bashō, who had passed through the hard school of practice under the Zen master Butchō, carried this silence within and listened to the deepest ground of nature, where all sounds lapse into stillness and thereby merely accent its awesomeness. In his travel book *Oku no Hosomichi* he tells how one day in his wanderings he encountered a perfect silence in nature. It was then that he composed his most beautiful song on silence, which we can savor in his introductory lines:

> In the district of Yamagata is located a mountain temple named Ryūshakuji, which was founded by Jikaku Daishi, and is an unusually pure and quiet spot. . . . We ascended to the temple hall on the mountain. Rock towers upon rock, pines and oaks are primeval, earth and stones are ancient and covered with slippery moss. The sliding doors of the rock-based temple buildings were closed. Not a sound could be heard. We wandered through the rocky expanse, crept over the boulders, and worshipped before the sacred Buddha images. The glorious landscape and the far-reaching silence pierced straight to our hearts.

Shizukasa ya	Only silence alone—
iwa ni shimiiru	Into the rocky cliff penetrates
semi no koe	The sound of the cicada.

The noise of the cicadas does not disturb the tranquillity of nature. The motion of life is no hindrance to the one who knows, but rather heightens the inner silence. "Stillness in motion, motion in stillness," is the ancient Oriental word of

wisdom which Zen has made its own. Bashō enters into the
stillness of Nature as he also enters into her motion. He is an
eternal wanderer, whom the "longing for wind and clouds"
constantly keeps on the road. His travel diaries are everywhere
interspersed with exquisite *haiku*. He experiences the uncertainty of life, survives its dangers and exertions, yet without the
spirit of adventure or the gestures of heroism. In all that trans-
pires in his mind he preserves the quiet clarity of the knowing
one. Human life is for him a single peregrination without beginning or end, from somewhere to somewhere, in keeping
with the Buddhist doctrine of the cycle of rebirths and the
Middle Way which sways between being and nonbeing, between the eternal and the transient. All nature is changeable—
sun and moon, wind and clouds. Should not man join them in
wandering? Thus he begins his famous book *Oku no Hosomichi*:

> Sun and moon are eternal wanderers. So also do the years
> journey, coming and going. He who passes his life in the floating
> ship and, as he approaches old age, grasps the reins of the horse,
> journeys daily. The journey is his abode. In ancient times many
> people died while on the road.
>
> I, too, enticed by the clouds and the winds, felt for some time
> the desire to wander. Last autumn I had returned from the sea-
> shore to my dilapidated house on the river, and as I brushed
> aside the cobwebs, the old year as well had passed. I was driven
> irresistibly by a demon in my heart to cross the barrier at Shira-
> kawa under the fog-veiled spring sky. I heard the inviting call of
> the gods of the road and could undertake no further work . . .

And so the poet sets out from his miserable hut by the ba-
nana tree from which he received the name by which he is
known in history. He wanders through the country and visits
the scenic spots of his island homeland. He venerates the places
made famous by legend, meets friends, and speaks with small
and great. Everywhere, human life is dear and precious to
him. Everywhere he is close to his mother Nature. In this way he

journeys through the length and breadth of the land till his staff falls from his weary hand and with his brush he writes down his last *haiku:*

Tabi ni yande	Sick from the journey;
yume wa kareno wo	Chasing on the dry field
kakemeguru	Dreams go round.

Bashō's poetry embraces a wide circle of things. It is not easy to determine whether in his selection of themes his poetic bent or his Zen world-view was the more decisive. His tastes inclined toward small animals and flowers, toward the wind, the clouds, and the moon, which last as it is mirrored in the water is reminiscent of the mind of man. In every particle of dust he grasps the universe, in the frog, the cuckoo, and the sparrow, in the chirping cicada and in the nightingale which soils the rice cakes on the veranda—in all he feels the life of the Buddha. Suzuki interprets Bashō's most famous *haiku* in the light of the Zen experience.[16] The frog, which with a plunge into the pond vivifies the universe, discloses the final meaning of reality. "What is life other than a noise that breaks the silence, a noise of foolish origin and soon to pass?" This is Gundert's interpretation of the *haiku:*

Furu ike ya	The old pond, ah!
kawazu tobikomu,	A frog jumps in:
mizu no oto	The water's sound.[17]

Bashō is one of the greatest lyric poets of all time. Because of their intimate fusion with language, as is the case with all lyric poetry, Bashō's verses can hardly be assessed without an adequate knowledge of the Japanese language. The charm of his humanity comes through in many simple poems which brighten the happenings of everyday life. His is the innocent eye of the child. He loves children as he loves flowers:

Ko ni aku to	"I do not like children"—
mosu hito ni wa	For him who says this
hana mo nashi	No flowers bloom.

Though of a thoroughly religious nature, Bashō shows little interest in the various forms of Buddhist doctrine.

Tsukikage ya	The gleam of the moon!
shimon shishū mo	The four entrances, the four doctrines
tada hitotsu	Are all but one.

His nature-loving religiosity lacks the personal note. No exuberant passion explodes in his lines. Men and their works in history remain outside the scope of his vision. The man Bashō is completely immersed in the contemplation of nature. He is merged with cosmic life. The limitation of his poetic utterances is conditioned by his naturalistic world-view which does not do justice to the personal character of man. Nowhere does man assume a towering and masterful position in the universe, nor is he possessed of a "royal nature" (Gregory of Nyssa) that subdues the earth to its will and lifts its eyes to heaven.

Human life is divested of its character of decision. It is not a unique, nonrecurrent event, but rather a mere moment in the course of nature. The Absolute also is absorbed into the cosmic process of becoming. This undiscriminating consciousness of nature is the expression of a naturalistic world-view that is incompatible with personal religion, as has been pointed out by the Japanese Barthian theologian Kitamori Kazō, who analyzed the aesthetics of Bashō's religious feelings in terms of the categories of Kierkegaard. Kitamori exposes the "pseudoreligion" of Bashō, which he calls the "enemy" of true religion.[18]

"I have observed that monism always reverts to naturalism and intellectualism," Karl Vossler wrote in a letter to his friend Benedetto Croce.[19] Zen Buddhism, which detached itself from the intellectualism of monist Mahāyāna, provides us with a stirring spectacle of relapse into naturalism. Among the great

Zen masters of the T'ang and Sung periods in China it was a naturalism of Taoist coloring. Thanks to the subtle appreciation of nature in the Japanese, Zen here found a new and highly artistic expression, nowhere more perfectly translated into words than by Bashō.

In Japan this naturalistic world-view is not limited to the adherents of Zen. Though nurtured on Confucianism, the noble educator and forerunner of the Meiji Restoration, Yoshida Shōin (1830-1859), drew strength at his last hour from a turning back to nature. From prison he wrote: "However men may judge, I give myself up to nature. I do not desire death. I do not refuse death." [20] And the pioneer of the Kokugaku school, Kamo Mabuchi (1697-1769), who devoted himself energetically to the renewal of Shinto, sees in the "harmony with heaven and earth" the highest ideal of life, which is to be accomplished in conformity to the spontaneous course of nature.[21]

Kitamori cites the widely read modern novelist Natsume Sōseki as a further representative of aesthetic naturalism.[22] It would be easy to list other names from all areas of religion and art. Zen is not the only element, nor perhaps the primary one, responsible for the naturalistic trend which runs through all of Japanese intellectual life, but it strongly corresponds to the innate Japanese feeling for nature. It was therefore possible for Zen to strike deep roots in Japan and to produce, in its alliance with the Japanese genius, a rich artistic tradition.

14 *The Zen Mysticism of Hakuin*

Next to Dōgen, Hakuin (1685-1768) was the greatest of the Japanese Zen masters. His efforts toward renewal in the Rinzai sect laid the foundation for the modern development of Japanese Zen. In his personality certain traits of Zen come to the surface for the first time. He was a dynamic character, prone to ecstatic states. By means of daring exercises he attained extraordinary mystical experiences which he describes in his writings. His accounts give evidence of a sharp mind, penetrating introspection, and great literary gifts. We find in the writings of Hakuin perhaps the most detailed descriptions of the mystical experience in all Zen literature. His personal experiences contributed to his formulations of doctrine. The rich, as yet little explored materials in his writings reveal him to be one of the most interesting characters in the history of religion.

Life and Work[1]

Hakuin began and ended his life in the nondescript village of Hara in the district of Suruga. His mother's family belonged to the Nichiren sect. His father was of noble birth and was adopted through marriage by his mother's family. The child, called Iwajiro, was the youngest in the family of five children, physically frail but intellectually highly gifted. From earliest childhood he displayed unusual religious responsiveness. The mere view of clouds rapidly changing over the sea made him sorrowful, and as early as the age of five he had inklings of the transiency of all earthly things. His parental home was frequented by an aged ascetic named Kyūshimbo, who, recognizing the genius of the child, was drawn to him and exhorted him to become a "land of bliss" for mankind.

Hakuin received his strongest spiritual impressions from his devout mother. She once took him along to a temple where he heard a famous bonze explain the writings of Nichiren. His sermon on the Eight Hot Hells completely shook the lad, who delighted in catching and killing insects and small birds. But now he was so smitten by fear of the terrible retribution awaiting such deeds that he was seized with a fit of trembling.

For a long time the fear of hell did not leave him. Once when he accompanied his mother to the bath, he underwent a deathly terror. Since his mother loved hot water, the maid had kindled a crackling fire, fed by logs of wood. To the ears of the imaginative boy the sound of the flames was as the roar of waves and the peal of thunder. He could only think of hell, and implored his mother to tell him how to escape its flames. She comforted him by promising to explain later when they were at a clean place. On another occasion he played with some boys from the village, trying to catch a young crow. But then he remembered that to kill a living being is punishable by hell. So he hurried home to his mother and again inquired how he might escape hell. While combing his hair she calmed him, saying that he should only venerate his guardian god, Temman Tenjin, the name by which Sugahara Michizane is worshipped in the Shinto cult. This god would deliver him from the painful *karma*.

With increasing zeal Hakuin now devoted himself to Buddhist piety. He was especially impressed by the *Lotus Sutra*, which claims that the ascetic who is protected by magic formulas can be harmed by neither fire nor water. For several days he zealously recited the *dhāranī* of the sutra. Then, trying his luck, he took a glowing iron rod from the hearth and touched his thigh. But the smarting pain informed him that no change had transpired.

Convinced now that his pious exercises were of no avail as long as he remained "in the world," he determined to leave his home and take up the monastic life. He was in his fifteenth year when he received permission from his parents to follow his bent, and sought out the Zen temple of his native village, Shōinji. There the master Tan Reiden guided his first steps in the religious life and ordained him a monk. He was given the name Ekaku. When shortly after Tan Reiden fell ill, Ekaku journeyed to the Daishōji temple in the nearby town of Numazu, there to continue his training under the master Sokudō. But here too he remained unsatisfied. Life at the temple proved to be a disappointment and the parables of the *Lotus Sutra* no sufficient answer to his soul. He began to doubt whether the Buddha Law could bring him liberation. His inner distress increased; in his nineteenth year he read the story of the tragic death of the Zen master Yen-t'ou, which intensified his despair. He was later to describe this crisis in his religious life in connection with his mystical experiences.

Driven by inner unrest and a thirst for knowledge, Hakuin now took up the staff of the wanderer. In the Zuiunji temple in the province of Mino he encountered the poet Baō (1704), who effectively stimulated his literary talent. A religious experience there aroused him to renewed seeking. On a summer day the poet had carried the many volumes of his library out of doors to air them in the sun. At the sight of these treasures of diverse wisdom Hakuin suddenly felt at a complete loss. Whom should he choose as a guide: Master Kung, Buddha, or the sages of Taoism? Praying fervently to all the guardian gods of the Dharma he took up a volume. It turned out to be a collection of Zen stories from the Ming period, a storehouse of precious ancient wisdom. He read of the famous Rinzai master Shih-shuang Ch'u-yüan who meditated day and night without interruption and who, when threatened by drowsiness, bored his flesh with a sharp awl in order to arouse his mind through the pain.

Hakuin's zeal for the practice of Zen was aroused. He determined to return to the Zen hall and to persevere until he attained full enlightenment. At that time the news of his mother's death reached him. His first impulse was to go home to her grave. But on second thought he felt that it would be more in keeping with her spirit if he would dedicate himself completely to the realization of his religious ideal. Accordingly he set out again to visit temples, with no other thought in mind but that of progress on the way to enlightenment.

This period of his itinerant life came to a close when he entered the Eiganji temple in the province of Echigo, to hear the discourses of the master Shōtetsu. Here he attained his first, as yet imperfect, experience of enlightenment. He next approached the master Etan of the Shōjuan hermitage (1708), who trained him with merciless rigor. He was spared no pain nor humiliation. But Hakuin was thankful to the aged monk for the rest of his life for the "great kindness" of his relentless severity, which helped him to higher levels of enlightenment.

Hakuin's stay at Shōjuan, however, was of but short duration, since he was soon summoned back to the Daishōji temple in Numazu to care for his sick old master, Sokudō.[2]

He continued to practice with the greatest intensity. His ecstatic experiences now multiplied, but his weak bodily constitution was not equal to the demands he made upon it. He suffered a series of nervous breakdowns which brought him to the verge of despair. And so in 1710 he visited the hermit

Hakuyū, who taught him a psychological treatment for the so-called "Zen sickness," by means of which he was restored to health. As he journeyed through the country his mystical experiences became more profound and frequent.

The news of his father's death now brought him back to his native village. In 1716 he settled permanently at the Shō-inji temple not far from his birthplace, a temple surrounded, as the name indicates, by a pine grove. This was where he had begun his religious career. Hakuin found the temple in a state of disrepair, but under his guidance it was destined to become the center of the strongest Buddhist movement of the Tokugawa period. The Myōshinji temple having accorded him rank, the right to succession, and the name Hakuin, his fame now spread throughout all Japan. While he cared for the small rural temple of Shōinji and counseled the humble peasants of the vicinity in both worldly and spiritual matters, disciples congregated from far and wide to be guided by him on the way to enlightenment.

Some of the more zealous novices met with an early death owing to the rigors to which they subjected themselves. Made wise by his own experience Hakuin admonished his charges to spare their bodily strength, while he ministered to their sicknesses. His warnings are underscored impressively by the long row of tombstones of disciples, whose remains rest beside those of the master in the cemetery of Shōinji. A number of unpublished sutra texts preserved there, with glosses from his hand, testify to his tireless zeal in study. But in addition to this he also painted and wrote poetry. Many of his Zen paintings are genuine expressions of his enlightened vision. The large radiant eyes which look out at us from his self-portraits speak of the deep insights which in his hours of ecstasy he gained into the nature of reality.

Hakuin continued to work tirelessly to an advanced age among his disciples and among the people. His annual lectures attracted a multitude of seekers. His eightieth year was marked by a new peak as more than seven hundred disciples gathered at Shōinji to take part in the spring exercises. The impact of his personality was widened through the numerous writings which he composed in the simple *kana* style for the common people. He liked to intersperse his treatises with songs and poems which could be easily retained and conveyed his teachings even to the illiterate. He translated Buddhist piety into everyday morality, inculcating obedience to the commandments and admonishing to virtue in home and state. The peasants he taught to cut off their passions at the roots like grass, in the song "While Hoeing Weeds." For the children he composed a "Song of Filial Piety of the Child," which in true Confucian manner teaches: "Be grateful to your parents, be aware that the child receives his body from his parents." In a "Song of the Old Woman Grinding Grain" he compares her to the consciousness which is identical with the Buddha, and has her begin her song: "How thankworthy is the grace of heaven and earth, the heat and the cold, the day and the night, all of which are needful." At the end of the song he has her say: "If the old woman searches her heart rightly, the true way of the patriarchs cannot fail. Persevere; keep well! The old woman now parts from you." Through his undemanding goodness, his candor and religious enthusiasm, Hakuin won the hearts of the common people; he belongs among the greatest religious reformers of Japanese history.

Mystical Experiences

As with all mystical experience, enlightenment in Zen is inexplicable and unutterable. But whereas the Christian mystics tirelessly seek to explain the inexplicable and to utter the unutterable, information about personal Zen experience is generally scarce. The *kōan* accounts usually close with the simple assertion: ". . . and he attained enlightenment." At most the effects of the experience are praised in a few words, such as "the clarity of the spiritual vision," "the feeling of liberation," and "the sense of power in the universe." But what the enlightenment consists of is not mentioned. As a rule, the steps on the Way of Enlightenment are not closely described either. In view of this scarcity of personal records, Hakuin's detailed descriptions of his inner experiences are especially valuable. In his writings he often refers to his own experiences, and with a good sense for psychological processes is able to utter a great deal of the "unutterable." For our present sketch we will follow his main report in the third book of his work *Orategama*, which consists of a number of extensive epistolary treatises.

Hakuin, as we already mentioned, was first set on the Way of Enlightenment by a religious crisis in his nineteenth year brought on by his chance reading of the tragic end of the Chinese Zen master Yen-t'ou. When he was murdered by robbers, Yen-t'ou cried out so loudly that he was heard for three miles and more. The young Hakuin brooded: "If a master of the rank of Yen-t'ou must come to such a pitiful end, of what good is Zen? How then can anyone escape the torment of the demons of hell after his death? Is not the whole Buddha Law a falsehood?" For three days he lay in greatest affliction without eating, for a time giving up all hope in the Buddha and regarding the Buddha images and sutras as worthless trash.

To drown his grief, Hakuin turned to worldly literature. But his anxiety could not be stilled and drove him to a restless search. Some insights came to him during a Zen exercise in which he participated three years later at a country temple in the province of Wakasa. From there he traveled to the island of Shikoku. He now combined reading of the sutras with practice of the *kōan,* devoting himself day and night to meditation on Master Chao-chou's "nothingness," which is the famous first exercise in the *kōan* collection of *Wu-mên-kuan.* Despite unremitting efforts he was unable to maintain a uniform state of concentration in waking and sleeping alike. He attributed this failure to his own lack of inner purity. But not long afterward he finally attained his first experience of enlightenment, which he describes as follows:

> During the spring of my twenty-fourth year I was staying at the Eiganji temple in the province of Echigo where I practiced assiduously. I slept neither by day nor by night, and forgot both to rest and to eat. Suddenly I was overcome by the Great Doubt. I felt as though freezing in an ice field extending thousands of miles. My bosom was filled with an extraordinary purity. I could neither advance nor retire. It was as if I were out of my mind and only the word "nothing" remained. During the lecture I heard, indeed, the explanations of the master, but it was as if I heard a discourse from afar in a distant Zen hall. Sometimes I felt as if I were floating through the air. This state continued for a number of days until one night while hearing the striking of the temple bell I experienced the transformation.
>
> It was like the smashing of a layer of ice, or the pulling down of a crystal tower. As I suddenly awakened and came to my senses, I felt myself to be like Master Yen-t'ou, who all through the three times (past, present, and future) encountered no suffering. All former doubts were fully dissolved like ice which melted away. With a loud voice I called out, "How glorious, how glorious!" We need no escape from the cycle of life and death, nor need we strive after enlightenment. The seventeen hundred *kōan* exercises are not worthy of being posed. My pride rose up like a mountain and my exaltation welled up like a flood. To myself I thought that for two or three hundred years there had been no sudden breakthrough like mine, with such great ecstasy. With this vision I immediately set out on the road to Shinano.[3]

In this description two phases of the psychic process can be clearly discerned. In the practice of the *kōan* there is first attained a state of great tension, which Hakuin describes as the "Great Doubt." The mind is under pressure to the point of explosion until the tension can mount no higher. The solution comes in an ecstatic experience which Hakuin explains by analogies. The breakthrough brings liberation, clarity, and delight.

Convinced that he had attained the enlightened state, Hakuin set out to report the good news to Etan, the aged hermit at Shōjuan in the district of Shinano. The master received him, and Hakuin described the experience for his approval and handed over his verses on enlightenment. What followed is one of those unique scenes, full of originality, wit, and crudeness, which have belonged to the Zen tradition since the days of the great masters of the T"ang era. Master Etan took up the verses in his left hand and said, "This you have learned. This is your theoretical knowledge. Now show me your own intuitive insight, your enlightenment," and at the same time he held out his right hand. Without hesitation Hakuin rejected the master's verdict that his enlightenment was inadequate. A sharp argument followed, at the end of which the old monk twisted Hakuin's nose, saying, "You poor child of the devil in a dark dungeon!" At last Hakuin inquired as to the points of inadequacy in his enlightenment, whereupon the aged master recounted the *kōan*-like story of the death of the Chinese master Nan-ch'üan. Hakuin stopped his ears and was about to leave the room. The master called him back and scolded him once more, saying, "You poor child of the devil in a dark dungeon!" And so the interview ended in frustration.

Hakuin practiced further. Had not the fame of the unyielding strictness of the highly enlightened old master drawn him to his hermitage? How could he give up when he had reached only the halfway mark? The following scene shows us the high point of the merciless training which Hakuin had to undergo. He writes:

> One evening the master sat cooling himself on the veranda. Once more I brought him my verses on enlightenment. The master said, "Confusion and nonsense!" I likewise called out, "Confusion and nonsense!" The master grabbed me and struck me twenty or thirty times with his fist and finally threw me off

the veranda. It was on the evening of the 4th of May, after the rainy season. I fell into the mud, almost unconscious, with all my thoughts fleeing away. Nor was I able to move. But the master only stood on the veranda and laughed aloud. After a while I regained my senses, and rose up and bowed to the master. My whole body was bathed in perspiration. The master called with a loud voice, "This poor child of the devil in a dark dungeon!" Thereupon I intensified my study of the *kōan* of the death of Nan-ch'üan and gave up sleeping and eating.[4]

Hakuin now entered the final phase of painful and pene-trating practice. He had gained some enlightenment, but the results did not yet satisfy Master Etan. Repeatedly he had to hear the invective of the devil's child in a dark dungeon which hints vaguely at the cause of the imperfection of his enlighten-ment. Like the devil in the dark dungeon, so his mind without his knowing was still imprisoned in his own ego. He trained in deadly despair. When his efforts remained fruitless he secretly thought of leaving the hermitage to try his luck elsewhere. But while he was begging alms in a neighboring village the change suddenly came. In his autobiography, *Itsu-made-gusa*, Hakuin gives a detailed description of the event:

The next morning I took up the alms bowl with exceeding anxiety and arrived in a village in the district of Iiyama where I began to beg. Without relaxing, however, I was constantly en-gaged with the *kōan*. Immersed in concentration I stood at the corner of a house. Someone called from within, "Go away, go away!" But I did not hear it. Thereupon the angry householder seized a broom, turned it around, hit me on the head, and then started beating me. My monk's hat was torn and I fell to the ground. Without consciousness, I was as one dead and could not move. The neighbors now came in alarm from all directions. "This is only the usual nuisance," said the householder, closing the door and showing no further interest in the matter.

Three or four of the passers-by wondered at what went on and asked what had happened. I returned to consciousness and opened my eyes. While I pursued the difficult *kōan* to its roots and penetrated to its bottom, a *kōan* which, up to then, I could neither understand nor grasp, the enlightenment flashed upon my mind. Jubilantly I clapped my hands and laughed aloud. The onlookers spoke in alarm, "A mad bonze! A mad bonze!" All hastened away without looking at me further. I stood up, cleaned my clothes, and put on my torn hat.

Laughing I wandered on at a slow pace toward the hermitage. On the way an old man invited me in to his house. "The honorable bonze was like dead," he said. I smiled and answered nothing. He gave me rice and tea and sent me on my way. I arrived at the gate of the hermitage laughing and full of joy. The master stood on the veranda, cast a glance at me, and said, "Speak! What is the good news?" I approached him and related my experiences in full. The master now stroked my back with his fan . . .[5]

Master Etan recognized the enlightenment of his disciple and admonished him to continue on the way without relaxing his exercises. In his *Orategama*, Hakuin describes the same episode more briefly and closes with the comment that henceforth the master did not again call him the "poor child of the devil in a dark dungeon." [6] He had now attained full enlightenment.

As he relates further in the *Orategama*, Hakuin underwent two or three more enlightenment experiences which could not be fully described in words, and he wandered as in a dim light. After his recovery from another serious affliction of the lungs and nervous system, his rich mystical experiences resumed. Toward the end of the *Yasen Kanna* he remarks:

Not only were my illnesses healed, but I also comprehended depths which are difficult to believe, difficult to penetrate, difficult to understand, difficult to enter upon, which prior to this I could not grasp with hands and feet, could not attain with my teeth—these I grasped in one instant, penetrating to their roots and piercing to their bottom. Thus I experienced the Great Joy six or seven times and in addition countless lesser enlightenments and delights, by which one forgets that one is dancing . . ." [7]

These experiences Hakuin describes more fully in the third book of the *Orategama*. Once with great joy he read a verse by the Chinese master Hsi-kêng. As a ray of light in a dark night illumines the way, so light fell upon his soul. In rapture he shouted loudly for joy. In another instance he wandered during the rainy season in the vicinity of Ise. The rain fell in torrents and the water reached to his knees. There he suddenly understood the deep meaning of some verses of Hsi-kêng which he had read earlier. So enraptured that he could not stand upright, he fell into the water. In amazement a passer-by looked at him and helped him to his feet. Hakuin laughed aloud for joy, so that once more the passers-by took him for a madman. Then, again, sitting in winter in nightly meditation in the Zen hall at a rural temple, he heard the snow falling outside and experienced states of enlightenment. On other occasions while wandering in the country of Mino he had ecstatic experiences which surpassed all that he had known previously.

In these hasty sketches, Hakuin appears as an ecstatic in an almost constant state of emotion. Enlightenment falls upon him whether in walking, in standing, or in meditation. Suddenly the rapture is upon him. The word *oboezu,* meaning "unexpectedly" or "unconsciously," recurs frequently in his writings. In the enlightened state he is as though beside himself. Immeasurable jubilation wells up in his heart and breaks out in involuntary shouts and spontaneous dancing. The degrees of intensity in these experiences vary, but every time Hakuin is astounded anew at the great force with which the experience grips him. But there was one experience which Hakuin himself regarded as peculiar. Whereas in his other experiences the emotional element predominated, this particular experience led him to a higher level of understanding. This account may be the most rare and informative of them all:

In my thirty-second year I took up residence in a dilapidated temple. One night in a dream my mother handed me a violet robe. As I lifted it up I felt a great weight in both sleeves. I investigated these and found in each sleeve an old mirror about five or six inches in diameter. The reflection of the mirror on the right side penetrated to the bottom of my heart. My own mind as well as mountains and streams, yes, the whole earth, became alike transparently clear and bottomless. The whole surface of the mirror on the left had no focal point of light. The surface was like that of a new skillet not yet touched by fire. Suddenly there flashed a light from the mirror on the left that surpassed the light of the mirror on the right a millionfold. Now the vision of all things was like the beholding of one's own face. For the first time I understood the meaning of the words "The perfected one beholds the Buddha-nature in his eye." [8]

The mystical experience here described begins as a dream, which then passes over into an awakened state of extraordinary clarity. The mother, the violet monastic robe, the two mirrors, and the light—all these elements of the mystic dream are of high significance for Hakuin's inner life. In an overwhelming flood of light he beholds the nature of all things, a vision which, according to the presuppositions of his Buddhist faith, he understands as beholding his own countenance which is identical with the Buddha-nature.

Following the account of this experience in the *Orategama* Hakuin, without indicating the time, tells of further insights which came to him later. Once he was reading from the *kōan* collection of *Pi-yen-lu* and in his intuitive comprehension he discovered a new answer to the *kōan* which was radically different from his previous understanding. He also tells of an experience belonging to his forty-second year, one of the major enlightenments of his life.[9] One autumn evening, as he was reading in the *Lotus Sutra*, he was aroused from his concentration by the humming of an insect, and came suddenly to new understanding.

Immediately I saw through the perfect true mystery [of the sutra] and broke through all initial doubts. I comprehended the error of my earlier greater or lesser enlightenments. Unexpectedly I called out and wept. One must realize that the practice of Zen is by no means easy.[10]

Only in the light of this mature enlightenment did Hakuin believe that he understood perfectly what the old monk of Shōjuan had told him.

We may conclude from Hakuin's reports that in Zen enlightenment there are degrees and stages. Present-day Zen masters distinguish between earlier and weaker stages of enlightenment, which can be fully lost again, and the permanently effective vision of full enlightenment. They are slow to judge an experience and even then opinions differ. Hakuin's reports seem to indicate that in the imperfect states of enlightenment the emotional elements, namely concentration and ecstasy, predominate, while as the mystical experiences mature deeper intuitive insights open. Once he had risen to higher levels, he comprehended the inadequacies and errors of his first experiences. The precise determination and characterization of the several stages in Zen enlightenment can contribute much to a fuller understanding of natural mysticism.

The Great Doubt and the Great Enlightenment

Hakuin's theoretical teachings concerning the Way of Enlightenment rest on his own experiences as well as on his view of the nature of Zen. These two elements mutually condition each other. He interprets his experiences in terms of the Buddhist world-view which he realizes in practice and experience. Buddhism is to him a monistic view. Not only is the inner meaning of all Buddhist schools ultimately the same, but in the final analysis Taoism and Confucianism as well conform to Buddhism. The core of the *Lotus Sutra*, which takes a central position in the Tendai and Nichiren schools, is not the proclamation of the single vehicle as opposed to the two or three vehicles in earlier Buddhism, but rather the revelation of the Buddha-mind which signifies the Absolute intended by all religions. Likewise the Pure Land of Amida is, in the last analysis, "void" and identical with one's own nature and the cosmic Buddha-body. Hakuin displayed unlimited tolerance toward doctrinal differences, tracing them all back to the monistic standpoint of Zen. His interest in metaphysics, however, is minor; everything hinges on the realization of this unity in experience.

In practical life, many roads lead to the same goal.[11] One can kill with a sword, but one can also finish off one's enemy with a spear. Buddhism stipulates meditation and concentration, but it also recognizes the recitation of the sutras, the invocation of the name of Buddha, and magic formulas (*mantra* and *dhāranī*). All exercises can aid in the attainment of the monistic vision, provided that they are practiced wholeheartedly and with strict concentration of the mind. He who practices the *kōan* halfheartedly will not reach the goal in ten or even twenty years, even if the *kōan* is as effective and incisive as the "nothingness" of Chao-chou. On the other hand, one can reach concentration in a short time only by invoking the name of Buddha.

To practice earnestly is to give up all clinging to passions and ideas and to eliminate all desire; even the wish for enlightenment or the possession of the Pure Land, since these are basically none other than a vision of one's own nature. All deceptive tricks have to be exposed. Whoever practices with the ulterior motive of calling upon the name of Buddha so that he may attain the joy of paradise in the world beyond, if not enlightenment itself, can never reach the goal. Like the practice of the *kōan* in Zen, so also the calling upon the name of Buddha by the Amida faithful, or of the name of the sutra by the followers of Nichiren, serve only as means and aids on the way to the enlightened view of the One Reality.

Hakuin complained about the growth of the Amida sects. He recognized the saints who attained enlightenment by means of *nembutsu*, but emphasized strongly the incomparable power of Zen meditation and the *kōan* exercises. If the "easy way" of faith in Amida were adequate, the indescribable efforts of the great patriarch Bodhidharma would be incomprehensible. Many Chinese masters, he noted, risked their lives in the practice of Zen and attained deep insights. These heroes of Zen brooked no compromise with belief in the Pure Land and the practice of *nembutsu*.

According to Hakuin, the superiority of Zen derives from the *kōan*, the practice of which constellates intensive psychic states which lead to great enlightenment. He esteemed Chao-chou's *kōan* of "nothingness" above all others. This was the *kōan* he himself had once practiced so intensively, and now for forty-five years he placed it before those of his disciples who desired the Great Enlightenment. The problem of this *kōan* is simple and direct. The Chinese master Chao-chou, when asked about the Buddha-nature of a dog, replied, "Wu (nothingness)." This utterance cannot be grasped logically but, like the pointing of the finger to the moon, signifies the presence of the Absolute in concrete things, in a manner which transcends both affirmation and negation.

Hakuin was an old man when he himself devised a problem which he believed would penetrate into one's consciousness with incomparable sharpness and would readily lead to the awakening of doubt and to progress in the exercises. His *kōan* of the "single hand" reads: "If someone claps his hands, one hears a sound at once. Listen now to the sound of a single hand!" [12] He who lifts one hand and while listening quietly can hear a sound which no ear hears, can surpass all conscious knowledge. He can leave the world of distinctions behind him; he may cross the ocean of the *karma* of rebirths, and he may break through the darkness of ignorance. In the enlightenment he attains to unlimited freedom. "In this moment the bottom of mind, will, consciousness, and feeling is broken through and the *karma* ocean of change is turned into submerging and arising." [13]

Between the intensity of the doubt nourished by the *kōan* and the value of the subsequent experience of enlightenment there is a proportionate relationship. "If your doubt measures ten degrees, so will the enlightenment." Enlightenment is brought on forcibly through doubt. Of this Hakuin was fully convinced. "Once the Great Doubt arises, out of a hundred who practice, one hundred will achieve a breakthrough; and of one thousand, a thousand will break through." He describes the state of doubt with reference to his own experience:

> If a person is confronted with the Great Doubt, then in the four directions of heaven [the four cardinal points] there is only wide, empty land, without birth and without death, like a plain of ice ten thousand miles in expanse, as if one sat in an emerald vase. Without there is bright coolness and white purity. As if devoid of all sense one forgets to rise when he is sitting, and forgets to sit down when he is standing. In his heart there remains no trace of passion or concept, only the word "nothingness," as if he stood in the wide dome of heaven. He has neither fear nor knowledge. If one progresses in this fashion without retrogression, he will suddenly experience something similar to the breaking of an ice cover or the collapse of a crystal tower. The joy is so great that it has not been seen or heard for forty years. [14]

Hakuin prodded on the hesitant among his disciples to daring exertions. The state of concentration of the Great Doubt is within reach of everyone. No special outward circumstances are necessary. One must only undertake the exercises with real energy.

> To evoke the state of Great Doubt one need not seek out a quiet place nor need one avoid the places of activity in daily life. Think: this ocean of my breath, below my navel, is the "nothingness" of Chao-chou. What does "nothingness" signify? If one casts off all passions, concepts, and thoughts and only practices,

the Great Doubt will certainly arise. In hearing of the pure and unclouded state of this Great Doubt, one may be overcome by a feeling of anxious, horrendous fear. And yet nothing affords greater joy than to break through the many-storied gateway of endless rebirths in the cycle of birth-and-death, and the inner realization of the original enlightenment of all the perfected ones of the four directions of heaven. Obviously one must be prepared for some pain in the training.[15]

The transition from the Great Doubt to the Great Enlightenment is indescribable. Hakuin also calls this event the "Great Dying." He elucidates the process by analogy:

If you wish to attain the true Nonego you must release your hold over the abyss. If thereafter you revive you will come upon the true ego of the four virtues. What does it mean to release one's hold over the abyss? A man went astray and arrived at a spot which had never been trodden by the foot of man. Before him there yawned a bottomless chasm. His feet stood on the slippery moss of a rock and no secure foothold appeared around him. He could step neither forward nor backward. Only death awaited him. The vine which he grasped with his left hand and the tendril which he held with his right hand could offer him little help. His life hung as by a single thread. Were he to release both hands at once, his dry bones would come to nought.

Thus it is with the Zen disciple. By pursuing a single *kōan* he comes to a point where his mind is as if dead and his will as if extinguished. This state is like a wide void over a deep chasm and no hold remains for hand or foot. All thoughts vanish and in his bosom burns hot anxiety. But then suddenly it occurs that with the *kōan* both body and mind break. This is the instant when the hands are released over the abyss. In this sudden upsurge it is as if one drinks water and knows for oneself heat and cold. Great joy wells up. This is called rebirth [in the Pure Land]. This is termed seeing into one's own nature. Everything depends on pushing forward and not doubting that with the help of this concentration one will eventually penetrate to the ground of one's own nature.[16]

Hakuin repeatedly compares the enlightened view with the immediate perception of the senses which is free from all deception. The enlightened one is sure of his experience in the same way that the person drinking water perceives both heat and cold. But it must be noted that the infallibility and certainty of knowledge acquired by the senses is limited to the moment of perception and that this perception is restricted to the immediate experience. Later reflections on the experience as well as its rational explanation are subject to mistake and error. The same must be said of mystical experiences. All mystics are certain of their possession of truth in the moment of their experience, and yet their interpretation and explanation of the insights thus attained are conditioned by their philosophy, and frequently bound up with falsehoods. Therefore the mystical experience can never suffice as a demonstration of objective truth.

Conversely, erroneous intellectual judgments do not invalidate the previous experience. Just as the senses do not err, but rather reason which judges the sense perception, so too the mystical experience itself is true. Its interpretation, however, must be subjected to objective standards. The certainty of the experience is enough to call forth the great joy which accompanies enlightenment. The ecstatic expresses his joy by spontaneous cries and movements of the body. The Great Doubt, the Great Enlightenment, and the Great Joy—this trio of mystic states constitutes the core of Hakuin's doctrine of enlightenment, a doctrine which rested on his own experience.

Zen Sickness

In the eventful life of Hakuin a major illness, diagnosed as tuberculosis of the lungs and a nervous ailment, which overcame him soon after his first great experience of enlightenment, played an important role. With the exertion of all his physical and psychic powers he sought to force further realizations. As with so many of the mystics it mattered little to him for his body to be broken if only his mind would be liberated for the ascent. But he too had to experience the interdependence of body and mind. Through his sickness the whole man was affected and along with his physical health his mental security was endangered.

At first he attached little importance to his psychic disturbances, but continued unremittingly his severe exercises until he collapsed. Hakuin now sought the advice of doctors and teachers. No one was able to help him until finally he found Hakuyū, an old hermit, in the lonely mountains near Shirakawa in the district of Yamashiro, who taught him a psychic remedy. In his late work *Yasen Kanna*, Hakuin graphically describes this visit and his subsequent recovery.[17] He depicts the course of his illness as follows:

> . . . On reflecting on my daily life I found the two domains of movement and rest torn asunder. I could not freely decide for one of the two sides, either to release or to grasp. So I thought to myself: I will devote myself earnestly to spiritual practices. Once more I shall stake my life on it. I gritted my teeth, opened both eyes wide, and gave up sleeping and eating. Before another month had passed, fever rose above my heart, my lungs dried up, both hands and feet became cold as though plunged in ice and snow, and both ears roared as if I were walking between cataracts in the valley. My liver and lungs were completely enervated. Many anxieties beset me, my mind was depressed and exhausted. In sleeping and waking I saw a thousand phenomena. My armpits broke out in perspiration continuously and my eyes were constantly filled with tears. Now I sought for able masters everywhere and looked all over for famous doctors . . .[18]

The thousand phenomena which Hakuin beheld night and day point to the state of visions and hallucinations, a state of psychic overstimulation which is well known in Zen and of which the Zen masters warn, calling it the "domain of the devil" (*makyō*). In the description of the symptoms of this illness old Chinese physiological concepts are combined with the doctrine of the cosmic elements according to which in the healthy person the head is cool while the lower body is warm. In this sickness, however, the bodily fire moves up and heats the head while the lower body, the legs, and the feet become cool. Therefore in recovery everything depends upon thoroughly heating the lower part of the body by strong, deep breathing, in order to overcome the natural tendency of fire to rise and of water to sink.

The hermit Hakuyū had taken the quintessence of his medical wisdom from the Chinese Taoists. He was strongly influenced by Taoism, as witnessed by his keeping the works of Lao-tzǔ on the table of his otherwise bare hut. His medical treatment placed the major emphasis on psychic efforts. Hakuin explains various methods which are at the same time means to mental concentration. Autosuggestions have played an important role in Buddhism from its beginnings. Dōgen was taught by his master Ju-ching to bring his heart into his left hand at the time of the exercise. Sometimes the pupil imagines he has a bean in the middle of his navel.

Hakuin emphatically recommends the method of introspection (*naikan*), to which he devoted himself totally and to which he was indebted for his recovery. Through deep breathing one fills the navel and the lower body with the breath of life and permits the invigorating energy to permeate down to the soles of the feet. At the same time one repeats the following words with the most intense concentration and identification, and tries to come as close as possible to an inner realization of their content:

This ocean of breath below my navel,
　These my loins and limbs down to the soles of my feet:
These are verily my original countenance—
　There is no need of nostrils in my face.

This ocean of breath below my navel,
　These my loins and limbs down to the soles of my feet:

These are verily my true abode—
  There is no need to visit far from home.

This ocean of breath below my navel,
  These my loins and limbs down to the soles of my feet:
These are verily my only Pure Land—
  There is no need of ornaments in that Land.

This ocean of breath below my navel,
  These my loins and limbs down to the soles of my feet:
These verily are the Amida of my body—
  There is no need to preach the Dharma.[19]

The "ocean of breath" is located three centimeters below the navel, man's center of gravity, in which his vital powers are collected by meditation and from which the healing of the sick organism must proceed. According to the teaching of Zen, the "original countenance," the true home, the Pure Land, and Amida are all identical with the Buddha-nature. They are not to be sought somewhere without, but are to be made actual in one's own self.

The most remarkable method of autosuggestion is the so-called "butter method," which Hakuin often explained and urgently advised. The process begins with the mental image of a pure, soft, and sweet-smelling lump of butter the size of a duck's egg, which, if placed on the head, would arouse a pleasant sensation. One's head would become moist, and the cool moistness would run down to the shoulders and arms, thence to the two breasts and the inner organs of lungs, liver, and stomach, and down to the end of the appendix. Pain in the loins and intestines would have to flow downward like water until the feeling of strong, vital energy would flood the entire body and warm the feet down to the very toes and soles. . . . Through a process of identification, one has to become fully permeated with this idea, and then repeat the experiment until body and soul feel in harmony and vital energy is restored.

At the end of his treatise *Yasen Kanna*, Hakuin assures us that by steady practice of the psychic healing processes which he was taught by the hermit Hakuyū his bodily powers were soon fully restored. All his illnesses disappeared, and until the ripe age of eighty-two years he enjoyed good health.

Personality and the Japanese Character

Hakuin is the last great figure in Zen of the present study, the last figure in a long line of eminent religious men who made a notable contribution to our understanding of the natural religiosity of Asia. These Buddhist mystics of the three great Asian cultures developed variants corresponding to the respective national characters. In India the mysticism of Hīnayāna and Mahāyāna showed tendencies toward escape from the world. Early Buddhism further took over much of the concentration scheme of Yoga, while the Mahāyāna sutras showed strong similarities to the Vedānta in their metaphysical interest and their intuitive monism. All this was dominated by the basic conviction of all mystics that Absolute Being transcends all categories of thought and is accessible only to the immediate vision of the mind.

Zen itself originated in China, where the concrete experience of reality was forced by ruthless frontal attack and was experienced with unparalleled immediacy. What the Zen masters of the T'ang and Sung eras accomplished with inimitable virtuosity has been compared, perhaps not without justification, to the *mi-atari*, the fighting method adopted by the suicide pilots during the late Pacific war—a physical and spiritual collision with the Absolute. This mysticism was combined with the naturalistic philosophy of Taoism and extended into cosmic dimensions. "Nature" became the central concept of Chinese Zen, while *zazen* and the *kōan* were developed as the chief methods. The many able masters who are immortalized in Zen literature assured the survival of the Chinese (Ch'an) flavor of Zen, and its influence on coming generations.

The Japanese masters contributed nothing substantial to the teachings and methods of Zen, and yet in Japan Zen assumed a peculiar new form whose value is demonstrated today by its unbroken vitality. We have encountered these special traits in many personalities of Japanese Zen history. At the end of our study these qualities emerge clearly once more, since perhaps no other Japanese master expressed the traits peculiar to his people as purely as did Hakuin, who for this reason is highly esteemed by all Zen adherents.

In a symposium recently reported by a Japanese daily newspaper, three well-known representatives of Buddhism commented on the popular religiosity of the Japanese people. The first speaker defended his countrymen against the frequent accusation of irreligiousness, an impression which a brief stay in Japan can easily give, particularly when this country is compared with Christian countries. Japanese religiosity, he maintained, takes a different form of expression. "In the center of the room stands a single table. In the *tokonoma* [niche] there is a single flower in a vase and above it hangs an ink brush-painting. Everything is scrupulously clean. For the unobservant eye there is nothing to be seen. In this room there is not a single Buddhist object. And yet here in the cleanliness and sparsity conducive to concentration of mind, Buddhism shines through. . . ." [20] He went on to speak of the tea ceremony and flower arrangement as expressions of the Zen religious spirit; but the second speaker countered that the naturalistic secularization of Buddhism constitutes a falling away from true piety. Whatever the truth, the tendency toward aesthetic-artistic transfiguration of life can certainly be said to belong to the religious peculiarity of the Japanese people which found in Zen its highest development.

Hakuin, it is true, cannot be regarded as the greatest artist in

Zen, but he is unique in his combination of superior enlightenment and genuine artistic ability. Hakuin's art is nourished by
his mystic vision and is oriented toward it. Even in his prose
writings his language vibrates and is full of imagery and originality. Again and again he breaks out into poetry. His famous
song on enlightenment discloses the monistic world-view of
the mystic. Like all pantheistic poetry it is monotonous and yet
it burns with strong spiritual passion.

> All sentient beings are from the very beginning the Buddhas:
> It is like ice and water;
> Apart from water no ice can exist,
> Outside sentient beings, where do we seek the Buddhas? . . .
>
> For them opens the gate of the oneness of cause and effect.
> And straight runs the path of non-duality and non-trinity.
> Abiding with the Not-particular in particulars,
> Whether going or returning, they remain for ever unmoved;
> Taking hold of the Not-thought in thoughts,
> In every act of theirs they hear the voice of Truth.
> How boundless the sky of Samādhi unfettered!
> How transparent the perfect moonlight of the Fourfold Wisdom!
> At that moment what do they lack?
> As the Truth eternally calm reveals itself to them,
> This very earth is the Lotus Land of Purity,
> And this body is the body of the Buddha.[21]

This festive hymn streams from the higher consciousness
which Hakuin attained in his ecstasies. In everyday life he
sang in *haiku*, projecting, as it were, with one stroke of the
brush ordinary little things into the universe. Even more impressive than his poems are his paintings, in which he brings
celestial things down to earth and lifts earthly things into the
realm beyond the senses.[22] He painted Kwannon (Chin.: Kuan
Yin), the Buddhist goddess of Wisdom and Compassion, with
solid human femininity. His landscapes approach the *haiga* in
which the spirit of tea is wed to the *haiku*. Only rarely does

Hakuin descend to the purely secular. Even when his paintings deal with no immediate religious theme, one can feel his deep inwardness which stems from Zen. His quiet and thoughtful humor radiates a friendly warmth. Ripe humanity and deep piety combine with an artistic sensibility that is close to nature and gives his Zen its special Japanese character.

The ascetic-ethical philosophy of the Japanese, which is also characteristic of Japanese Zen, stands in remarkable contrast to their aesthetic bent. The religiously transfigured art of life could have easily degenerated into inanity had it not possessed an ethical dimension. In taking upon himself with relentless rigor and persistent patience an ascetic training which in the strictness of its discipline equaled that of the Christian mystics, Hakuin followed the impulse of his higher nature. It was clear to him that without *abstine et sustine*, without "abstaining and sustaining," no great spiritual fruit could be gathered.

During his years of wandering, his "holy madness" brought him to the limits of his physical and psychic strength. After he was restored to health there was no counteraction as is usual with pseudomystics. In full possession of his mental and physical powers he held on to a strong ethical pattern of life. His illness left no inner weakness behind. His own distress taught him the potential value of illness. Once he admonished a sick bonze to turn his sickbed into a Zen hall and to imitate that early master who experienced enlightenment in his sickness and praised the Buddha. In Hakuin's view all infirmities can be healed through the power of the mind.

Hakuin's ethical outlook enabled him to exert considerable pedagogic influence. Admittedly the monist doctrine of Zen cancels the distinction between good and evil, but in a manner similar to that of all good popular educators Hakuin admonished the simple peasants to lead a good life. He is one of those masters through whose work Zen reached in Japan a degree of popular influence unequaled in its Chinese history.

Japan, also, had its enlightened ones who in stern aloofness guided only a restricted circle of the chosen, but at the same time there is in Japanese Zen a strong element of genuine folk religiosity. Both tendencies can still be noted in Japanese Zen today, and it is not yet clear which tendency will eventually prevail. As mysticism, Zen displays aristocratic tendencies, and yet without accommodation to the psychology of the people a stronger effect on society is impossible.

15 *The Essence of Zen*

History and Form

Is there a form which is featureless and wordless, where "gatelessness becomes the gate"? [1] D. T. Suzuki presented Zen to the Western world as pure mysticism, as a paradox beyond all categories, as a phenomenon outside history and metaphysics, without affiliation to a religious community. In contrast to this, we have tried in this book to describe the actual features of Zen mysticism in their historical development, to present the character and activity of its adherents, to describe its history, and to clarify its evolution. Wherever man exists, there is history, there is becoming and change, form and figure. A quintessence of Zen may indeed be likened to a colorless white cloud floating in the sky, without history or metaphysics, and without relationship to an existing religion. But in reality, Zen is subject to the general laws of mankind, and its history manifests its form.

Since as a rule nothing can give more insight into the substance of a phenomenon than a deep penetration into its inception and its roots, the historical study of Zen seeks to trace its origins. Japanese historians likewise usually begin their presentation of Zen history with the ancient Buddhist Dhyāna which they call "Hīnayāna Zen." The roots of Zen, however,

are to be found more immediately in the soil of the great
Mahāyāna sutras. The creative beginning in China is as difficult to trace by way of sources as are the Indian backgrounds.

Nevertheless, though clarity of detail is lacking, the major
lines can be adequately ascertained. The great personalities of
Buddhism, who stand out in the long lists of patriarchs, stamped
on Zen the imprint of their characters. Further, practically all
the religious currents of East Asia came in contact with Zen
and left their mark, especially Taoism. The obvious relationship of Taoism to Zen appears in their numerous and deep
similarities. The current of Zen throughout many countries
and centuries shows no lack of unexpected deviations and
developments induced by strong personalities and remarkable
coincidences.

Historical study repeatedly stands baffled, but the other effect
of historical research, namely the disenchantment of history,
will also be met in the study of Zen. Inappropriate attitudes of
mystery must give way to clear knowledge. Certain repetitions
and schemes, indeed, spiritual "mechanisms," permit us to
place Zen in the established categories of the history of ideas.
This original mysticism is not always as new and fresh as it may
appear at first sight. The suppression of the personal element
in pantheistic Zen caused the unique, concrete, and creatively
new forces to flow into the unchanging cosmic cycle of nature.

The moment Zen is approached in the context of the history
of ideas, its metaphysical moorings call for consideration. Repeatedly, Suzuki denies all metaphysical bonds. Thus he writes
in his *Introduction to Zen Buddhism:*

> We may say that Christianity is monotheistic, and the
> Vedānta pantheistic. But we cannot make a similar assertion
> about Zen. Zen is neither monotheistic nor pantheistic, Zen de-
> fies all such designations. Hence there is no object in Zen upon
> which to fix the thought. Zen is a wafting cloud in the sky. No
> screw fastens it, no string holds it. . . . Zen wants to have one's

mind free and unobstructed; even the idea of oneness or allness is a stumbling block and a strangling snare which threatens the original freedom of the spirit.[2]

Admittedly, as a mystical experience, Zen is no philosophical or religious doctrine. But Rudolf Otto, in his preface to the first German publication on Zen, already directs attention to its metaphysical roots: "No mysticism is merely a heavenly vault. Rather it rests on a foundation which it denies as far as it can, but from which it continuously receives its peculiar character, never identical with forms of mysticism developed elsewhere."[3] Zen mysticism is rooted in the pantheistic or cosmotheistic metaphysics of the Mahāyāna sutras, whose basic theses are repeated by the Chinese and Japanese Zen masters.

Suzuki's own works contain much material which refutes his thesis that Zen is without metaphysics, for he repeatedly emphasizes the close connection of Zen with the *Prajñāpāramitā Sutras* and the *śūnyatā* philosophy. Another name for *satori* is *prajñāpāramitā*, which signifies the supreme, impersonal wisdom. Suzuki cites a Chinese text attributed to Bodhidharma, apparently dating from the T'ang period, in which it is stated: "If you wish to seek the Buddha, you ought to see into your own Nature; for this Nature is the Buddha himself. . . . This Nature is the Mind, and the Mind is the Buddha, and the Buddha is the Way, and the Way is Zen."[4] Or a Zen master speaks to his disciples in the hour of death: "The Dharmakāya remains forever perfectly serene, and yet shows that there are comings and goings; all the sages of the past come from the same source, and all the souls of the world return to the One."[5] The experience of Zen, which in philosophical language is also called the "acquired enlightenment," permits the "inherent enlightenment," which is nothing other than the Buddha-nature dwelling in all sentient beings, or the cosmic body of Buddha, to flash into consciousness.

Another essential trait of Zen in its historical form is its total embeddedness in Buddhist religion. Zen sprouts from the Buddhist mother soil, and remains piously rooted in it. The great Zen masters are without exception spiritual men who are indebted for their best qualities to the Buddhist religion. The spiritual aspect of Buddhist doctrine directed toward the Absolute inspired their souls to the mystic ascent, and awakened their desire to grasp the Supreme Truth (*paramārtha*) in intuitive vision and to achieve, in enlightenment, unity with the Buddha.

Zen regarded itself as the most pure and genuine *dharma*, as the best form of Buddhism, and yet it incorporated itself into the family of Buddhist schools and regarded itself as only one of the possible means of salvation. Never did it sever itself fully from cult, scripture, and tradition. Otto rightly surmises that only after we have studied and understood all the holy writings "which 'must be burned' to come to knowledge" can Zen be rightly understood.[6] As it presents itself historically, Zen belongs to the many-branched tree of Buddhism.

The figure of Zen is rounded out by its manifold expressions in culture and art, which by no means are to be regarded as by-products, but rather as the outflow of its very essence. These expressions, inviting to tranquillity and leading into depth, are a genuine enrichment of human life. In its artistic creations, the naturalistic tendency dominates. The Zen perception of life is formed out of the experience of cosmic unity. Man is in harmony with the universe, a harmony which expresses itself in hints and symbols, but most fully in deep silence, pregnant with meaning. The cultural achievements of Zen issue from the still center to the various peripheral areas of human existence and promote the shaping of life in the here and now. And yet the heart of Zen is the experience of enlightenment, the so-called *satori*, on the right understanding of which everything depends.

The Experience of Satori

Psychological research in Zen must acquire a copious and well-rounded knowledge of the material, if it is to avoid short circuits and false judgments. We were able to include in our historical sketch various records of the experience of enlightenment. The mysticism of Hakuin seems especially important for the evaluation of the psychic processes in Zen. The following descriptions present various aspects, and can help to make vivid the totality of *satori*. Imakita Kōsen, one of the best-known Zen masters during the Meiji era, gives a fairly complete description of his experience:

> One night when I was engaged in *zazen* the boundary between before and after was suddenly cut off. I entered the blessed realm of the exceedingly wonderful. I found myself, as it were, on the ground of the Great Death, and no awareness of the being of all things and of the ego remained. I felt only how in my body a spirit extended itself to ten thousand worlds, and an infinite splendor of light arose. After a short while I breathed again. In a flash seeing and hearing, speech and motion, were different from every day. As I sought the supreme truth and the wonderful meaning of the universe, my own self was clear and things appeared bright. In the excess of delight I forgot that my hands were moving in the air and that my feet were dancing.[7]

Perhaps this description has been influenced by the expressions of Hakuin. The ecstatic state of being "outside one's self" places one in the exalted mood of supreme delight. The ordinary course of consciousness is interrupted and the activity of the senses is cut off. The Chinese Zen master Kao-fêng (1238-1285), who in painful exercises pursued Chao-chou's *kōan* of "nothingness" (Chin.: *wu*; Jap.: *mu*), beheld also a great brightness and clarity.

> I felt as if this boundless space itself were broken up into pieces, and the great earth were altogether levelled away. I forgot myself, I forgot the world, it was like one mirror reflecting an-

other. I tried several *kōan* in my mind and found them so transparently clear. I was no more deceived as to the wonderful working of Prajñā [Transcendental Wisdom].[8]

Tê-i of Mount Mêng likewise experienced the psychic state where the mind is clear like a mirror. As the moon retains its form while its beams shine upon the unmoved depths of a stream flowing swiftly on the surface, so the mind in composure remains clear and still.[9]

T'ien-shan Ch'iung, a disciple of Tê-i, had to traverse an unusually long and difficult path before he could attain enlightenment. The more joyfully, therefore, he praised his liberation:

> All the bonds that had hitherto bound my mind and body were dissolved at once, together with every piece of my bones and their marrow. It was like seeing the sun suddenly bursting through the snow-laden clouds and brightly shining. As I could not contain myself, I jumped down at once from the seat and running to the master took hold of him exclaiming, "Now, what am I lacking?" [10]

In the same way, Hsüeh-yen Tsu-ch'in (d. 1287) felt himself transported from darkness into sunlight, as in the enlightenment he gained a new insight into reality.

> The experience was beyond description and altogether incommunicable, for there was nothing in the world to which it could be compared. . . . As I looked around and up and down, the whole universe with its multitudinous sense-objects now appeared quite different; what was loathsome before, together with ignorance and passions, was now seen to be nothing else but the outflow of my own inmost nature which in itself remained bright, true, and transparent. This state of consciousness lasted for more than half a month.[11]

Consciously or unconsciously, the interpretation of this experience is influenced by Buddhist doctrine. How the experience suddenly breaks through and then fuses with the worldview of the mystic becomes evident in the following description by the renowned founder of the Engakuji temple of Kamakura, Tsu-yüan:

> All of a sudden the sound of striking the board in front of the head-monk's room reached my ear, which at once revealed to me the "original man" in full. There was then no more of that vision which appeared at the closing of my eyes. Hastily I came down from the seat and ran out into the moonlit night and went up to the garden house called Ganki, where looking up to the sky I laughed loudly, "Oh, how great is the Dharmakāya! Oh, how great and immense for evermore!"
>
> Thence my joy knew no bounds. I could not quietly sit in the Meditation Hall; I went about with no special purpose in the mountains walking this way and that. I thought of the sun and the moon traversing in a day through a space 4,000,000,000 miles wide. "My present abode is in China," I reflected then, "and they say the district of Yang is the centre of the earth. If so, this place must be 2,000,000,000 miles away from where the sun rises; and how is it that as soon as it comes up, its rays lose no time in striking my face?" I reflected again, "The rays of my own eye must travel just as instantaneously as those of the sun as it reaches the latter; my eyes, my mind, are they not the Dharmakāya itself?" [12]

A Japanese bonze from the Sōtō sect, whose integrity I cannot doubt, once described to me his experience of *satori* thus: "Enlightenment is an overwhelming inner realization which comes suddenly. Man feels himself at once free and strong, exalted and great, in the universe. The breath of the universe vibrates through him. No longer is he merely a small, selfish ego, but rather he is open and transparent, united to all, in unity. Enlightenment is achieved in *zazen*, but it remains effective in all situations of life. Thus everything in life is meaningful, worthy of thanks, and good—even suffering, sickness, and death. Enlightenment comes in *zazen*, where man becomes completely dedicated to the Buddha. But it does not come through the grace of the Buddha. Indeed, enlightenment does not come from without, but only from within. The self is delivered through its own effort. . . ." In this description also, experience and interpretation seem to merge. This same bonze held that the amount of enlightenment as well as the possibility of its attainment during this life depends on man's previous existences. For many people, passions which derive from sins committed during previous incarnations present insurmountable obstacles to enlightenment.

The Psychological Interpretation of Satori

The early reports about Zen which reached Europe were not adequate to impart a vivid knowledge of this most original form of Buddhist mysticism. Friedrich Heiler, under the spell of Indian wisdom, directed his loving attention to the concentration scheme of Hīnayāna mysticism, and treated Chinese-Japanese Zen as an inferior form of externalized quietist concentration. Significantly enough, he saw in this "decadent" form of Buddhist mysticism, as he regarded it, an approximation to psychotherapy, though he had no presentiment of the later rise of this discipline. Wrote Heiler: "In Japanese Buddhism, which rather remarkably designates itself by the term *dhyāna*, meditation becomes 'nonthinking' and contemplation becomes a concentration stripped of thought and feeling. The Zen disciple believes to find in this experience the full inner tranquillity which enables him to act with fresh vigor. The temporary suspension of thought and feeling serve as a nerve-strengthening, psychotherapeutic means. . . . Thus the same tragic fate befell Buddhist concentration as had befallen prayer. . . ." [13]

Since Heiler wrote in this vein, the appreciation of Zen mysticism in Europe and America, thanks especially to the influence of the works of Suzuki, has undergone a complete change. There developed quickly a body of psychological literature about Zen, generally filled with admiration for this precious phenomenon in Oriental spirituality, from which it was hoped that modern man in psychic danger might draw much good. Suzuki tried to make Zen's psychological peculiarity comprehensible to the Western reader. For this purpose he adopted, especially in his early writings, the categories of the American school of the psychology of religion. Taking as his point of departure the four well-known characteristics of the mystic state as formulated by William James (ineffability, noetic quality, transiency, and passivity),[14] he set forth eight characteristics of *satori*, which he analyzed individually. These were: irrationality, intuitive insight, authoritativeness, affirmation, sense of the beyond, impersonal tone, feeling of exaltation, and momentariness.[15]

These categories, however, are quite general, and apply equally to all types of mysticism, a fact readily recognized when one notes their origin in the scheme of James. It is in their elucidation that Suzuki seeks by word and example taken from the Zen masters to set forth the traits peculiar to Zen. He attaches prime importance to the "impersonal tone," as the chief distinguishing mark of *satori* in contrast to Christian mysticism. Heiler, in his studies in Hīnayāna, had already emphasized the striking difference between the cool, impassive concentration of Buddhism and the ardent consciousness of God in Christian mysticism.

In a crass oversimplification, Suzuki considers the essence of Christian mysticism to be "the personal and frequently sexual feelings" of the mystics, a conclusion which he draws from the fact that much of their terminology is derived from human love. This implied identification of "sexual" and "personal" can be maintained only on Freudian premises. Exact psychology, on the other hand, recognizes the high degree of spiritualization in the love of the classic Christian mystics. "Harmless religious motives" should not be attributed to "hidden sexual springs." [16]

Suzuki is seemingly indebted to James's celebrated *The*

Varieties of Religious Experience for yet another important suggestion in his psychological understanding of *satori*. James regards the hidden powers that break forth from the subconscious as a major source of religious energy. Without clearly defining the concept of the subconscious or subliminal, he calls it "the abode of everything that is latent and the reservoir of everything that passes unrecorded and unobserved"; it is "the source of our dreams" and the mother soil of "whatever mystical experiences we may have, and our automatisms, sensory or motor." The strongest formative powers, he believes, emerge from this vast unexplored territory into the realm of religious history.[17] These formulations must have inspired Suzuki when he wrote in the introduction to the first volume of his *Essays on Zen Buddhism:*

> Just as our ordinary field of consciousness is filled with all possible kinds of images, beneficial and harmful, systematic and confusing, clear and obscure, forcefully assertive and weakly fading; so is the Subconscious a storehouse of every form of occultism or mysticism, understanding by the term all that is known as latent or abnormal or psychic or spiritualistic. The power to see into the nature of one's own being may lie also hidden there, and what Zen awakens in our consciousness may be that.[18]

In this sense, Suzuki terms *satori*, in which the mature consciousness of Zen breaks through, "an insight into the Unconscious." [19] And he designates the driving power which leads to enlightenment as "a certain desperate will," which is "impelled by some irrational or unconscious power behind it." [20]

By his use of the term "unconscious," Suzuki introduced the keyword of modern depth psychology into Zen literature, without apparently recognizing fully the significance of his discovery. It is worthy of note that many words of the Zen masters who speak of "seeing into one's nature" or "the original countenance before birth" point in this direction. The same can be said of a good number of accounts of Zen experiences which disclose the eruption of a deep and unknown layer in the psyche and may have suggested to Suzuki the term "unconscious."

We encounter here a remarkable complexity of relationships. The unconscious, brought into the foreground of European thought through the science of depth psychology, has been recognized in Asia since antiquity. Not only did the Indian philosophers carefully observe dreams and subconscious states but they built the unconscious into their metaphysical systems. Especially among the Buddhists, in whose doctrine the "store-consciousness" (*ālayavijñāna*) with its content of hidden seeds plays an important role, one finds striking parallels to the views of modern depth psychology. It is therefore no mere coincidence that the introduction of the concept of the unconscious to Occidental thought, undertaken in the nineteenth century by the Romantic school which was so receptive to the Oriental mind, was preceded by a previous encounter with the spiritual world of Asia. It was the romanticists Schelling and especially C. G. Carus who, out of a full awareness of the deep psychic layers of the human soul, first spoke of the significance of the unconscious.[21] Eduard von Hartmann's *Philosophy of the Unconscious* (1869) was influenced by Buddhism by way of Schopenhauer. He understood the unconscious, not psychologically, but metaphysically. The renewed encounter between the psychology of the unconscious and Oriental thought in the interpretation of Zen by Suzuki and C. G. Jung can be viewed against this fascinating historical background.

On the basis of the material furnished by Suzuki, Jung interpreted the experience of Zen as the breaking forth of the unconscious forces of the human psyche which exhibits the totality of the nature of the soul, both its conscious and its unconscious strata. According to Jung, the "great liberation" of *satori* is nothing other than the liberation of the unconscious. For conscious psychic life is constantly limited and obstructed. "The world of consciousness is inevitably a world full of restrictions, of walls blocking the way. It is of necessity always one-sided, resulting from the essence of consciousness. . . ." [22] On the other hand, "the Unconscious is an unglimpsable completeness of all subliminal psychic factors, a total exhibition of potential nature. . . ." [23]

Jung's interpretation of the *satori* experience in terms of depth psychology sheds new light upon it, and provides us with the key to many natural mystical phenomena. This interpretation makes clear the specific changes which occur in the states of consciousness as well as in the psychic mechanisms they entail, but the mystical experience itself, which precisely in its mystical character points *beyond* the mere psychic realm, cannot be fully explained in this manner.

In similar fashion the French psychologist Benoit regarded *satori* as basically the integration or realization of man in his psychic totality. According to Benoit, the unconscious is the first and only motor of the psyche, and the Absolute Principle which in *satori* is regarded as identical with the universe. He names it "the Fundamental Unconscious (No-Mind or Cosmic Mind of Zen)." [24] His distinction between *satori* as a state and as an event corresponds roughly to the distinction between primordial and acquired enlightenment in Mahayanist metaphysics. As a state, *satori* has been here from eternity. There is no need of an actual liberation. Our condition is similar to that of a man in a room, where the door is wide open whereas the window is protected by bars. An inner compulsion holds our gaze fixed on the images outside the barricaded window.[25] By this comparison Benoit depicts the simultaneous freedom and inner bondage of man who is not first liberated by the *satori* experience, but who rather appropriates the freedom which can never be lost. Man lets go, escapes his inner tensions, and seizes the possibility of the open door.

Benoit mingles apt psychological observations with philosophic concepts which he derives in part from the Mahayanist metaphysical background of Zen and in part from his own thought. Thus he declares, with Nietzschean logic, that "man because he is virtually capable of living his identity with the Absolute Principle, cannot accept the sleep of this identity; he cannot allow that he is not the First Cause of the Universe." [26] The transcending of all dualistic opposition in an absolute monism is for him the summit of human wisdom. His thought moves clearly on the level of metaphysics. Philosophical monism cannot be derived from psychological presuppositions nor can it be based on human experience.

Modern psychology expects from Zen an enrichment of its therapeutic treatments. While the "minor therapy" seeks to heal neuroses by resolving complexes suppressed into the subconscious, the "major therapy" aims at the integration of personality by making use of the wisdom of humanity stored in the "collective unconscious." In stirring the subconscious layers of the human psyche, Zen appears to favor these tendencies. Those who practice it are aware that here they are on religious ground, but they believe they have discovered "not an individual substitute for religion," but "a genuine religious possibility." [27]

In the reception accorded to Zen in Europe and America, psychotherapeutic expectations played a large role. Zen was divested of its original religious character, and an effort was made to fit it into a therapeutic system. It may well be that psychotherapy is able indeed to gain help from Zen. And yet Zen is robbed of its soul if it is made to eke out its existence in the psychological laboratory. Born as it was from the primal religious urge of man, and nourished by religious resources, Zen for many centuries inspired great religious achievements. Therefore psychology cannot speak the final word regarding the value and usefulness of Zen.

Natural Mysticism

If at the end of our inquiry we seek to define the substance of Zen mysticism, we do not intend to pass judgment on the religious experiences, of which there are numerous records available. It is far from our purpose to test and to evaluate individual accounts,[28] which in any event are psychologically inaccurate. Rather we seek to determine the categories into which the Zen experience in its best and most genuine expressions, as disclosed in documentary materials, can be fitted. Thus the term "natural mysticism" seems to offer itself. This term indicates an immediate religious experience of reality or a psychic contact with the absolute being, and distinguishes Zen from the supernatural mysticism of grace as well as from the manifold phenomena of magic in the history of religion.

The question of the nature and genuineness of the mystical experience is to be distinguished from the philosophical question of truth. Following our natural inclination we are likely to expect from the mystical experience new insights into a hidden and otherwise inaccessible truth. Thus we are inclined to ask expectantly, "Does this mystic really possess the truth, and if so, which truth? Or is he only a dreamer, a deceived one, or perhaps himself a deceiver? But if his mysticism is genuine, how much truth dare we expect of him?" With these questions, however, we are not on the right track. For even where genuine mysticism reaches its highest perfection, namely in the mysticism of Christian revelation, the soul which is caught up by the truth of God is usually not capable of expressing it. Only in a few exceptional instances have mystics been charged to bring a message to men. Usually their view of truth is a purely personal matter. And when they seek to stammer something about their experience, words prove inadequate. Indeed, in using words they often mix falsehood with truth, so that it has been possible to compile a long catalogue of false sayings by true mystics. Generally, therefore, the mystical experience provides no guarantee of truth for the subsequent communication by word.

The import of the mysticism of supernatural revelation lies in the fact that the mystical experience is an expression of divine grace. Christian mystics, who glory in the immeasurable worth of the mystic pearl, praise the gift of eternal love which permits them to perceive the immortal God in their mortal bodies. The mystical experience is for them precious above all else, since they obtain it, not through their own ardent exertions, but as a gift from above. The clear and immediate perception of the presence and action of God in the soul, which is the heart of their experience, exceeds the natural cognitive powers of man.

Christian mysticism is thus a matter of grace and is essentially supernatural. As a supernatural manifestation it belongs to a higher order than natural mysticism, even though there may be a similarity in the psychological structure of the two experiences. It must be noted too that membership in the true Church of Christ is not necessarily a prerequisite for the reception of the supernatural mystical grace. Nothing prevents our assumption that God can bestow even His choicest gifts outside the visible body of Christ, if He so wills. And trustworthy witnesses testify to the fact that on occasion He has done so.[29] The mystical movement of Sufism in Islam has produced saints of prayer who ascended to high levels of mystic life. In countries that are still heathen, missionaries encounter elect souls who before their baptism, or even before contact with Christianity, received the grace of supernatural mystical experience. It may have been that God disclosed His existence and majesty by mystical grace to a person whom He thereby called to a life of union, or that a seeking soul, after long yearning, was granted certitude regarding the great invisible God through a clear awareness of His presence.

The minimal prerequisite of the soul for the reception of supernatural mystical grace is faith in a personal God. The mystical experience which, as in the case of Zen, occurs outside the intimate I-thou communion of the soul with its Maker, belongs by contrast to natural mysticism, a concept generally recognized today by Christian theologians. Admittedly, the individual manifestations of natural mysticism have been little studied as yet. Furthermore, the line of demarcation between natural mysticism and magic psychic processes is not easy to draw. Magic in this connection is the attempt of man to break through the order of nature by forceful means and to coerce the divinity or the supersensory demonic beings, as is frequently practiced in primitive religions.

In mysticism we speak of magic phenomena wherever the extraordinary state is forced into being by unnatural physical or psychic methods. Among such forms of magic can be included to some extent hypnosis, suggestion, and hallucinations, as well as ecstatic states adduced by intoxication, sexual incitements, or other stimuli. Just as the physician sometimes prescribes poison for the sick body, such means may, on occasion, heal the sick soul, but they are essentially unnatural and harmful. For the stream of genuine and strong life flows within the boundaries of natural psychic laws.

The technique of nonthinking carried out in the sitting meditation known as *zazen* and the violent mental effort used in the *kōan* exercise have given rise to the classification of Zen among magic or parapsychological phenomena. Similarly, Jung's interpretation of the *satori* experience points more to an artificially induced psychic explosion than to a genuine experience of reality. For the seizure of psychic substance which was sunk in the subconscious connotes no new insights or spiritual contact. It must be admitted that in the collections of *satori* and *kōan* texts one can point to much that is strange and distorted, indeed even morbid and unnatural. Not infrequently these materials border on magic. Nevertheless, Zen as a religious-mystical phenomenon belongs, not to the realm of magic, but to that of natural mysticism.

Mager defines natural mysticism as "the psychospiritual perception of the natural activity of God in the soul." [30] The possibility of this experience is not to be denied. "The soul by its very nature is spiritual, and has not first become so by revelation. Why then should it not be possible that the soul should rise to spiritual activity in a quite natural way? Such activity can be regarded as natural mysticism, and is to be distinguished from every sort of magic." [31]

August Brunner likewise recognizes "the possibility of a natural mysticism in which one becomes aware in a new way of the depths of one's own subjective spiritual being." [32] Gardet regards the self as the object of natural mysticism. Whereas in supernatural mysticism the soul reaches the depths of God, the terminal goal of natural mysticism is "the secret of the substantial existence of the soul as spirit, pervaded with the activity of the Creator." This, as Gardet observes, is likewise an absolute goal.[33]

Merton describes "a kind of natural ecstasy in which our own being recognizes in itself a transcendental kinship with every other being that exists and, as it were, flows out of itself to possess all being and returns to itself to find all being in itself." Merton distinguishes from this metaphysical intuition of being, which is perhaps similar to the Zen experience and which is "a very great thing," "the intuitive appreciation of the Absolute Being of God." The pagan philosophers regarded this intuition as "the highest beatitude, and indeed it is the highest beatitude that man could ever arrive at by his natural powers alone." [34]

Mager names as apparent examples of natural mysticism Sufism (which seems, at least in part, to belong to supernatural mysticism), Buddhism, Neo-Platonism, and the Neo-Indian phenomena of Ramakrishna and Vivekananda. These are all examples with an affinity to Zen.

Just as the genuineness of supernatural mysticism is to be determined chiefly by its results, so too the value of natural mysticism must be tested by its fruits. Zen seems to pass this test. Admittedly, it would be difficult to determine in each case the concrete role of mysticism in the formation of personality. But generally the religious men who matured in the practice of Zen are distinguished by prudence in conduct, by great resolution in difficult situations, and by unfailing courage in constant action. The great Zen masters of whom the Chinese chronicles speak are by and large energetic and intellectually developed personalities, robust at times perhaps to the point of crudity, but nonetheless in full possession of their spiritual faculties. In Japanese Zen we meet illustrious figures such as Dōgen and Hakuin whose religious genius was recognized by their contemporaries, and continues its influence by way of their writings. Zen also exerted an admirable influence on Japanese art and culture.

The extravagant praise of some authors is toned down by the awareness of the sad moral perversion which existed in Zen temples during certain periods of Japanese history. Zen shares in the responsibility for the general religious decay throughout the country and the resultant decline in the public esteem for Buddhism. But this does not diminish the worth of Zen mysticism as such. For this degeneracy came about precisely because ascetic practice and enlightenment fell into neglect. The spiritual tradition survived the periods of decay and resisted even extreme secularization. Even today the Zen temple is still a place of quiet dignity where a superior intellectual life and natural mysticism can unfold.

If Zen is indeed an experience of natural mysticism, enlightenment must be a matter of spiritual contact rather than mere sensory stimulation. For the immediate perception of spiritual reality is the hallmark of all true mysticism. The psychological descriptions of Zen experience hardly provide us with adequate information. They depict an exalted state of the soul, which is largely a matter of feeling, rather than disclosing new knowledge. The "impersonal tone" of *satori*, in which Suzuki glories, implies rather the imperfection of the mystical experience in Zen, since spiritual reality is perceived immediately but the supreme spiritual attainment of personality is not comprehended. The ecstatic states of Zen remind one of the psychic processes which James designated as "cosmic consciousness." [35] Man experiences himself in the unity of the universe, an experience which exhilarates and strengthens him.

There is no difficulty in assuming here—indeed, this is the real meaning of the thesis of natural mysticism—that the soul, which experiences its own spirituality in enlightenment, becomes aware, at the foundation of its own spiritual substance, of God's eternal creative spirit. But precisely at this crucial point the descriptions of the *satori* experience stop short. Only the spiritual and absolute character of the realization can be discerned with certainty. The soul in its spiritual self is aware of perceiving the realm of absolute being.

In accordance with Mahāyāna philosophy, Zen disciples interpret this experience in monistic terms. This confirms the general thesis of the history of religions "that non-Christian mysticism is to a high degree in danger of monism, pantheism, and theopanism." [36] The reason for this is, first, the predominance of monistic speculation in Far Eastern philosophy where, since the earliest times of the Upanishads, the monistic view of *Tat tvam asi* (That thou art) drew religious and metaphysical minds into the wake of its influence. Equally important is the second reason, that on the human side a clear concept of personality is lacking. Since in terms of his spiritual existence man is essentially a person, "only a mysticism of personal communion and not of impersonal diffusion in the universe, can truly fulfill his existence." [37]

If, therefore, Zen presents itself as a kind of natural mysticism, it must be emphasized that the pantheistic strain in its teaching stems, not from the experience, but from the philosophy of the Zen mystics. Experience itself can only permit the consciousness of contact between the spiritual self and the realm of the Absolute, and thus it is basically open to the theistic possibility. Indeed, one finds among the Zen mystics an oscillation between a faith which reaches out to a transcendent Other and the absolutizing of the ego believed to be identical with the All. In intimate contact with adherents of Zen, one finds inescapably a certain contradiction in the religious attitude of many a zealous Zen disciple.

The reader's indulgence is asked for the relation of several examples of personal encounter. During the early years of my residence in Japan I associated a great deal with young Zen students who diligently read Buddhist texts with me, explaining them and showing themselves helpful in every respect. They were convinced adherents of the pantheistic philosophy of Mahāyāna (the Great Vehicle) and looked with disdain on all dualistic views as belonging to Hīnayāna (the Lesser Vehicle). During the summer vacation they went into the country to practice *zazen,* but at the same time they were ardent in their veneration of the Buddha images and in their recitation of the sutras. They were genuinely devout. But how did their devotion tally with their pantheistic philosophy? Granted, in terms of their philosophy, that these exercises in devotion denoted only an "artificial means." And yet in these pious actions there was expressed a heartfelt faith which reached out to transcendence.

Later I was often impressed by the genuine simplicity and noble humanism of the older Zen masters. The master of a group of young novices once explained to me the major points of practice and enlightenment. At the outset I learned little that was new. Even for an enlightened one, he indicated, life remains within the limits of earthly existence, and bears no conspicuous peculiarity nor any trace of miracle or magic. Then I dared to ask what seemed to be the central question: "When a person achieves Buddhahood through enlightenment, thereby becoming one with the Absolute, does he become elevated to the realm of absolute being and thus become absolute himself?" As soon as the bonze understood the intent of my question, he replied, "No, after my enlightenment, I am by no means an absolute being. I am still living in the everyday world, engaged in work and ascetic practice, subject to inadequacies and weaknesses, even to death [in Buddhist terms: subject to the law of causality]. . . . We Buddhists do not know the concept of sin familiar to Christians, but to atone for the shortcomings in my life, I sweep out my room daily as well as the adjacent unclean toilet, and just as a novice, I must practice works until I die."

An elderly Zen master, whom I visited at his temple in the country, replied with simple directness to the same question about becoming identical with Buddha in the enlightenment: "No, I do not believe so. Whether perhaps a few exceptional superhuman personalities achieve absoluteness I do not know. But a person as sinful as I am can never become the Absolute. I practice *zazen*, and from moment to moment I am what I ought to be. This I have done for forty or fifty years, and believe that my exercises are not wrong. Therefore I am happy and at peace." Did not perhaps the light of supernatural grace enlighten this bonze on his long way to inner peace?

The two conspicuous virtues of the spiritual practitioners of Zen are kindness and humility. This is of no mean importance in our evaluation of Zen mysticism. All too easily one associates with the designation "pantheistic mysticism" an idea which does not do justice to the reality of Zen. It goes without saying that the truly enlightened ones are always few.

In their exercises, Zen disciples are motivated by religious interests, since enlightenment is their highest religious concern. As is the case with all persons stirred by religion, they are "pilgrims of the Absolute." They cannot express their experiences in words. When they seek nonetheless to communicate what they experience, they do so in the language of Mahāyāna philosophy. But experience and philosophy are always basically different. The experience of unity can be interpreted pantheistically as well as theistically. The criterion of the authenticity of a world-view never lies in subjectivity. Every genuine philosophy maintains vital contact with human experience, but its criterion and goal must always be sought in the objective realm. Therefore without disparaging the significance of Zen enlightenment for earnest Zen disciples, we are driven to question its claim to be the norm of truth. Furthermore, as a mystical phenomenon, the *satori* experience is imperfect. No human effort to attain enlightenment, no matter how honest and self-sacrificing, can ever lead to the perfect truth, but only the eternal Logos "who coming into the world enlightens every man" (John 1:9).

Notes

The Mystical Element in Early Buddhism and Hīnayāna

1. The controversy over the religious character of Buddhism can be regarded as resolved. Cf. Heiler, pp. 69 f.; also, Glasenapp (1) and Regamey.
2. Oldenberg held that, according to the character of the sources, "the calculations of historical criticism could not possibly lead to a definite result, to either a clear yes or a clear no" (pp. 127 f.). Thomas remarked, in his study of the historical sources for the life of the Buddha, that the Pali Canon is by no means more reliable than the Sanskrit sources. "We have nothing, even in the Pali, at all like 'the real facts of the Gospel history'. . . . We have merely other forms of the same legend, some earlier, some later" (1), p. xxiv.
3. Beckh (1), p. 122.
4. According to Heiler, Shākyamuni entered *nirvāna* from the fourth stage, since the fourth *dhyāna* is "the last step before complete deliverance" (p. 35). Thomas regards the entrance into *nirvāna* from the fourth *dhyāna* stage as the earliest form of the legend, which was retained even after the addition of other mystical episodes (1), p. 153.
5. *Mahāparinibbāna Sutta*, Chap. 1.
6. Thomas (2), pp. 42 ff.
7. This is especially the merit of Heiler's study. Beckh (2) likewise gives a sketch of the Buddhist way of enlightenment. Thomas briefly treats the mystic exercises in early Buddhism (2), pp. 44 ff. Conze gives a selection of translations of texts, with introductions, chiefly from the Pali Canon (1). The *Visuddhi Magga* of Buddhaghosa (Eng. tr.: Ñānamoli; Ger. tr.: Nyanatiloka) is the most important systematic presentation of the Hīnayāna Way.
8. The Japanese Buddhologist Ui rejects the view that the first seven steps are subordinate to the eighth stage, by citing other versions of the Eightfold Path. According to him, this path entails no mysticism, but

rather provides the Buddhist with a pure ascetic discipline for his daily religious life (1), pp. 99 f.

9. Also in the Upanishads and the *Yoga Sutra* (II, p. 38), *brahmacarya* is commended as conducive to meditation. Regarding the meaning of the term, see Thomas (2), p. 44.

10. Beckh interprets the Four Immeasurables as the mental state corresponding to the first commandment (*śīla*) in Yoga, namely, the commandment to protect life (*ahimsā*) (2), pp. 27-29. According to Heiler these four (stages), which appear also in the *Yoga Sutra* (I, p. 33), present "an independent and parallel scale of concentration, equal in value" (p. 81). However, Anesaki-Takakusu and Beckh take the Four Immeasurables as the exercise preliminary to *dhyāna*. Likewise Kern (p. 471) regards them as the first and introductory meditations. In the *Visuddhi Magga*, Buddhaghosa includes them among the forty subjects of meditation (*kammatthāna*) (Eng. tr.: Ñāṇamoli, pp. 354-71; Ger. tr.: Nyanatiloka, pp. 372-89). Against Heiler's view it can be said that in the Four Immeasurables we have to do with ascetic practices devoid of real mystical character.

11. P. 9.

12. See Glasenapp (3), pp. 44, 46. The seat (*āsana*) is the third stage (*anga*) in the *Yoga Sutra*. The seat (Pali: *pallanka*; Skt.: *paryanka*) is also the prerequisite of Buddhist meditation. The *Samaññaphala Sutta* presents the monk seated in meditation. See Rhys-Davids, pp. 82, 86.

13. Heiler, p. 9. Likewise Beckh regards consciousness as the primary element in the Buddhist breathing technique (2), p. 42.

14. The superhuman capacities which in Yoga are called *vibhuti* are also mentioned in the Buddhist formula for purification from sin (*pāti-mokha*), a fact which Thomas takes as evidence that "Yoga is an essential part of the primitive doctrine" (2), p. 17.

15. See Glasenapp (2), p. 108.

16. Beckh (2), p. 11.

17. For detailed evidence, see Heiler, pp. 44-47. Heiler believes that both traditions, namely Buddhism and Yoga, "go back to a common older root." In the same way Hauer concludes that "the two ways, Yoga and Buddhism, are different expressions of one and the same movement" (1), p. 39. Vallée-Poussin assesses the "predominantly psychic and hypnotic Yoga" (Heiler speaks similarly of the "mystic psychotechnique" of Yoga [p. 44]) and terms early Buddhism "a branch of Yoga" (1), p. 12. In comparing Buddhism and Yoga, see also Keith, pp. 143 ff.

18. Regarding the history and meaning of the term *nirvāna*, cf. Thomas (2), pp. 121 ff.; Ui (3), pp. 37 ff.; Vallée-Poussin (1), p. 54.

19. Quoted by Oldenberg, p. 305.

20. *Udāna* VIII, p. 9; in Oldenberg, pp. 307 f.

21. The chief exponents of the nihilist *nirvāna* interpretation are Childers, J. D. Alwis, J. A. Eklund, J. Dahlmann, and H. Oldenberg in the early edition of Oldenberg's work *Buddha*. Later Oldenberg came to the conclusion that *nirvāna* signifies something absolute, not in the sense of the cause of the universe but as an absolute final goal. Glasenapp writes: "Nirvāna is a relative, not an absolute nothingness" (3), p. 235.

Ui does not give a nihilistic interpretation to primitive Buddhism nor does he ascribe to it a mystic state. Rather he explains *nirvāna* (in the sense of the formula for dependent origination [*paticcasamuppāda*]) as the realization of the relativity of being. It is noteworthy that he, with many other exponents of Mahāyāna, finds a nihilistic version of *nirvāna* in Hīnayāna Buddhism (3), pp. 44 f. There is a strong note of negativism in the thirteen explanations of the word *nirvāna* in the *Vibhāshā* (28, 18), which Vallée-Poussin cites (1), p. 54.

22. Thus Keith, p. 63; Vallée-Poussin (2).
23. Ui (3), p. 40. The twelve-linked chain has been variously interpreted by Buddhists themselves. While the Mahāyāna Buddhologists such as Ui see in this formula the earliest Buddhist expression for the relativity of being, Hīnayāna Buddhists interpret it as the rise in causal dependence through the three times of past, present, and future. Which interpretation corresponds to the original meaning cannot be determined with certainty. The first explanation is more metaphysical, while the second corresponds to the Indian notion of the cycle of rebirths in *samsāra*.
24. *Mahāparinibbāna Sutta*, Chaps. 3, 5.
25. See Glasenapp (3), p. 224, and Rosenberg and Stcherbatsky (1), who present the Hinayanist philosophy in detail.
26. *Udāna* VIII, p. 3; in Oldenberg, p. 326.
27. *Samyutta-Nikāya* IV, pp. 374 ff.; quoted by Oldenberg, p. 321.
28. *Sutta-Nipāta*, pp. 1074 ff.; quoted by Oldenberg, p. 325.
29. Regarding the two *nirvāna*, see Thomas (2), pp. 131 f. The distinction between a this-worldly and an other-worldly *nirvāna*, which is common in Hinayanist literature, does not go back to primitive Buddhism, according to Ui, but belongs rather to the later Hinayanist thought. According to Ui, the true concept of *nirvāna* signifies the attainment of Buddhahood, which has no relationship to physical death. Since the attainment of Buddhahood in this life was beyond the understanding of later Buddhists, and they nonetheless demanded results from their ascetic exertions, Ui thinks that they distinguished between the perfect *nirvāna* without a remainder or substrate and the imperfect *nirvāna* in which a substrate remains. This distinction was combined with the doctrine of the transmigration of souls, which likewise did not belong to original Buddhism.

Mysticism Within Mahāyāna

1. Practically all recent treatments of Buddhism distinguish between the original doctrine of Shākyamuni and the later development of Hīnayāna. Regamey traces the development successively through precanonical Buddhism, the Lesser Vehicle, and the Great Vehicle. Conze includes in his book on Buddhism (2) an informative "Table of Dates." The first entry in this table under the heading "Hīnayāna" is put at 246 B.C., nearly three hundred years after Buddha. In the small edition of

his *History of Indian Philosophy*, Ui proposes the following division: 1) Primitive Buddhism until thirty years after Buddha's entrance into *nirvāna*; 2) Early Buddhism until 270 B.C. (coronation of Asoka); 3) Sectarian Buddhism from 270 to about 100 B.C.; and 4) Hīnayāna and Mahāyāna, 100 B.C. to A.D. 100. The total time-span of these four periods, however, as Ui sees it, belongs to the development of primitive Buddhism. In the same work Ui distinguishes three periods in the early history of Mahāyāna: 1) The rise of Mahāyāna in North and South India from the first century B.C. until the third century A.D., the beginnings and the early sutras; 2) elaboration of the Mahāyāna doctrines, *ca.* A.D. 250 to 400, with further sutras; and 3) the final sutras and the full development of Mahāyāna, A.D. 400 to 650 ([2], pp. 263 ff). The first century B.C. is today generally regarded as the period of the rise of Mahāyāna. Further classification is dependent on the uncertain dating of Mahayanist thinkers, and of sutras and shastras.

2. Sectarian developments in early Buddhism remain an obscure chapter. For a long time it was customary to distinguish between the southern (Pali) tradition, chiefly represented by the Theravādins, and the northern (Sanskrit) tradition, to which the Mahāsāmghikas and the Sarvāstivādins belonged. The Sarvāstivādins had their chief seat in Mathura and spread to the northwest as far as Kashmir. Cf. Thomas (2), pp. 37 ff., and his Appendix on the eighteen schools, pp. 288-92. The work of Vasumitra, which belongs to the Sautrāntikas and deals with the eighteen schools, was translated by J. Masuda. Cf. Walleser's study of the schools and sects in ancient Buddhism (1). For further details cf. the great work of Lamotte (3) on the history of Indian Buddhism.

3. Stcherbatsky (2), p. 36. Thomas contrasts this text with Rosenberg's remark that "there is no difference in the basic views. . . . The difference exists not in the theory but in the practice of salvation, in which Mahāyāna admits a greater number of ways which lead to the same goal" (p. 226). Thomas feels that Rosenberg "seems to underrate the importance of philosophical principles" (2), p. 213. In the assessment of the differences between Hīnayāna and Mahāyāna, the student's dominant approach—philosophical or religious as the case may be—is the decisive factor. Since the coherence of Buddhism rests not on philosophical theories but in the religious realm, Stcherbatsky's final judgment goes astray when he says, "It must be allowed that the Mahāyāna is a truly new religion, so radically different from Early Buddhism that it exhibits as many points of contact with later Brahmanical religions as with its own predecessor" (2), p. 36.

4. Thus Filliozat writes, "*Le passage insensible des idées anciennes à celles du Mahāyāna a pu s'opérer ainsi grace à un développement progressif naturel de speculations nouvelles dans les écoles anciennes elles-mêmes . . .*" (p. 564).

5. Stcherbatsky (2), pp. 26, 28.

6. According to Thomas (2), pp. 169 f., it is certain that the development of Mahāyāna began in Sarvāstivādin schools, where the Bodhisattva still appears as a possibility alongside the Arhat, who is the ideal saint of Hīnayāna Buddhism, one who has obtained for himself

the highest stage of monastic asceticism. While in the Theravādin teachings the term "Bodhisattva" signifies only a preliminary stage on the way to Buddhahood and is applied especially to Shākyamuni, the Sarvāstivādins combine with the Bodhisattva ideal new ideas, which are pregnant with the future, especially the two concepts of the inherent Buddhahood of all living beings and the helping of living beings on their way to deliverance. As an offshoot of the Sarvāstivādins, the Sautrāntikas, whose further development prepared the way for the doctrine of Mahāyāna, arose. A strong Mahayanist tendency is to be found also in the Lokottaravādins, who arose as an offshoot of the Mahāsāmghikas. Among these is to be found the Mahāvastu school which, in the Daśabhūmika chapter (not to be confused with the Mahayanist *Daśabhūmika Sutra*), deals with the ten stages (*bhūmi*) of the Bodhisattva career.

7. Thus D. T. Suzuki remarks appropriately: "It is to be remembered that the spiritual vitality of Buddhism lies in its sutras and not in its shastras so-called, which are philosophical treatises, and this is what we naturally expect of religious literature. Whoever the compilers of the Mahāyāna sutras may be, they are genuine expressions of the deepest spiritual experiences gone through by humanity as typified in this case by Indian minds." (Introduction to B. L. Suzuki, p. xxx)

8. Thomas (2), p. 167.

9. A detailed description of the ten Bodhisattva stages is to be found in the *Daśabhūmika Sutra*, quoted by Thomas (2), pp. 205-10. Filliozat presents the same stages according to the *Mahāyāna Sūtralankāra* (pp. 571 f).

10. The list of the Ten Perfect Virtues in the Pali Canon differs from the ten Mahayanist *pāramitā*. See Filliozat, p. 555.

11. See B. L. Suzuki, p. 60. The Chinese characters used in the translation point in the direction of this distinction.

12. German translation of Walleser (2), p. 99.

13. *Ibid.*, p. 98.

14. Conze (4), p. 33.

15. In Suzuki (4), p. 95.

16. Suzuki (3), p. 314.

17. *Ibid.*, pp. 31 f.

18. *Ibid.*, p. 299.

19. In Mahāyāna Buddhism the concept of the Bodhisattva was broadened. In addition to the heavenly Beings of Enlightenment, great historical personalities such as Nāgārjuna, Asanga, and others were venerated as Bodhisattvas. Finally, every enlightened and saintly person, whether bonze or layman, came to be called a Bodhisattva because of his great knowledge and virtue. Nonetheless the distinction between the three named kinds of Bodhisattvas remains alive in the religious consciousness. The heavenly Beings of Enlightenment and the historical personalities are not placed on the same level of veneration.

20. See Ui (1), pp. 160 f.; cf. B. L. Suzuki, pp. 36 f.

21. Thomas calls attention in his depiction of the Bodhisattva career to the fundamental difference between the standpoint of Buddhism and that

of Western docetism. He writes: "This is unlike the Gnostic docetism which represented the essentially divine as assuming the mere appearance of the human. Indian thought never conceived any fundamental difference in kind between the human and the divine. Whether as in Vedic thought they started with the One and reached the individual, or as in Buddhism extended the individual into a universal principle, the conception always resulted in pantheism or pancosmism according to the aspect emphasized" (2), p. 203.

22. Cf. the brief presentation of the doctrine of the Three Buddha-Bodies by B. L. Suzuki, pp. 36-48.

23. The Mahayanists therefore also designate their doctrine as "deep" in contrast to the "shallow" Hinayanist doctrine. See Ui (1), p. 160.

24. Cf. the enlightening study of D. T. Suzuki on the *kōan* exercise and the *nembutsu* (calling upon the name of Buddha) (2), pp. 135-88.

The Mahāyāna Sutras and Zen

1. Suzuki (5), pp. 3 f.; cf. p. 32.

2. Of the group of at least twelve sutras, the three following are the most important: *Ashtasāhasrikā Prajñāpāramitā Sutra*, in eight thousand verses, translated in part into German by Walleser (2); the *Vajracchedikā Prajñāpāramitā Sutra* (*Diamond Sutra*), most frequently translated into Chinese and widely read, with German translation by Walleser (2); and the *Prajñāpāramitā-hridaya Sutra* (*Heart Sutra*), the briefest text, of late date, especially loved by Zen adherents and translated into English by Suzuki (6), pp. 26-30. Concerning the *Prajñā-pāramitā* literature, cf. (in addition to the introduction of Walleser) D. T. Suzuki (3), pp. 234-36; B. L. Suzuki, pp. 89 f.; T. Matsumoto (in German); and Conze (3). For the dating of these texts see Thomas (2), p. 212; Conze (2), p. 204; and Conze (3), p. 117. The *Diamond Sutra* and the *Heart Sutra* are quoted according to the new translation by Conze (4).

3. Suzuki explains the eighteen forms of emptiness taught in the *Prajñā-pāramitā* in (3), pp. 248-54. For the following, see his two essays (3), pp. 215-323.

4. Conze (4), pp. 28, 39 f., 52 f.

5. *Book of Emptiness*, in *Ashtasāhasrikā Prajñāpāramitā Sutra*, quoted by Walleser (2), p. 110.

6. Suzuki (3), pp. 283 ff.

7. *Book of Thusness*, in *Ashtasāhasrikā Prajñāpāramitā Sutra*, quoted by Walleser (2), pp. 96 f.

8. *Book of Emptiness*, quoted by Walleser (2), p. 112; cf. p. 110.

9. *Book of the Benevolent Friends*, quoted by Walleser (2), p. 129.

10. For Nāgārjuna, see Grousset (pp. 200-344), Murti, and Schulemann (Chap. 5). Nāgārjuna's great treatise on Transcendental Wisdom was translated into French by Lamotte (1). The biography of Nāgārjuna is uncertain. Cf. Lamotte (2), pp. 383 ff., 390.

11. *Wu-mên-kuan,* Kōan No. 7, in Dumoulin (1), pp. 18 f.
12. Suzuki (3), p. 280.
13. *Ibid.,* p. 122 f.
14. *Ibid.,* pp. 228 ff.
15. For the following, see Suzuki (3), pp. 21-214.
16. D. T. Suzuki, in the Introduction to B. L. Suzuki, p. xxxiv.
17. *Ibid.,* pp. xxxii f.
18. Cf. the passage in Suzuki (3), pp. 88 f.
19. *Ibid.,* p. 147 n.
20. Dumoulin (2), pp. 41 f.; (3), p. 5.
21. See Dumoulin (2), pp. 63 f.; (3), pp. 31 f.
22. Seckel (1), p. 47.
23. English translation by H. Idumi, in the *Eastern Buddhist,* Vol. III (1924-1925) and Vol. IV (1926-1928); German translation by Jakob Fischer in collaboration with Yokota Takezo and E. Naberfeld. The following page numbers are from the English translation (with a few slight alterations according to the Chinese version in order to bring out more clearly the paradox of the sutra).
24. *Ibid.,* Vol. III, p. 142.
25. *Ibid.,* p. 144.
26. *Ibid.,* pp. 146 f.
27. *Ibid.,* pp. 152 f.
28. *Ibid.,* p. 145.
29. *Ibid.,* Vol. IV, p. 352.
30. *Ibid.,* p. 183.
31. *Ibid.,* Vol. III, p. 146.
32. *Ibid.,* Vol. IV, p. 350.
33. Tao-hsüan, *Hsü Kao-seng-chuan (Biographies of Famous Buddhist Monks).* See Suzuki (4), p. 44; cf. p. 4. Regarding the relationship of Bodhidharma and Hui-k'o to the *Lankāvatāra Sutra,* see Ui (4), p. 25.
34. Suzuki (4), pp. 48 ff.
35. Suzuki assumes that this sutra appeared before the formation of the two major Mahayanist philosophical schools, the Mādhyamika and the Yogācāra. He finds in it tendencies toward both schools. See (4), p. 170.
36. *Ibid.,* pp. 421-27.
37. Cf. *ibid.,* pp. 97 f., 247 f. Miyamoto interprets the reversal dialectically as a transition from consciousness (*vijñāna*) to wisdom (*prajñā*), a contrast which is anticipated in the doctrine of the Sarvāstivādins (in the *Abhidharma-mahā-vibhāshā*). See pp. 501-3.
38. Suzuki (4), pp. 418, 159 ff.
39. Ui (1), pp. 158, 281 f.
40. Suzuki (4), p. 207, and n. 1.
41. *Ibid.,* p. 107.
42. *Wu-mên-kuan,* Kōan No. 6, Dumoulin (1), pp. 17 f.
43. Suzuki (4), p. 109.
44. Preface, in Dumoulin (1), pp. 7 f.
45. *Sūtralankāra* XII, 2, in Suzuki (4), p. 110, n. 3.
46. Suzuki (4), p. 90; cf. p. 229.

The Anticipation of Zen in Chinese Buddhism

1. In Suzuki (7), p. 130; see Suzuki's reply, pp. 135 ff.
2. The most important chronicle is the *Ching-tê chuan-têng-lu* (thirty volumes) of Tao-yüan (1004). Likewise belonging to the Sung era are: *Tsung-ching-lu* (961), *Kuang-têng-lu* (1036), *Chuan-fa-chêng-tsung-chi* (1061), *Hsü-têng-lu* (1101), *P'u-têng-lu* (1201), and *Wu-têng hui-yüan* (1252). These chronicles, often dependent on one another, are historically unreliable.
3. Hu Shih bases his radical correction of traditional Zen history on these writings. A summary of his Chinese studies appeared in Japan under the title *Changes in Chinese Zen.*
4. Cf. Ui (4), (5), and (6), and Masunaga (1) and (2).
5. Liebenthal (1), pp. 116-29. Liebenthal bases his studies on the two-volume pioneering Chinese work of T'ang Yung-t'ung entitled *Han-Wei-liang-chin nan-pei-ch'ao fo-chiao shih.*
6. *Ibid.*, p. 120. See Nakamura (3), p. 276.
7. Cf. Eliot (1), p. 247; Fung Yu-lan, pp. 242 f.
8. Ui believes that the rendition of the word *dhyāna* by two Chinese ideographs is of later date. Many similar examples show that in early times there was a tendency to omit the final sound in writing. Hence he holds that *ch'an* is not, as is commonly assumed, an abbreviation of *ch'an-na*, but that this *na* is a later addition which philologically is not justifiable. See Ui (4), p. 2 (Preface).
9. Fung Yu-lan, p. 241, n. 2; also Eliot (1), pp. 313 ff.
10. In Liebenthal (2), p. 249.
11. Nanjio lists fifty translations (in Appendix II, No. 59, pp. 406-8).
12. Cf. Ui (7), p. 29; Sakaino, pp. 502 ff. See the list of the canonical works translated by Buddhabhadra, in Nanjio, Appendix II, No. 42, pp. 399 f.
13. Letter of Seng-chao cited by Liebenthal (3), p. 98.
14. Cf. B. Matsumoto, p. 237. Matsumoto, in the second half of his not wholly reliable book, treats meditation in China before Bodhidharma in detail.
15. Liebenthal (3), p. 8.
16. In Fung Yu-lan, p. 268; cf. Liebenthal (3), p. 109.
17. In Fung Yu-lan, p. 269.
18. Liebenthal (3), p. 40.
19. *Ibid.*, p. 130.
20. *Ibid.*, p. 137.
21. *Ibid.*, p. 138.
22. From Hu Shih, cited by Liebenthal (4), p. 310. Liebenthal does not adopt this term itself, but in general does accept Hu Shih's view of the history of Zen in China.
23. Fung Yu-lan, p. 388.
24. Cf. Liebenthal (4), pp. 303 ff.
25. Liebenthal (5), pp. 97 f. See Fung Yu-lan, pp. 270 f.

26. In Liebenthal (5), p. 98; (6), p. 266.
27. Regarding Hsieh Ling-yün and his work (*Pien-tsung-lun*), see Liebenthal (4), pp. 301-3.
28. See Fung Yu-lan, pp. 275 f.
29. *Ibid.*, pp. 276 f.
30. In Liebenthal (5), p. 88.
31. *Ibid.*, p. 80.
32. See Appendix III in Liebenthal (3), pp. 169-90.
33. See Liebenthal (5), p. 87.
34. Liebenthal reports the views of T'ang Yung-t'ung (4), pp. 311 f.
35. See Ui (7), pp. 59 f.

Zen Patriarchs of the Early Period

1. In the treatise *Shih-mên-cheng-t'un* (1237), these verses are attributed to Nan-chüan P'u-yüan (748-834), a Zen master of the T'ang era. See Suzuki (1), p. 176.
2. Cf. *Wu-mên-kuan*, Kōan No. 6, Dumoulin (1), pp. 17 f.
3. Suzuki lists the names of the twenty-eight Indian Zen patriarchs (1), p. 170. The list begins with Shākyamuni, while Kāshyapa comes second and Nāgārjuna fourteenth.
4. We have sought to distinguish between history and legend. See Dumoulin (4) for details and evidence on the following. Ui (4) and Masunaga (1) deal with Bodhidharma and the early Zen patriarchs.
5. Ui (4), pp. 15 f., seeks to salvage the nine-year period of "wall-gazing" by connecting it with the nine-year apprenticeship of Hui-k'o under Bodhidharma, mentioned in the epigraph of Fa-lin (572-640) as recorded in the *Pao-lin-chuan*. But the *Pao-lin-chuan*, which was found among the Tun-huang manuscripts, is historically unreliable.
6. Regarding meditation in China during the time of Bodhidharma, see Ui (4), pp. 136 ff.
7. According to the general consensus of historians, the "Six Treatises of Bodhidharma" are spurious, with the exception of the brief text of *Two Entrances and Four Acts*, a fact which Suzuki also admits (1), pp. 178, 232 f. Suzuki translates the presumably authentic text from the later chronicles of Tao-yüan (1004) (1), pp. 179-83. However, this text too, after the analyses of P. Demiéville and Liebenthal (8), cannot be regarded as authentic. Further historical research is required to come to a definite conclusion with regard to the historicity of Bodhidharma. In the meantime, in opposition to Liebenthal (in the review of the German edition of my Zen history in *MS*, Vol. XVIII, p. 485, 1959), I do think it is "still permissible to deal with Bodhidharma as a historical person."
8. The *Vajrasamādhi Sutra* (Nj. No. 429) is regarded as one of the Mahāyāna sutras early translated from the Sanskrit, according to Ui (4), p. 24, by an unknown translator, before the year 374. According to Mizuno the translation of this sutra is simply the forgery of an

anonymous author of the T'ang era, between 650 and 665, who is said to have assimilated the teachings of Bodhidharma.

9. Pelliot notes that the expression had "not yet for Tao-hsüan the literal and somehow material meaning which legends later attributed to it" (p. 258).

10. Ui (4), pp. 20 f.

11. Eliot thinks Bodhidharma may have belonged to a transitional school between Buddhism and Vedantism, so strong does he feel the relationship to be of his teaching to the Indian mysticism of the Upanishads and the Vedānta. This remark is instructive insofar as it underscores the fact that the Indian character of Mahāyāna was retained on Chinese soil. Besides this, in the further development of his discussion Eliot emphasizes the Chinese-Taoist element in Bodhidharma (2), pp. 163 ff.

12. Cf. Dumoulin (4). Japanese Buddhologists seek to salvage the historicity of the story of Hui-k'o's sacrifice of his arm by giving the epigraph of Fa-lin precedence over the historical work of Tao-hsüan.

13. In the *Ching-tê chuan-têng-lu*, Vol. III.

14. In Suzuki (1), pp. 194 f.

15. In his biography of Fa-ch'ung, Tao-hsüan names a Zen master, Ts'an, who according to Ui (4), p. 63, can have been none other than Seng-ts'an. In the epigraph of Fa-lin, it may also benoted, Seng-ts'an is attested as a disciple of Hui-k'o.

16. The *Hsin-hsin-ming* (Jap.: *Shinjinmei*) consists of 624 Chinese characters. There is an English translation in Suzuki (1), pp. 196-201, and a free German translation in Ōhasama-Faust, pp. 64-71. Because of the remark in the *Lêng-chia-shih-tzu-chi* that Seng-ts'an is said to have left no writings, the genuineness of this text has been doubted. Ui proposes as a solution that Seng-ts'an may only have spoken the poem (4), p. 71. The quotation below is reprinted from *Essays in Zen Buddhism* (Series I) by Daisetz Teitaro Suzuki, by permission of the Hutchinson Publishing Group, London, and Grove Press, Inc., New York.

17. Concerning this, see the informative chapter of Ui (4), pp. 81-90, to which I am much indebted in the following.

18. Cited by Masunaga (2), p. 13.

19. The "five manners" and the "five exercises" of Tao-hsin provide schemes for concentration. In the five manners the ascent leads from the knowledge of the mind and its activity through enlightenment and the vision of emptiness to changeless unity. See Masunaga (1), p. 64.

20. The *Liu-tsu-ta-shih-fa-pao-t'an-ching* speaks of more than eleven hundred disciples. The Japanese historians Ui and Masunaga assume that from the time of Tao-hsin on there were constantly five hundred and more disciples practicing together in the temple district of the East Mountain.

21. Concerning the treatise *Tsui-shang-ch'êng-lun* (Jap.: *Saijōjōron*) which is attributed to Hung-jên and, like the *Vajrasamādhi Sutra*, teaches the original purity of one's own nature and the identity of the mind with the Buddha, see Masunaga (1), p. 65.

22. Many names are given by Ui (4), pp. 72 ff., with tables of the branch-

ing-off after Bodhidharma, Hui-k'o, Hung-jên, Shên-hui, and Shên-hsiu (pp. 90, 127, 167 f., 181 f., 373 f.).

23. Ui treats this Niu-t'ou sect, which was named for the home of its founder, in detail, and gives the names of its representatives down to the eighth generation (4), pp. 91-134.

24. These three treatises are the *Mādhyamika Shastra* and *Dvādasanikāya Shastra* of Nāgārjuna, and the *Śata Shastra* of Deva. Regarding the relationship of Fa-yung to the Three Treatises, see Ui (5), pp. 511-17.

25. *Liu-tsu-ta-shih-fa-pao-t'an-ching*. The authorship and date of this treatise are uncertain. In the tradition of the southern sect, it is attributed to Fa-hai, a disciple of Hui-nêng. Hu Shih gives four arguments favoring the authorship of Shên-hui. Apparently it comes from the second half of the eighth century. In later renditions one finds many additions and modifications, but even the earliest accepted version is not historically reliable. See Gernet (1), pp. 37 f. Rousselle translated the first chapters of this sutra into German. The English translation is a free one. The two *gāthā* are to be found in the *Sutra of the Sixth Patriarch* and in the later writings of the southern sect, but not in the *Shên-hui yü-lu*. From this Ui concludes that Shên-hui did not yet know them, since they would have been grist for his mill (4), pp. 348 ff. Likewise the *Lêng-chia-shih-tzu-chi* (*ca.* 708) and *Li-tai-fa-pao-chi* (*ca.* 774) do not contain these stanzas.

26. The birth date of Shên-hsiu is fixed by reckoning back. Little is known regarding his youth. In 625 he received the monastic ordination at the temple of Tien-kung-ssŭ at Lo-yang. At the age of fifty he became a disciple of Hung-jên, with whom he stayed for six years, apparently from 656 to 661. In addition to his knowledge of Buddhist writings he was also well acquainted with Confucianism and Taoism.

27. This story is recorded in the first chapter of the *Sutra of the Sixth Patriarch* and is cited by Rousselle (1), pp. 180 ff., and Suzuki (1), pp. 205 ff. See also *Wu-mên-kuan*, Kōan No. 23, Dumoulin (1), pp. 35 ff.; Watts (2), pp. 67, 68; and Chang Chen-chi, pp. 10, 169.

28. Shên-hsiu was invited to the court in the year 700, when he was ninety-four years old. As a learned man and monk he was highly esteemed. He died in 706 at the Tien-kung-ssŭ temple at Lo-yang, where he had received his ordination in his early years. See Ui (4), pp. 273-75. Shên-hsiu's recommendation of Hui-nêng to the court is recorded in Vol. XVII of the *Annals* of the early T'ang period (Ui [4], p. 106).

29. Tsung-mi (780-841) tells of a stay of Shên-hui with Shên-hsiu, which Ui fixes at 699-701. Since he infers that Shên-hui was at one time a disciple of Shên-hsiu, Ui sees in Shên-hui's later attack on the disciples of his own erstwhile master an act of shameful ingratitude. Ui dates at 701 the acceptance of Shên-hui into the circle of Hui-nêng, and his journey to the north at 704-709. During the years following the death of Hui-nêng (713-720), Ui surmises that Shên-hui engaged in solitary ascetic exercises (4), pp. 198-210, 228 f. Gernet, on the other hand, gives Shên-hui's attachment to Hui-nêng as 708-713, while he regards his stay with Shên-hsiu as unlikely. For the following also see Ui and Gernet.

30. French translation by J. Gernet.
31. Gernet (1), p. 41.
32. Ui (4), p. 226.
33. This expression can be understood to imply nothing derogatory, but rather, merely to state a psychological fact. Gernet thinks that Shên-hui "was no such firm exponent of the doctrine of sudden enlightenment," but that as in life so also in doctrine he made concessions (1), p. 68. Liebenthal argues on the other hand ([7], p. 136) by appealing to a word of Shên-hui in his *Sermon from the High Seat*. The further development of the Ho-tse sect, as it can be seen especially in Tsung-mi, appears to support Gernet's view. Ui likewise points to the inconsistency in the standpoint of Shên-hui (4), pp. 219-21, 274 f.
34. Ui (4), pp. 222-24.

The High Period of Chinese Zen

1. Ui examines fifteen primary sources of the biography of Hui-nêng (5), pp. 173-84. Liebenthal regards the epigraph of Wang Wei (composed before 759; see Ui [5], p. 176) as the only reliable source (7), p. 135.
2. According to the first chapter of the *Liu-tsu-ta-shih-fa-pao-t'an-ching*, which relates the career of the Sixth Patriarch.
3. Among them, the *Prajñāpāramitā-vajraccheda*, the *Vimalikīrti*, the *Lankāvatāra*, and the *Saddharma-pundarīka Sutras*. See Ui (5), p. 188.
4. In the following we limit ourselves to the most important events which Ui presents in his exhaustive biography (5), pp. 184-248.
5. Cf. Ui's critical study of the *Sutra of the Sixth Patriarch* (5), pp. 1-172. Ui regards the doctrinal lectures of Hui-nêng, which are the core of the sutra, as having been written down by his disciple Fa-hai. The first chapter, which relates the career of the patriarch, is legendary.
6. The citations from the *Sutra of the Sixth Patriarch* which follow are taken from the translation of Rousselle (*Sutra*, Chap. I, Rousselle [1], p. 178).
7. *Sutra*, Chap. V, Rousselle (4), p. 136.
8. Shên-hui, *Sermon from the High Seat*, in Liebenthal (7), p. 149.
9. *Sutra*, Chap. II, Rousselle (2), p. 78.
10. In Gernet (1), p. 65; cf. *Shên-hui yü-lu*, Book IV.
11. Shên-hui, in Gernet (2), p. 107.
12. *Sutra*, Chap. VI, Rousselle (5), pp. 208 f.
13. *Sutra*, Chap. III, Rousselle (3), p. 32.
14. *Sutra*, Chap. VI, Rousselle (5), p. 205.
15. *Ibid.*, p. 206.
16. *Ibid.*, p. 207.
17. *Ibid.*, p. 208.
18. *Enneads*, VI, 7, 39; V, 3, 5, 6.
19. *Sutra*, Chap. II, Rousselle (2), p. 81. Likewise Shên-hui recommends the study of the doctrine of Transcendental Wisdom in the Mahāyāna sutras. See Liebenthal (7), pp. 138, 153.

20. Cf. the introduction to the sermon of Shên-hui by Liebenthal (7), p. 137. Similarly, Hui-nêng's *Sutra*, Chap. IV, Rousselle (4), p. 132.
21. See Liebenthal (7), pp. 136 f.
22. Rousselle regards "the application of the doctrine of the so-called Buddha-mind (*bodhicitta*)" as "a basic innovation," though he admits that "certain anticipations had already prepared the way for this development." (Prefatory remarks to the translation of the *Sutra*, Chap. I, by Rousselle [1], p. 3.) With regard to metaphysics, "a basic innovation" cannot be discovered in Hui-nêng.
23. *Sutra*, Chap. I, Rousselle (1), p. 188.
24. *Sutra*, Chap. II, Rousselle (2), p. 78.
25. Shên-hui includes the comparison to a mother giving birth in the third book of *Sermons*. Tsung-mi also takes it up, adding others such as the rising of the sun. Cited by Gernet (2), p. 92.
26. See Gernet's Introduction (2), pp. iv f.
27. *Sutra*, Chap. IV, Rousselle (4), p. 133.
28. For this section see Dumoulin (2) and (3).
29. *Ching-tê ch'uan-têng-lu*, Vol. VI, Dumoulin (2), p. 43; (3), p. 6.
30. Regarding the succession of Zen masters during the T'ang and Sung periods, see the tables in Dumoulin (2) and (3). The dates are in part uncertain. A few in the following section have been ascertained.
31. *Ching-tê ch'uan-têng-lu*, Vol. V., Dumoulin (2), p. 46; (3), p. 9.
32. *Ibid.*, Dumoulin (2), p. 46; (3), pp. 9 f.
33. *Ibid.*, Vol. VI, Dumoulin (2), p. 47; (3), p. 10.
34. *Wu-mên-kuan*, Kōan Nos. 30 and 35, Dumoulin (1), pp. 43 f., 47 f.
35. *Collected Sayings of the Master Nan-ch'üan*, Dumoulin (2), p. 48; (3), p. 11.
36. *Wu-mên-kuan*, Kōan No. 14, Dumoulin (1), pp. 25 f.
37. *Ibid.*, Kōan No. 7, Dumoulin (1), pp. 18 f.
38. *Collected Sayings of Master Chao-chou*, Dumoulin (2), p. 49; (3), p. 12.
39. *Ibid.*
40. Supplement of the *Collected Sayings of Master Chao-chou*, Dumoulin (2), p. 49; (3), p. 12.
41. *Wu-mên-kuan*, Kōan No. 28, Dumoulin (1), pp. 40-42; (2), p. 44; (3), pp. 7 f.
42. *Wu-têng hui-yüan*, Vol. VII, Dumoulin (2), p. 45; (3), p. 8.
43. *Wu-mên-kuan*, Kōan No. 3, Dumoulin (1), pp. 13 f.; (2), pp. 51 f.; (3), pp. 15 f.
44. See Nakamura (1).
45. *Ching-tê ch'uan-têng-lu*, Vol. VI, Dumoulin (2), p. 51; (3), p. 15.

Peculiarities of the "Five Houses"

1. For this section see also Dumoulin (2) and (3).
2. *Wu-mên-kuan*, Kōan No. 40, Dumoulin (1), pp. 51 f.

3. *Wu-têng hui-yüan*, Vol. IX, Dumoulin (2), p. 53; (3), p. 18. Cf. Suzuki (1), pp. 242 f.
4. *Ching-tê ch'uan-têng-lu*, Vol. XI, Dumoulin (2), p. 55; (3), p. 20.
5. *Jên-t'ien yen-mu*, Vol. II, Dumoulin (2), p. 62; (3), p. 30.
6. Quoted by Suzuki (1), p. 117.
7. In the translation and explanation of this *kōan* from the *Pi-yen-lu* (Jap.: *Hekiganroku*) collection, I follow the Japanese Zen master Ya- sutani Ryōkō, who presented the *kōan* orally in this fashion.
8. *Jên-t'ien yen-mu*, Vol. II, Dumoulin (2), p. 63; (3), pp. 30 f.
9. *Ibid.*, Vol. IV, Dumoulin (2), p. 64; (3), pp. 31 f.
10. Ui regards this explanation of the name of the Ts'ao-tung sect as the most likely. According to another explanation the first ideograph was taken directly or indirectly from the name of the residence of the Sixth Patriarch, Ts'ao-ch'i. Apparently the name was first used by outsiders. See Ui (6), pp. 138, 232, 321 f. The following information regarding the main stages of the life and work of Tsung-shan is taken from the detailed chapter of Ui (5), pp. 137-222. Ui also tests the historical value of the *Collected Sayings of Tung-shan and Ts'ao-shan*, which are the primary sources for the beginning of the Ts'ao-tung sect, to which Ui himself belongs. See (6), pp. 65-136.
11. For the biography of Ts'ao-shan, see Ui (6), pp. 223-52.
12. For the biography of Yün-chü, see Ui (6), pp. 321-72.
13. Ui treats the Five Ranks in (6), pp. 253-320.
14. One finds many details regarding Lin-chi and his teaching in the first two volumes of essays by Suzuki, who himself belongs to the Rinzai sect. Further, in a Japanese work on the "basic ideas of Rinzai," Suzuki deals extensively with the dialectic of Lin-chi. See also the essay on Rinzai by Asahina Sōgen, abbot of the Engakuji temple in Kamakura.
15. *Lin-chi-lu*, quoted by Suzuki (1), pp. 295 f.
16. *Lin-chi-lu*, Dumoulin (2), pp. 56 f.; (3), p. 22.
17. *Ibid.*, p. 57; (3), p. 22.
18. *Lin-chi-lu*, free translation according to the Japanese rendition of Asa- hina, p. 72. Cf. a similar lengthy text in Suzuki (1), pp. 347 f., where Lin-chi speaks thus: "Inwardly or outwardly, if you encounter any ob- stacles, lay them low right away. If you encounter the Buddha, slay him; if you encounter the Patriarch, slay him; if you encounter the Arhat or the parent or the relative, slay them all without hesitation; for this is the only way to deliverance."
19. *Lin-chi-lu*, according to Asahina, p. 72.

Spread and Methodological Development During the Sung Period

1. For this section see Dumoulin (2) and (3).
2. *Jên-t'ien yen-mu*, Vol. II, Dumoulin (2), p. 69; (3), p. 38.
3. Regarding the meaning of the *kōan*, see Gundert, who presented the first thirty-three *kōan* of the *Pi-yen-lu* collection in excellent German

translation. See Bibliography, Gundert, tr. (7). I am indebted to him for the terms "accounts of the fathers," "models of the elders," and "public notice" or "public announcement."

4. Regarding the origin of the *Wu-mên-kuan*, see the Introduction to Dumoulin (1), pp. 1-6.
5. See Ui (6), pp. 308-20.
6. Suzuki (2), pp. 83 f.
7. *Wu-mên-kuan*, Preface, Dumoulin (1), p. 7.
8. *Ibid.*, Kōan No. 18, Dumoulin (1), p. 31.
9. In Suzuki (5), pp. 59, 62.
10. In Suzuki (2), p. 66.
11. Herrigel, p. 50.
12. Ui deals extensively with the historical development of the Ts'ao-tung sect during the Sung period (6), pp. 373-475.
13. The treatise is entitled *Mo-chao-lu* (Jap.: *Mokushōroku*).
14. In the treatise *Tso-ch'an-cheng* (Jap.: *Zazenshin*), which is contained in the sixth volume of the *Collected Sayings of the Master T'ien-t'ung*.
15. In Suzuki (2), pp. 96 f.

The Transplanting of Zen to Japan

1. Eliot (2) places Dōshō's journey to China in the year 654. I am following the Buddhist lexicon of Ui (8), p. 782, from which the following dates of the history of Japanese Buddhism are generally taken. Regarding the encounter of Dōshō with Zen during his stay in China, see Ui (4), pp. 75 f., 167.
2. See Ui (4), p. 307 f.
3. Regarding Eisai, see the essay by Takeda Ekushū.
4. The temple was built according to the model of the Chinese Po-chang-shan temple (see Ponsonby-Fane, p. 151). Ponsonby-Fane deals extensively with the Zen temples of Kyoto and includes information regarding the size of the grounds and the incomes. Most temple buildings were repeatedly the victims of flames, especially during the civil war, Ōnin no ran (1467-1477), so called from the era of Ōnin.
5. Regarding the Chinese "Five Mountains"—five magnificent Zen temples of the Sung period—see Dumoulin (2), p. 66, and (3), p. 35. The first list of "Five Mountains" in Japan includes temples in Kyoto and Kamakura. Later, two series of "Five Mountains" each emerged in Kyoto and Kamakura. The Shogun Ashikaga Yoshimitsu finally fixed the list in 1386. For details see Ponsonby-Fane, pp. 215 f.
6. Suzuki (9), p. 66.
7. *Kamikaze*, for which the well-known Japanese suicide squads during World War II were named.
8. Tōkeiji is one of the "Five Mountains" of the Zen nuns in Kamakura. The nuns of the Rinzai sect also had five main temples in Kamakura and in Kyoto which were designated the "Five Mountains."
9. Regarding the layout of the Zen temple, see Yokoyama, pp. 40-45. In

other Buddhist sects there are other enumerations of the "seven halls." The number seven, according to various commentators, signifies the completeness of the layout.

10. According to the information given by Ponsonby-Fane (p. 153), the *sammon* is a work of the Muromachi period (fifteenth century). It is ascribed by tradition to the Katei era (1235-1238). In 1585 it collapsed, but Hideyoshi immediately restored it. From the Katei era only the *tōsu* and the *yūshitsu* have survived. The Zen hall dates from the Kenchō period (1249-1256), and the Treasure Hall of the Sutras from the Tenju period (1375-1381). All the buildings underwent a thorough restoration during the Kan'ei period (1624-1644) of the Tokugawa era.

11. In 1334 the Nanzenji temple was accorded the rank of Tenka Daiichi, or the first in the empire. The buildings of this temple burned repeatedly. But at the beginning of the Tokugawa period it received the gift of two valuable buildings dating from the Momoyama period, the Seiryōden and the Momoyama palace of Hideyoshi. The gate for the imperial messenger (*chokushimon*) was the east gate (*nikkamon*) of the old imperial palace. See Ponsonby-Fane, pp. 154 f.

12. For Kakushin see the Introduction to the Wu-mên-kuan, Dumoulin (1), pp. 3-5.

13. Cf. Eliot (2), pp. 285, 296 f.

14. In Masunaga's judgment, "Sōtō Zen flourished most in Japan. Rinzai Zen developed according to the Chinese style, and was unable to achieve much growth as a religion in Japan" (3), p. 41.

The Zen Master Dōgen

1. Citations in Masunaga (4), Preface, p. 3. The following biographical sketch follows this work in the main. Dōgen's youth is treated by Benl (1). See also Tanaka. For the teachings of Dōgen see especially Akiyama.

2. From the *Denkōroku* in Masunaga (4), p. 7. The *Denkōroku*, in two volumes, is the major historical work of the Sōtō sect. It contains biographies of Indian, Chinese, and Japanese representatives of the Zen tradition, from Shākyamuni down through fifty-three generations. These were selected by Keizan, a noted abbot of the Eiheiji in the line of Dōgen (1300). Regarding the life and work of Keizan, see Dumoulin (9), pp. 329-32.

3. Masunaga weighs the evidence pro and con and concludes that the meeting did take place (4), pp. 16 ff.

4. *Denkōroku*, in Masunaga (4), p. 22.

5. *Shōbōgenzō Zuimonki*, Vol. I, No. 6, Dōgen (4), p. 17. After the death of Dōgen his disciple Ejō collected sayings and anecdotes from his life in the six volumes of the *Shōbōgenzō Zuimonki*. Iwamoto has translated excerpts from this work into German, and some chapters of the *Shōbōgenzō* have been translated into English by Masunaga (5).

6. The *Shōbōgenzō* consists of ninety-five chapters, whose origin is spread

over half the life of Dōgen (1231-1253). Regarding the genesis of the
individual chapters, see Masunaga (4), pp. 105-9.
7. Six short treatises on life in the Zen hall are assembled in the volume
Eihei Dōgen Zenji Shingi. The following directives are taken from the
fifth chapter of the *Shōbōgenzō* with the title "Jūundōshiki."
8. See Nanjio, Nos. 122, 1209, 1597.
9. Quoted by Masunaga (4), pp. 97 f.
10. See Akiyama's chapter (pp. 223-31) on "*zazen* only."
11. *Shōbōgenzō,* section "Butsudo," Dōgen (2), p. 217.
12. *Fukanzazengi,* Dōgen (5), pp. 8-11; English translation in Masunaga
(5); German translation, Dumoulin (10).
13. In the seventh book of the *Mahāprajñāpāramitā Sutra* (Jap.: *Daichi-doron*).
14. *Shōbōgenzō,* section "Bendōwa," Dōgen (1), p. 60.
15. *Shōbōgenzō Zuimonki,* Vol. II, No. 20, Dōgen (4), p. 55.
16. *Shōbōgenzō,* section "Bendōwa," Dōgen (1), p. 69.
17. *Ibid.,* section "Zazenkan," Dōgen (1), p. 69.
18. *Ibid.,* section "Shōji," Dōgen (3), p. 240.
19. *Ibid.,* section "Bendōwa," Dōgen (1), pp. 65 ff.
20. *Fukanzazengi,* Dōgen (5), p. 8.
21. See *Shōbōgenzō,* section "Busshō," Dōgen (1), pp. 315 ff.
22. *Ibid.,* section "Zammai-ō-zammai," Dōgen (3), p. 14.
23. *Ibid.,* section "Genjō Kōan," Dōgen (1), pp. 83 ff.
24. *Ibid.,* section "Busshō," Dōgen (1), p. 315.
25. *Ibid.,* section "Uji," Dōgen (1), p. 159.
26. *Ibid.,* section "Kuge," Dōgen (2), p. 171.
27. *Shōbōgenzō Zuimonki,* Vol. II, No. 14, Dōgen (4), p. 44.
28. See the revealing study of Nakamura (2).
29. See the supporting quotations from Dōgen in Nakamura (2),
pp. 116 f.; see also Nakamura (3), pp. 370 f.
30. *Shōbōgenzō Zuimonki,* Vol. III, No. 7, Dōgen (4), pp. 63 f.
31. *Ibid.,* Vol. I, No. 11, Dōgen (4), pp. 20 f.
32. *Shōbōgenzō,* section "Genjō Kōan," Dōgen (1), pp. 83 f.
33. *Ibid.,* section "Shizen Biku," Dōgen (3), p. 215.
34. *Ibid.,* section "Shizen Biku," Dōgen (3), p. 211; cf. Nakamura (2)
p. 118. Beyond this, I am indebted to Professor Nakamura personally
for valuable information regarding Dōgen.

The Cultural Influence of Zen in the Muromachi Period

1. The temple of Daitokuji is designated in a contemporary decree as "the
Zen temple of the court par excellence." See Ponsonby-Fane, p. 156.
See there also the description of the buildings.
2. Ponsonby-Fane regards the Myōshinji temple today as "the most complete and best example of the big Zen foundations." Because of their

artistic value, its numerous buildings have been placed under special government protection (p. 200).

3. See the study by Benl (2), which, in addition to a biographical sketch of the master, presents the translation of a number of chapters from his most important work, *Muchū-mondō*.

4. According to the definitive list, the "Five Mountains" of Kyoto include: Tenryūji, Shōkokuji, Kenninji, Tōfukuji, and Manjuji; of Kamakura: Kenchōji, Engakuji, Jūfukuji, Jōchiji, and Jōmyōji. Manjuji in Kyoto is today a full dependent of Tōfukuji and of no significance. Similarly, in Kamakura, Jōchiji has become a dependent of Engakuji, while Jūfukuji and Jōmyōji have lapsed into insignificance.

5. Not infrequently a famous master who himself did not live at a given temple was, because of special ties to it, designated as founder (*kaisan*), even though another bonze actually held the first abbacy. The precious building of the Kinkakuji, after escaping the destruction of the recent war, burned down, but by 1955 it had already been reconstructed. For historical details regarding the Kinkakuji and the Ginkakuji, see Ponsonby-Fane, pp. 203-7.

6. Furuta has described the development of Zen among the populace in an interesting essay.

7. In Furuta (1), p. 63.

8. Down to the present time, Zen masters repeat these same thoughts and analogies, but with the authority coming from their own personal experience.

9. *Twenty-three Questions and Answers*, No. 1, Musō, p. 71.

10. Regarding the doctrine of the relation between the primal substance (Jap.: *honji*) and its earthly *avatar* (Jap.: *suijaku*), see Gundert (2), pp. 76 f. Their relationship is later reversed in favor of Shinto. See Dumoulin (5), pp. 37 f.

11. *Twenty-three Questions and Answers*, No. 19, Musō, pp. 88 f.

12. Bassui, "Kana-hōgo," No. 8, p. 124.

13. *Ibid.*, p. 125.

14. *Ibid.*, No. 4, pp. 114 f.

15. Gettan, "Kana-hōgo," pp. 241 f.

16. *Ibid.*, p. 249.

17. Regarding Ikkyū, compare the essay of Ichikawa.

18. This is the judgment of the Buddhist historian Furuta (1), p. 68.

19. In Ikkyū's treatise on the "Skeleton" (*gaikotsu*), pp. 287 f.

20. Quoted by Ichikawa, pp. 183 f.

21. In Ikkyū's treatise *Amida hataka monogatari*, in Ichikawa, p. 182.

22. For this whole section see Suzuki (9), Anesaki (1), Seckel (2), Tsuda, and Tsutzumi.

23. On the art of Japanese gardening see *Pageant of Japanese Art* (2), Newsom, and Tamura.

24. Okakura, in his brilliant essay on tea, pp. 59 and 3. Cf. the new book on the Way of Tea by Hammitzsch (6).

25. Cf. *Pageant of Japanese Art* (1), Kümmel, Cohn, and Fischer.

26. Seckel (1) gives an excellent interpretation of the painting of Mu-ch'i, "Six Kaki Fruits [Persimmons]."

27. Suzuki interprets Josetsu's painting in *kōan* fashion. Just as it is impossible to catch the catfish with a gourd, so rational thought is incapable of grasping enlightenment. Suzuki (9), explanation to plate xiv (first edition); see p. 15 in the revised edition.
28. The date of Sesshū's death is uncertain. Perhaps it was 1502, when he was eighty-three years old. See the essay of Matsushita.
29. Cohn, p. 99.
30. Kümmel, p. 43.

The First Encounter Between Zen and Christianity

1. Schurhammer-Voretzsch, p. xvii.
2. Regarding this, cf. the testimony of the letters of Francis Xavier and many missionaries, in Schurhammer-Wicki, ed., p. 188; Schurhammer-Voretzsch, tr., pp. 9 f., 338 f.; Torres in Schurhammer (1), p. 47; Valignano in Schütte, p. 112. The Portuguese captain Jorge Alvarez, a good observer and one of the few Europeans to visit Japan (1547) before the arrival of the missionaries, "was horrified by the prevalence of sodomy, especially in the precincts of Buddhist temples." See Boxer, p. 35. This matter is discussed most fully by Schurhammer (2), pp. 80-97. Various missionaries, citing Japanese sources, attribute the introduction of pederasty in Japan to Kōbō Daishi (Kūkai, A.D. 774-834). See Schurhammer (2), p. 89; cf. Schurhammer (3), pp. 206-28. Tsuji, the historian of Japanese Buddhism, asserts that pederasty was widespread in Zen temples. The earliest mention of this abuse is found in a decree of the Shogun Hōjō Sadatoki to the Engakuji temple in Kamakura in the year 1303. Subsequent to this, instructions were issued repeatedl regarding the living arrangements, clothes, etc., of the handsome boy.. The literature of the "Five Mountains" (*Gozan Bungaku*) contains many love songs addressed to boys. See Tsuji (1), pp. 335-37.
3. Schurhammer-Wicki, ed., pp. 189 f.
4. Schurhammer-Voretzsch, tr., p. 7.
5. *Ibid.*
6. Ninshitsu died in 1556. He had been abbot of the Sōtō temple Fukushōji. Nothing further is known concerning his death. See Laures (1).
7. Schurhammer-Voretzsch, tr., pp. 122 f. Frois writes "Nanriji," but the correct rendition is "Nanrinji."
8. *Ibid.*, pp. 94 f.
9. *Ibid.*, p. 100.
10. *Ibid.*, pp. 96-98 ff.
11. *Ibid.*, pp. 87 ff.
12. Schütte, p. 284.
13. Schurhammer-Voretzsch, tr., p. 9; cf. Schurhammer-Wicki, ed., pp. 188 f., 204.
14. Schurhammer-Voretzsch, tr., p. 99; cf. p. 90.
15. Schurhammer-Wicki, ed., p. 186.
16. *Ibid.*, p. 259.

17. Schurhammer (1), p. 12.
18. Schurhammer-Wicki, ed., p. 288.
19. Schurhammer (1), p. 48.
20. *Ibid.*, p. 52.
21. Schurhammer cites three letters of Torres and the detailed report in a letter of Fernandez. Frois also reports on these disputations. See Schurhammer-Voretzsch, tr., pp. 21-26.
22. Schurhammer (1), p. 50.
23. *Ibid.*, p. 67.
24. *Ibid.*, pp. 66 f.
25. Regarding the origin and contents of the catechism of Valignano see Schütte, pp. 90-120.
26. *Ibid.*, p. 94.
27. *Ibid.*, p. 107.
28. *Ibid.*, p. 108.
29. Schurhammer-Voretzsch, tr., pp. 4 f.
30. Boxer, p. 221.
31. Anesaki (2) was the first to report on Fabian. Pierre Humberclaude translated the Christian apologetical work *Myōtei Mondō* into French.
32. Humberclaude, tr., p. 529.
33. *Ibid.*, p. 530.
34. *Ibid.*, p. 533.
35. Schurhammer-Voretzsch, tr., p. 168.
36. *Ibid.*, p. 15.
37. Schurhammer (1), p. 62; cf. Schurhammer-Voretzsch, tr., p. 21.
38. Quoted by Schurhammer (4), p. 42.
39. *Ibid.*, p. 34.
40. For the following see Schütte, pp. 219-63.
41. Schütte, p. 222.
42. *Ibid.*, p. 223.
43. On this entire section see the study of Nishimura on Christianity and tea.
44. Juan Rodriguez Tçuzzu, Álvarez-Taladriz, ed., pp. 39 f. *Arte del Cha* covers Chaps. 32 to 35 of the still unpublished Japanese Church history of Rodriguez Tçuzzu (manuscript *Ajuda* 49-IV-53).
45. *Ibid.*, p. 38.
46. Thus the wealthy patrician, Diogo Hibiya Ryōkei, in whose house in Sakai Francis Xavier found a haven. See Nishimura, p. 38, and cf. Schurhammer-Voretzsch, tr., p. 245.
47. See the long list of ten utensils in the possession of Ōtomo Yoshishige as listed in the Japanese chronicle *Ōtomo Kōhaiki*, pp. 292-96.
48. Schurhammer-Voretzsch, tr., p. 469. Concerning the events in Bungo, see the presentation of Schurhammer (5).
49. *Ōtomo Kōhaiki*, pp. 307 f.
50. See Kataoka (1), p. 459. According to Kataoka the following were Christians: Takayama Ukon, Gamō Ujisato, Oda Yūraku, Seta Kamon, and Shibayama Kenmotsu. As Laures points out, nothing is said of Shibayama in the *Jesuit Letters* (2), p. 313. Nishimura discusses the other four Christian tea masters in detail.

51. In Laures (2), pp. 177 f.
52. See Nishimura, p. 101. See also the essay on Ukon as tea master by Kataoka (2). Minaminobo is Ukon's name as artist.
53. See Nishimura, pp. 102 f.
54. See Laures (2), p. 310.
55. In *ibid.*, p. 312.
56. Father Organtino described him thus on the basis of the statement of a Christian nobleman. *Ibid.*, p. 173.
57. See Nishimura, p. 159.
58. *Ibid.*, pp. 136 f.
59. *Ibid.*, p. 95.
60. See Dumoulin (6), pp. 115 f.
61. See the account of her conversion in Kleiser, p. 612.
62. See Nishimura, pp. 99 f.
63. *Ibid.*, p. 67.
64. See Laures (2), p. 174.
65. In Nishimura, p. 150.
66. See Nishimura, p. 223. Nishimura deals extensively with the peculiar character of Furuta Oribe. The following treatment is based on his presentation.
67. Nishimura treats the question from all sides and comes to a negative conclusion. The case for the adherence of Rikyū to Christianity is advanced because of the need to find an explanation for the noted tea master's falling into disfavor with Hideyoshi, which drove him to suicide. See Nishimura, pp. 177 ff.
68. Nishimura regards Furuta Oribe as a Christian (see pp. 209, 213, 234, 238), but still admits uncertainty. Conclusive evidence which would permit a definite conclusion is wanting.
69. On this the Japanese historian Ebizawa writes very revealingly. He relates how Seyakuin Zensō, the personal physician and advisor of Hideyoshi, sought a mistress for his master in the Hizen district of Kyushu, after his military campaign there against Satsuma, but encountered the intransigent opposition of the Christian girls who turned down this honor so highly prized throughout the whole empire (pp. 22 f.). Also, he relates how the first modern scientific knowledge was brought to Japan by the Christian mission.

Zen in the Modern Japanese Age

1. In his great history of Japanese Buddhism, the Japanese historian Tsuji deals extensively with the various factors which led to the congealing of Buddhism during the Tokugawa era. See Tsuji (2), Vol. III, pp. 1-284. According to his judgment: "Thus it came to a point where the heart of the people was alienated from Buddhism during the Edo period. The temples of the bonzes became the objects of the hatred and disdain of the people . . ." ([2], Vol. IV, p. 443).
2. Regarding Sōden, see Tsuji (2), Vol. II, pp. 26-88. Sōden apparently

participated in the drafting of the persecution edict against Christianity of January 27, 1614. See Boxer, p. 318.

3. See Tsuji's chapter on "Takuan and the Shogun Iemitsu" (2), Vol. II, pp. 448-92.

4. Suzuki (9), pp. 150 ff.

5. The political achievements of Iemitsu hardly compensate for his pernicious character (see Boxer, pp. 362 ff.). Indeed, the Way of the Warrior loses much of its glory when one compares ideal and practice. During the Tokugawa era the warrior class sank to a low level and the many masterless samurai were a scourge to the country. Even the vengeance of the forty-seven *rōnin*, so celebrated in literature, shows clearly the limits of the ethics of Bushido. Cf. Sansom, pp. 488 ff.

6. Tsuji treats the Ōbaku sect (2), Vol. III, pp. 285-416; cf. the essay of Shimmyō.

7. Regarding Tetsugen, see Furuta (2), pp. 162-69.

8. See Tsuji (2), Vol. III, pp. 442 ff.

9. See Furuta (1), pp. 79 f.

10. *Ibid.*, pp. 71 f.; also for the following quotations.

11. *Ibid.*, pp. 73-75; also for the following quotations.

12. Suzuki (1), p. 254; cf. (2), p. 100. Since December is both the birth- and death-month of Hakuin, both dates are shifted one year in accordance with the new calendar.

13. In his history of Japanese literature ([3], pp. 121-23) Gundert gives a good introduction to Bashō. Some of his more important travel books have been translated into German by Hammitzsch. A partial German translation of the travelogue *Oku no Hosomichi* has been done by Übeschaar. Cf. further Suzuki (9), pp. 253-62. According to Suzuki, "the spirit of Bashō is the spirit of Zen expressing itself in seventeen syllables" (first edition, p. 264). Blyth presents a large number of Bashō's *haiku*, and considers him "the world's greatest poet" (p. viii).

14. At the beginning of *Utatsu Kikō* (*Travel Book of the Years of Utatsu*).

15. Translation by Gundert (3), p. 122.

16. See Suzuki (9), pp. 227 ff. (See also the first edition, pp. 147 f.) Blyth likewise interprets this *haiku*, pp. 217 f.

17. Gundert (3), p. 123.

18. Kitamori, p. 119.

19. Salditt, p. 294.

20. See Dumoulin (7), p. 375.

21. Especially in the major work *Kokuikō*. See Dumoulin (5), pp. 268-303.

22. Kitamori, pp. 123 ff.

The Zen Mysticism of Hakuin

1. For Hakuin's biography see, in addition to autobiographical data in his writings (especially regarding his mystical experiences), his autobiography composed late in life and entitled *Itsu-made-gusa* (3 vols.) and the chronicle of his life compiled by his disciple Tōrei (d. 1792). The

following sketch is based chiefly on these two sources. Naoki presents a brief and easy-to-read sketch of his life, pp. 3-20.

2. I follow here the autobiographical remark in Hakuin's treatise *Orategama*, which I later quote. According to the chronicle of Tōrei, Hakuin first returned to the Shōinji temple in Hara, where he became ill. His stay in Numazu is reported for the year 1711.
3. Hakuin (2), pp. 204 f.
4. *Ibid.*, pp. 205 f.
5. Hakuin (1), pp. 196 f.
6. Hakuin (2), p. 206.
7. Hakuin (3), p. 364.
8. Hakuin (2), p. 207.
9. The chronicle of the disciple Tōrei emphasizes the importance of this enlightenment by having it mark the end of the first period of Hakuin's life (pp. 42 f.).
10. Hakuin (2), p. 207.
11. For the following see Hakuin's debate with Amidism on *kōan* and *nembutsu* in the Appendix to the *Orategama* (2), pp. 211-44.
12. Hakuin tells of his invention of the *kōan* of the "single hand" in his treatise *Sekishū Onjō* (4).
13. *Ibid.*, p. 391.
14. Appendix to the *Orategama*, Hakuin (2), p. 232.
15. *Ibid.*, pp. 232 f.
16. *Ibid.*, pp. 221-23.
17. English translation by R. D. M. Shaw and W. Schiffer.
18. Hakuin (3), p. 349.
19. *Ibid.*, pp. 343 f.
20. Masutani Fumio, in *Mainichi Shimbun*, June 24, 1957.
21. From the English translation of Suzuki (1), pp. 336 f. Reprinted by permission of the Hutchinson Publishing Group, London, and Grove Press, Inc., New York.
22. See the book of Kurt Brasch on the Zen painting of Hakuin, which is illustrated with twenty-eight excellent reproductions of paintings.

The Essence of Zen

1. *Wu-mên-kuan*, Dumoulin (1), p. 7.
2. Suzuki (5), p. 41.
3. Ōhasama-Faust, p. ix.
4. Suzuki (1), pp. 233 ff.
5. Suzuki (10), p. 58.
6. Ōhasama-Faust, p. ix.
7. In Kishimoto (1), p. 448.
8. In Suzuki (1), pp. 251 ff.
9. See Suzuki (2), pp. 105 ff.
10. *Ibid.*, p. 115; cf. pp. 112 ff.
11. *Ibid.*, p. 111; cf. pp. 109 ff.

12. In Suzuki (1), p. 257. Reprinted by permission of the Hutchinson Publishing Group, London, and Grove Press, Inc., New York.
13. Heiler, p. 50.
14. James, pp. 380-82.
15. Suzuki (2), pp. 30-36. In an essay on Zen and *nembutsu*, Kishimoto (2) undertook a comparison of the eight characteristics of Suzuki and the four characteristics of James and found wide agreement between the two series. Suzuki's "affirmation" may have been suggested by James's "yes-function."
16. Girgensohn, p. 603. On the basis of his psychological data, obtained by experiments, Girgensohn challenges the "style of the Freudian school."
17. James, pp. 483 f.; see also p. 207.
18. Suzuki (1), p. 32.
19. Suzuki (2), pp. 62 f.
20. *Ibid.*, p. 31.
21. C. G. Carus, *Psyche: Zur Entwicklingsgeschichte der Seele* (1846). Carus writes: "The key to the knowledge of the substance of the conscious life of the mind lies in the region of the unconscious."
22. Suzuki (5), Introduction, p. 21.
23. *Ibid.*, p. 22.
24. Benoit, p. 134, according to the English edition, which is revised and considerably improved. In the English edition an entirely new chapter is given to "The Zen Unconscious," pp. 72-78.
25. *Ibid.*, p. 175.
26. *Ibid.*, p. 209.
27. Schmaltz, p. 30.
28. The material presently available on the mystical experiences in Zen by no means meets the conditions stipulated by experimental psychology. To obtain precise data for a psychological definition of Zen it would be necessary to have inquiries and experiments conducted by professional psychologists, following the methods of Gruehn. Such material could readily be collected in Japan. Cf. Gruehn's experimental-psychological analysis of the mystic process, pp. 122-42.
29. Cf. Dumoulin (8) and Ohm, pp. 399 ff., both of which include further bibliographical information.
30. Mager (1), p. 407.
31. Mager (2), p. 270.
32. Brunner, p. 129.
33. Gardet, Preface to the German translation, p. 11. Cf. the section on the "Realization of the Self," pp. 20-23.
34. Merton, pp. 197 f.
35. James, pp. 398 f.
36. Ohm, p. 398.
37. Brunner, p. 193.

Bibliography

AKIYAMA, H. Dōgen no kenkyū (Studies in Dōgen). Tokyo, 1935.
ALVAREZ-TALADRIZ, J. L. (ed.). Juan Rodriguez Tçuzzu, Arte del Cha. Series Monumenta Nipponica Monographs No. 14. Tokyo, 1954.
ALWIS, J. D. Buddhist Nirvāna. Colombo, 1871.
ANESAKI, M. (1) Buddhist Art in Its Relation to Buddhist Ideals with Special Reference to Buddhism in Japan. Boston, 1915.
————. (2) "The Writings of Fabian the Apostate Irman," in Proceedings of the Imperial Academy, VIII, pp. 307-10 (1929).
ANESAKI-TAKAKUSU. "Dhyāna," in ERE, IV, pp. 702-4, New York, 1912.
ASAHINA, S. "Rinzai," in Gendai Bukkyō Kōza, V, pp. 66-72, Tokyo, 1955.
BASSUI. "Kana-hōgo," in Zenmon hōgoshū, 6th edn. Tokyo, 1910.
BECKH, H. (1) Buddhismus, Einleitung, Der Buddha, 3rd edn. Berlin-Leipzig, 1928.
————. (2) Buddhismus, Die Lehre, 3rd edn. Berlin-Leipzig, 1928.
BENL, O. (1) "Der Zen-Meister Dōgen in China," in NOAG, Nos. 79-80, pp. 67-77, Hamburg, 1956.
————. (2) "Musō Kokushi. Ein japanischer Zen-Meister," in OE, II, pp. 86-108 (1955).
BENOIT, H. La Doctrine suprême, Études psychologiques selon la Pensée Zen, Paris, 1952. English translation: (The Supreme Doctrine, Psychological Studies in Zen Thought), with Foreword by Aldous Huxley. New York, 1955, 1959.
BERVAL, R. de (ed.). "Présence du Bouddhisme," in France-Asie, No. 153, Tokyo, 1959.
BLOFELD, F. The Zen Teaching of Huang Po on the Transmission of Mind. London, 1958.

BLYTH, R. H. *Zen in English Literature and Oriental Classics.* Tokyo, 1942; (paperback), New York, 1960.

BOXER, C. R. *The Christian Century in Japan.* London, 1951.

BRASCH, K. *Hakuin und die Zen-Malerei.* Tokyo, 1957.

BRUNNER, A. *Die Religion. Eine philosophische Untersuchung auf geschichtlicher Grundlage.* Freiburg, 1956.

CHANG CHEN-CHI. *The Practice of Zen.* New York, 1959.

COHN, W. *Stilanalysen als Einführung in die japanische Malerei.* Berlin, 1908.

CONZE, E. (1) *Buddhist Meditation.* London, 1956.

————. (2) *Buddhism.* Oxford, 1951.

————. (3) "The Ontology of the Prajñāpāramitā," in PEW, III, 2, pp. 117-29 (1953).

————. (4) (tr.). *Buddhist Wisdom Books Containing the Diamond Sutra and the Heart Sutra.* London, 1958.

DAHLMANN, J. *Nirvāna.* Berlin, 1896.

DŌGEN. (1) *Shōbōgenzō,* I. Iwanami Bunko (ed.). Tokyo, 1939.

————. (2) *Shōbōgenzō,* II. Iwanami Bunko (ed.). Tokyo, 1942.

————. (3) *Shōbōgenzō,* III. Iwanami Bunko (ed.). Tokyo, 1943.

————. (4) *Shōbōgenzō Zuimonki,* Iwanami Bunko (ed.). Tokyo, 1937.

————. (5) *Fukanzazengi,* Iwanami Bunko (ed.). Tokyo, 1940.

DOI, T. "Das Kegon Sutra. Eine Einführung," in MOAG, XXXIX, C, Tokyo, 1957.

DUMOULIN, H. (1) (tr.). *Wu-mên-kuan. Der Pass ohne Tor.* Series Monumenta Nipponica Monographs No. 13. Tokyo, 1953.

————. (2) "Die Entwicklung des chinesischen Ch'an nach Hui-nêng im Lichte des Wu-mên-kuan," in MS, VI, pp. 40-72 (1941).

————. (3) (tr. of [2]). *The Development of Chinese Zen after the Sixth Patriarch in the Light of Mumonkan.* Translated into English, with additional notes and appendices, by Ruth Fuller Sasaki. New York, 1953.

————. (4) "Bodhidharma und die Anfänge des Ch'an-Buddhismus," in MN, VII, pp. 67-83 (1951).

————. (5) *Kamo Mabuchi, Ein Beitrag zur japanischen Religions- und Geistesgeschichte.* Series Monumenta Nipponica Monographs No. 8. Tokyo, 1943.

————. (6) "Die Erneuerung des Liederweges durch Kamo Mabuchi," in MN, VI, pp. 110-45 (1943).

————. (7) "Yoshida Shōin, Ein Beitrag zum Verständnis der geistigen Quellen der Meijierneuerung," in MN, I, pp. 350-77 (1938).

————. (8) "Östliche und westliche Mystik," in GL, XX, pp. 133-47, 202-22 (1947).

————. (9) (tr.). "Das Merkbuch für die Übung des Zazen des Zen-Meisters Keizan," in MN, XIII, pp. 329-46 (1957).

————. (10) (tr.). "Allgemeine Lehren zur Förderung des Zazen von Zen-Meister Dōgen," in *MN*, XIV, pp. 429-36 (1958).

EBIZAWA, A. *Kindai Nippon Bunka no tanjō* (The Origin of Modern Culture in Japan). Tokyo, 1956.

EKLUND, J. A. *Nirvāna*. Upsala, 1899.

ELIADE, M. *Yoga. Immortality and Freedom*. New York, 1958.

ELIOT, C. (1) *Hinduism and Buddhism*, III. London, 1921.

————. (2) *Japanese Buddhism*. London, 1935.

FILLIOZAT, J. "Le Bouddhisme," in *Manuel des Études Indiennes*, II. Hanoi, 1953.

FISCHER, O. "Chinesische Landschaftsmalerei." Munich, 1921.

FISCHER-YOKOTA (tr.). *Das Sutra Vimalikīrti*. Tokyo, 1944.

FUNG YU-LAN. *A History of Chinese Philosophy*, II. Princeton, 1953.

FURUTA, S. (1) "Nihon-zen no hattatsu" (The Development of Japanese Zen), in *Gendai Zen-kōza*, II, pp. 49-81, Tokyo, 1956.

————. (2) "Tetsugen," in *Gendai Bukkyō Kōza*, V, pp. 162-69, Tokyo, 1955.

GARDET, L. *Expériences Mystiques en terres non-chrétiennes*. Paris, 1953. German translation: *Mystische Erfahrungen in nicht-christlichen Ländern*. Alsatia, 1956.

GERNET, J. (1) "Biographie du Maître Chen-Houei du Ho-tsö," in *JA*, pp. 29-68 (1951).

————. (2) (tr.). *Entretiens du Maître du Dhyāna Chen-Houei du Ho-tsö*. Hanoi, 1949.

GETTAN. "Kana-hōgo," in *Zenmon hōgoshū*, 6th edn. Tokyo, 1910.

GIRGENSOHN, K. *Der seelische Aufbau des religiösen Erlebens*. Gütersloh, 1930.

GLASENAPP, H. v. (1) *Die fünf grossen Religionen*, I. Düsseldorf, 1952.

————. (2) *Buddhistische Mysterien*. Stuttgart, 1940.

————. (3) *Die Religionen Indiens*. Stuttgart, 1943.

GROUSSET, R. *Les Philosophies Indiennes*, I. Paris, 1931.

GRUEHN, W. *Die Frömmigkeit der Gegenwart. Grundtatsachen der empirischen Psychologie*. Münster, 1956.

GUNDERT, W. (1) (tr.). *Bi-yän-lu, Meister Yüan-Wu's Niederschrift von der smaragdenen Felswand*. Munich, 1960.

————. (2) *Japanische Religionsgeschichte*. Tokyo, 1935.

————. (3) *Die japanische Literatur*. Wildpark-Potzdam, 1929.

HAKUIN. (1) *Itsu-made-gusa*, in *Hakuin Oshō Zenshū*, I, pp. 149-230, Tokyo, 1935.

————. (2) *Orategama*, in *Hakuin Oshō Zenshū*, V, pp. 105-246.

————. (3) *Yasen Kanna*, in *Hakuin Oshō Zenshū*, V, pp. 341-400.

————. (4) *Sekishū Onjō*, in *Hakuin Oshō Zenshū*, IV, pp. 385-404.

HAMILTON, C. H. *Buddhism. A Religion of Infinite Compassion*. New York, 1952.

HAMMITZSCH, H. (tr.). Translations into German of the travel books of
Bashō:
————. (1) "Wegbericht einer Wanderung nach Kashima (Kashima-
Kikō)," in N., II (1936).
————. (2) "Ein Reisetagebuch des Matsuo Bashō (Kasshi-ginkō)," in
NOAG, No. 75, Hamburg, 1953.
————. (3) "Vier Haibun des Matsuo Bashō," in Sl, IV, 2 (1954).
————. (4) "Das Sarashina-kikō des Matsuo Bashō," in NOAG, Nos. 79-
80, Hamburg, 1956.
————. (5) "Wegbericht aus den Jahren U-tatsu (U-tatsu-kikō)," in Festschrift A. Wedemeyer. Leipzig, 1956.
————. (6) Cha-Dō—Der Tee-Weg. Munich-Planegg, 1958.
HAUER, J. W. (1) Der Yoga als Heilsweg. Stuttgart, 1932.
————. (2) Der Yoga. Ein indischer Weg zum Selbst. (Revised and enlarged ed. of [1]). Stuttgart, 1958.
HEILER, F. Die buddhistische Versenkung. Eine religionsgeschichtliche Untersuchung. Munich, 1918.
HERRIGEL, E. Zen in der Kunst des Bogenschiessens. Konstanz, 1948. English translation: Zen in the Art of Archery, by R. F. C. Hull, with an
introduction by D. T. Suzuki. New York, 1953.
HOFFMANN, H. Die Religionen Tibets. Freiburg-Munich, 1956.
HUMBERCLAUDE, P. (tr.). "Myōtei Mondō," in MN, I, pp. 515-48 (1938);
II, pp. 237-67 (1939).
HUMPHREYS, C. Zen Buddhism. London, 1949.
HU SHIH. (1) "Development of Zen Buddhism in China," in SPSR, XV,
4 (1932).
————. (2) Shina Zengaku no hensen (Developments in the Study of
Zen). Tokyo, 1936.
ICHIKAWA, H. "Ikkyū," in Gendai Bukkyō Kōza, V, pp. 178-84, Tokyo,
1955.
IDUMI, H. (tr.). Vimalikīrti's Discourse on Emancipation, in EB, III,
pp. 55-69, 138-53, 224-42, 336-49 (1924-1925); IV, pp. 48-55, 177-
190, 348-66 (1926-1928).
IKKYŪ. "Gaikotsu" (Skeleton), in Zenmon hōgoshū, 6th edn. Tokyo, 1910.
IWAMOTO, H. (tr.). Shōbōgenzō Zuimonki Wortgetnene Niederschrift der
lehrreichen Worte Dōgens über den wahren Buddhismus. Tokyo, 1943.
JAMES, W. The Varieties of Religious Experience. New York-London,
1902.
KATAOKA, Y. (1) "Takayama Ukon," in MN, I, pp. 451-64 (1938).
————. (2) "Chajin Takayama Minaminobō" (Tea Master Takayama
Minaminobō), in KK, XXIV, 5-6, pp. 123-39 (1944).
KEITH, A. B. Buddhist Philosophy in India and Ceylon. Oxford, 1923.
KERN, H. Der Buddhismus und seine Geschichte in Indien, I. Leipzig,
1882.

KISHIMOTO, H. (1) "Gyō no shinri" (Psychology of Asceticism), in *Gendai Shinrigaku*, IV, Tokyo, 1942.

———. (2) *Shūkyō to shinri no mondai to shite no Zen to Nembutsu* (Zen and Nembutsu as a Religious and Psychological Problem), in *SK*, XIV, pp. 133-44 (1937).

KITAMORI, K. "Nihon ni okeru dendō no shōgai" (Obstacles to Missionary Work in Japan), in *Asia ni okeru Kiristokyō* (Christianity in Asia). Tokyo, 1955.

KLEISER, A. "Doña Gracia Hosokawa. Ihre Bekehrungsgeschichte nach einem Originalbericht des P. Antonio Prenestino," in *MN*, II, pp. 609-16 (1939).

KÜMMEL, O. *Die Kunst Ostasiens*. Berlin, 1922.

LAMOTTE, E. (tr.). (1) *Le Traité de la grande vertu de sagesse (Mahā-prajñāpāramitāśāstra)*. 2 Vols. Louvain, 1944, 1949.

———. (2) "Sur la formation du Mahāyāna," in *Asiatica, Festschrift Friedrich Weller*, pp. 377-96, Leipzig, 1954.

———. (3) *Histoire du Bouddhisme Indien. Des Origines à l'Ère Śaka.* Louvain, 1958.

LAURES, J. (1) "Notes on the Death of Ninshitsu," in *MN*, VIII, pp. 407-11 (1952).

———. (2) *Takayama Ukon und die Anfänge der Kirche in Japan.* Münster, 1954.

LIEBENTHAL, W. (1) "Was ist chinesischer Buddhismus?" in *AS*, pp. 116-29 (1952).

———. (2) "Shih Hui-yüan's Buddhism as Set Forth in His Writings," in *JAOS*, LXX, pp. 243-59 (1950).

———. (3) (tr.). "*The Book of Chao*. A Translation from the Original Chinese, with Introduction, Notes and Appendices," Series Monumenta Serica Monographs No. 14. Peking, 1948.

———. (4) "A Biography of Chu Tao-sheng," in *MN*, XI, pp. 284-316 (1955).

———. (5) "The World Conception of Chu Tao-sheng," in *MN*, XII, pp. 65-103 (1956).

———. (6) "The World Conception of Chu Tao-sheng Texts," in *MN*, XII, pp. 241-68 (1956).

———. (7) "The Sermon of Shên-hui," in *AM*, pp. 132-55 (1952).

———. (8) "Notes on the 'Vajrasamādhi,'" in *TP*, XLIV, pp. 347-86 (1956).

MAGER, A. (1) "Mystik," in *Lexikon für Theologie und Kirche*, VII. Freiburg, 1935.

———. (2) *Mystik als Lehre und Leben*. Innsbruck, 1934.

MASUDA, J. (tr.). "Origins and Doctrines of Early Buddhist Schools," in *AM*, II, 1925.

MASUNAGA, R. (1) "Shoki zenshūshi to Dōgen zenji no buppō" (The Early History of the Zen School and the Buddhism of Dōgen), in *KDKK*, No. 13, pp. 58-75 (1955).

————. (2) "Koitsu Shozenseki no Kenkyū" (Studies of the Sources of the Early History of Zen), in *NBGN*, No. 15, Tokyo, 1949.

————. (3) "Zengaku nyūmon" (An Introduction to the Study of Zen, 2), in *D*, XXII, 6, pp. 38-46 (1955).

————. (4) *Eihei Shōbōgenzō—Dōgen no shūkyō* (The Religion of Dōgen). Tokyo, 1956.

————. (5) *The Sōtō Approach to Zen.* Tokyo, 1958.

MATSUMOTO, B. *Daruma no Kenkyū* (Studies on Bodhidharma). Tokyo, 1942.

MATSUMOTO, T. *Die Prajñāpāramitā-Literatur.* Stuttgart, 1932.

MATSUSHITA, T. "Sesshū. His Life and Art," in *JQ*, III, pp. 460-67, Tokyo, 1956.

MERTON, T. *The Ascent to Truth.* New York, 1951.

MIYAMOTO, S. *Chūdō shisō oyobi sono hattatsu* (The Philosophy of The Middle Way and Its Development). Tokyo, 1944.

MIZUNO, K. "Bodai-daruma no ninyū shigyōsetsu to Kongō-sammaikyō" (Bodhidharma's Doctrine of the Two Entrances and Four Acts and the Vajrasamādhi Sutra), in *KDKK*, No. 13, pp. 33-57 (1955).

MORGAN, K. W. (ed.). *The Path of the Buddha, Buddhism Interpreted by Buddhists.* New York, 1956.

MURTI, T. R. V. *The Central Philosophy of Buddhism, A Study of the Mādhyamika System.* London, 1955.

MUSŌ KOKUSHI (Sōseki). "Nijūsan mondō" (Twenty-three Questions and Answers), in *Zenmon hōgoshū*, 6th edn. Tokyo, 1910.

NAKAMURA, H. (1) "Zen ni okeru seisan to kinrō no mondai" (The Question of Production and Labor in Zen), in *ZB*, I, 2, pp. 27-35; 3, pp. 7-15 (1955).

————. (2) "Une Charactéristique de la Pensée Japonaise. La Dévotion Absolue à une Personnalité Déterminée," in *MN*, VIII, pp. 99-120 (1952).

————. (3) *The Ways of Thinking of Eastern Peoples.* Tokyo, 1960.

ÑĀNAMOLI (tr.). *The Path of Purification (Visuddhimagga) by Bhadantā-cariya Buddhaghosa.* Colombo, 1956.

NANJIO, B. *A Catalogue of the Chinese Translation of the Buddhist Tripitaka.* Oxford, 1883.

NAOKI, K. *Hakuin no kenkōhō to itsuwa* (Hakuin's Medical Treatment and Anecdotes). Tokyo, 1955.

NEWSOM, S. *A Thousand Years of Japanese Gardens.* Tokyo, 1953.

NISHIMURA, T. *Kirishitan to Sadō* (Christianity and the Way of Tea). Kyoto, 1948.

NYANATILOKA (tr.). *Visuddhi-magga oder der Weg zur Reinheit, aus dem Pali*, 2nd edn. Konstanz, 1952.

ŌHASAMA-FAUST. *Zen, der lebendige Buddhismus in Japan*. Gotha, 1925.

OHM, TH. *Die Liebe zu Gott in den nichtchristlichen Religionen*. Krailing vor München, 1950.

OKAKURA, K. *The Book of Tea*, 2nd edn., with foreword by E. Grilli. Tokyo, 1958.

OLDENBERG, H. *Buddha*, 10th edn. Stuttgart-Berlin, 1926.

Ōtomo Kōhaiki, I (The Flowering and Decline of the Ōtomo Family, I). Oita, 1936.

Pageant of Japanese Art:
(1) II (Painting). Tokyo, 1952.
(2) VI (Gardening). Tokyo, 1952.

PELLIOT, P. "Notes sur quelques artistes des six Dynasties et des T'ang," in *TP, XXII* (1923).

PONSONBY-FANE, R. A. B. *Kyoto—The Old Capital of Japan*. Kyoto, 1956.

PRATT, J. B. *The Pilgrimage of Buddhism*. New York, 1928.

REGAMEY, C. "Der Buddhismus Indiens," in *Christus und die Religionen der Erde*, III. Freiburg, 1951.

RHYS-DAVIDS, T. W. "Dialogues of the Buddha," in *SBB*, II, London, 1899.

ROSENBERG, O. *Die Probleme der buddhistischen Philosophie*. Heidelberg, 1924.

ROUSSELLE, E. (tr.). *Sutra des Sechsten Patriarchen:*
———. (1) Chap. 1, in *S*, V, pp. 174-91 (1930).
———. (2) Chap. 2, in *CDA*, pp. 76-86 (1931).
———. (3) Chap. 3, in *S*, VI, pp. 26-34 (1931).
———. (4) Chaps. 4 and 5, in *S*, XI, pp. 3-4, 131-37 (1936).
———. (5) Chap. 6, in *S*, XI, pp. 5-6, 202-11 (1936).

SAKAINO, K. *Shina Bukkyō Seishi* (Detailed History of Chinese Buddhism). Tokyo, 1935.

SALDITT, M. "Karl Vossler und Benedetto Croce," in *H*, 49, pp. 293-95 (1957).

SANSOM, G. B. *Japan—A Short Cultural History*. London, 1931.

SASAKI, R. FULLER. (1) *Zen—A Religion*. New York, 1958.

———. (2) *Zen—A Method for Religious Awakening*. Kyoto, 1959.

SCHMALTZ, G. *Östliche Weisheit und westliche Therapie*. Stuttgart, 1953.

SCHULEMANN, G. *Die Botschaft des Buddha vom Lotos des guten Gesetzes*. Freiburg, 1937.

SCHURHAMMER, G. (1) *Die Disputationen des P. Cosme de Torres mit den Buddhisten in Yamaguchi im Jahre 1551*. Tokyo, 1929.

———. (2) "Kōbō Daishi, nach den gedruckten und ungedruckten Missionsberichten des 16. und 17. Jahrhunderts," in *ZM*, XII, pp. 80-97 (1921).

————. (3) "Die Yamabushis," in ZM, XII, pp. 206-28 (1922).

————. (4) *Der hl. Franz Xaver in Japan.* Schöneck-Beckenried (Schweiz), 1947.

————. (5) "Ein fürstlicher Gönner des heiligen Franz Xaver: Ōtomo Yoshishige," in *KM*, No. 47, pp. 25-29 (1918).

SCHURHAMMER-VORETZSCH (trs.). *Die Geschichte Japans von P. Luis Frois, übersetzt und kommentiert.* Leipzig, 1926.

SCHURHAMMER-WICKI (eds.). *Epistolae S. Francisci Xaverii,* II. Rome, 1945.

SCHÜTTE, J. *Valignanos Missionsgrundsätze für Japan,* I-II. Rome, 1958.

SECKEL, D. (1) "Mu-hsi, Sechs Kaki-Früchte. Interpretation eines Zen-Bildes," in *NOAG,* No. 77, pp. 44-55, Hamburg, 1955.

————. (2) *Buddhistische Kunst Ostasiens.* Stuttgart, 1957.

SHAW-SCHIFFER (trs.). "Yasen Kanna. A Chat on a Boat in the Evening by Hakuin Zenji," in *MN,* XIII, pp. 101-27 (1957).

SHIMMYŌ, A. "Ōbaku no shimpū" (The New Style of Ōbaku), in *D,* pp. 74-80, May, 1957.

STCHERBATSKY, T. (1) *The Central Conception of Buddhism and the Meaning of the Word "Dharma."* London, 1923.

————. (2) *The Conception of Buddhist Nirvāna.* Leningrad, 1927.

SUK, C. *Ch'an and Zen Teaching.* London (1960).

SUZUKI, B. L. *Mahāyāna Buddhism,* with Introduction by D. T. Suzuki. London, 1948.

SUZUKI, D. T. (1) *Essays in Zen Buddhism,* I. London, 1927. New edns. London, 1949, 1958.

————. (2) *Essays in Zen Buddhism,* II. London, 1933. New edns. London, 1950, 1958.

————. (3) *Essays in Zen Buddhism,* III. London, 1934. New edns. London, 1953, 1958.

————. (4) *Studies in the Lankāvatāra Sutra.* London, 1930. Repr. 1957.

————. (5) *An Introduction to Zen Buddhism.* Kyoto, 1934. New edn., with a Foreword by C. G. Jung. London, 1949, 1960.

————. (6) *Manual of Zen Buddhism.* Kyoto, 1935. New edns. London, 1950, 1951.

————. (7) *Studies in Zen.* London, 1955.

————. (8) *Rinzai no komponshisō* (The Central Ideas of Rinzai). Tokyo, 1949.

————. (9) *Zen Buddhism and Its Influence on Japanese Culture.* Kyoto, 1938. Revised and enlarged second edition under the title *Zen and Japanese Culture.* New York, 1959. (Quotations from the revised edition.)

————. (10) *The Training of the Zen Buddhist Monk.* Kyoto, 1934.

————. (11) (tr.). *The Lankāvatāra Sutra. A Mahāyāna Text.* Translated for the first time from the original Sanskrit. London, 1956 (first published 1932).

TAKAKUSU, J. *The Essentials of Buddhist Philosophy.* Honolulu, 1947.

TAKEDA, E. "Eisai," in *Gendai Zen-Kōza,* II, pp. 198-205, Tokyo, 1956.

TAMURA, T. *Art of Landscape Gardens in Japan.* Tokyo, 1935.

TANAKA, T. "Dōgen," in *Gendai Zen-Kōza,* II, pp. 206-12, Tokyo, 1956.

THOMAS, E. J. (1) *The Life of Buddha as Legend and History.* London, 1927. Rev. edn. London, 1949. Repr. London, 1952, 1956.

———. (2) *The History of Buddhist Thought.* London, 1933. Repr. New York, 1951.

TŌREI ENJI. "Shinki-dokumyō Zenji Nempu-ingyōkaku" (Chronicle of Hakuin), in *Hakuin Oshō Zenshū,* I, pp. 1-78, Tokyo, 1935.

TSUDA, N. *Handbook of Japanese Art.* Tokyo, 1935.

TSUJI, Z. (1) *Nihon Bukkyōshi* (History of Japanese Buddhism), Middle Ages, V. Tokyo, 1951.

———. (2) *Nihon Bukkyōshi,* Modern Times, I-IV. Tokyo, 1954, 1955.

TSUTZUMI, T. *Die Kunst Japans.* Leipzig, 1929.

ÜBERSCHAAR, H. (tr.). "Bashō und sein Tagebuch 'Oku no hosomichi'," in MOAG, XXIX/A, Tokyo, 1935.

UI, H. (1) *Indo Tetsugakushi* (History of Indian Philosophy), 3rd edn. Tokyo, 1935.

———. (2) *Indo Tetsugakushi* (small edn.). Tokyo, 1936.

———. (3) "On Nibbāna," in *Studies on Buddhism in Japan,* I. Tokyo, 1939.

———. (4) *Zenshūshi Kenkyū* (Studies in the History of the Zen School), I. Tokyo, 1939.

———. (5) *Zenshūshi Kenkyū,* II. Tokyo, 1941.

———. (6) *Zenshūshi Kenkyū,* III. Tokyo, 1943.

———. (7) *Shina Bukkyōshi* (History of Chinese Buddhism). Tokyo, 1936.

———. (8) *Konsaisu Bukkyō Jiten* (Concise Buddhist Dictionary). Tokyo, 1938.

VALLÉE-POUSSIN, L. DE LA. (1) *Nirvāna.* Paris, 1925.

———. (2) "Nirvāna," in ERE, IX, New York, 1917.

WALLESER, M. (1) *Die Sekten des alten Buddhismus.* Heidelberg, 1927.

———. (tr.). (2) *Prajñāpāramitā. Die Vollkommenheit der Erkenntnis.* Göttingen, 1914.

WATTS, A. W. (1) *The Spirit of Zen,* Wisdom of the East Series. London, 1936.

———. (2) *The Way of Zen.* New York, 1957.

WONG MOU-LAM (tr.). *The Sutra of Wei Lang* (or Hui Nêng), new edn. London, 1947.

YOKOYAMA, H. "Zenshū no shichi dō garan" (The Seven Halls of the Zen School), in ZB, II, 4, pp. 40-45 (1956).

Abbreviations of Titles
of Periodicals

Index